REIGNING CATS
AND DOGS

REIGNING CATS AND DOGS

Katharine MacDonogh

St. Martin's Press, New York

For Hortense

Wilfred & Gigi
& Monty

I owe an enormous debt of gratitude to the many friends and acquaintances who have helped me in one way or another with this book. Of these the following deserve a particular mention: la marquesa de las Almenas, Mr Michael Bloch, Mr Christopher Busby, Mr Keith Day, Mr Patric Dickinson, M Didier Girard, Mr Lucian Boyd Harte, Mr Christopher Howse, my brothers Jeremy and Giles MacDonogh, Dr Lauro Martinez, Mrs Diane Maxfield, Mr Terence McCarthy, Dr Charles C. Noel, Mr Nigel Perfect, Dr John Martin Robinson, Mrs Judy Russo, Miss Sue Simon, Dr Simon Thurley, Mr Alexander Titov and Miss Gilly Reed-Walker. The seminars organised by the Society for Court Studies have greatly broadened my understanding of court history and I am grateful to the committee and members for the ideas they have generated. The staff of the British, London and Kennel Club Libraries were indispensable, as were those at the Heinz Archive, particularly Jayne Shrimpton. Frau Doctor Gabriele Helke of the Kunsthistorisches Museum in Vienna was exceedingly generous with both her time and knowledge when she accompanied me around the collection in 1996. The Curator of Lyme Park, David W. Evans, also provided invaluable material.

The two borzoi portraits in the book will be included in the forthcoming Catalogue Raisonné of Portraits by Philip de László M.V.O., P.R.B.A., R.P., N.P.S., 1869–1937. I would like to thank Miss Emily Hayward for her assistance in procuring the illustrations and Mr Robert Updegraff for designing the book. One would have to search far and wide to find two more sympathetic people than Mr Christopher Potter at Fourth Estate and my agent, Mr Christopher Sinclair Stevenson, who, contrary to what I was led to expect of members of their profession, were ever at hand to offer support and advice. My husband, Mr Charles Sheppard, who showed great forbearance throughout the period this book took to write, not only read the text and made many valid suggestions but also offered unflagging encouragement. Dr Philip Mansel, who also read the manuscript, saved me from many an error of fact or judgement. Any mistakes that remain are entirely of my own making.

First published in Great Britain in 1999 by
Fourth Estate Limited, 6 Salem Road, London W2 4BU

ISBN 0-312-22837-6

Library of Congress Cataloging in Publication Data to be found at the Library of Congress.

First published by St. Martin's Press: 1999

1 3 5 7 9 10 8 6 4 2

Typeset by MATS
Designed by Robert Updegraff
Printed in Italy

HALF TITLE: *Photograph of the tombstone of Edward VII's dog Caesar at Marlborough House.*
TITLE PAGE: *The portrait by Nicolas de Largillière of* Louis XIV and his Heirs *includes a Bolognese and a pug.*

Contents

CHAPTER ONE

Royal Favourites

T HE TASTE FOR UNNECESSARY PETS began at court. During
the Renaissance they reflected the desire for conspicuous display and
were items of prestige, adding lustre to a princely house. Above all,
they constituted an important, and generally uncontroversial, emotional outlet. As the most loyal of all subjects, pets were incapable of betrayal and disinterested in their affections. They alone had constant access to the royal ear.
As Axel Munthe, the celebrated author of *The Story of San Michele*, put it:

> the dog cannot dissimulate, cannot deceive, cannot lie because he can-
> not speak. The dog is a saint . . . A dog gladly admits the superiority
> of his master over himself . . . He looks upon his master as his king,
> almost as his god . . . He knows by instinct when he is not wanted, lies
> quite still for hours when his king is hard at work, as kings often are,
> or at least ought to be. But when his king is sad and worried he knows
> that his time has come and he creeps up and lays his head on his lap.
> Don't worry! Never mind if they all abandon you, I am here to replace
> all your friends and to fight all your enemies.[1]

Most monarchs were raised with pets from birth and, in the loneliness of
their privileged childhood, formed a lifelong bond. They helped reduce the
strains of office and fill the vacuum at the heart of monarchy. They countered
the ennui and artificiality of court life with its insistence on etiquette and protocol. A species unto themselves, monarchs sometimes felt such a strong
symbiotic attachment to their pets that the lines distinguishing humans from
animals became blurred. For men, and more especially women, pets frequently
acted as surrogate children, receiving the parental affection denied to their bio-
logical issue. Pets were not merely humanised; they were superior to man.

CHILDREN

Royal children came into contact with animals from birth; indeed, Princess Victoria narrowly missed entering this world among lapdogs when her eight months pregnant mother, the Duchess of Kent, reached England in 1819 aboard a travelling coach brimming over with them. Familiarising their young with animals was natural for royal parents, themselves devoted to pets, but it was also policy. Princes had to learn to hunt, in order to train them for war, to overcome fear and harden their hearts against the dangers and accidents to which kings were prone. Their first riding lessons frequently took place astride dogs, progressing to ponies generally at the age of four. Princes were necessarily separated for much of their youth from children of their own age and were discouraged from forming close attachments to the few with whom they came into contact. This affective void was exacerbated by parental neglect. As the Duke of Windsor observed when recalling his own childhood: 'Kings and Queens are only secondarily fathers and mothers.'[2] Emotional deprivation frequently resulted in psychosomatic disorders to which pets alone remained indifferent.

The eldest son of Henri IV of France and Marie de Medici, the Dauphin Louis (Louis XIII, 1601–43, reigned from 1610), was hunting the stag by the age of six, accompanied by his page, Bompar, and could already discuss the subject with authority. By the age of seven, Louis was hunting with the King. Most of his early training took place indoors: young game would be released in the *galerie* at Fontainebleau or the *salle de bal* at St Germain and small dogs, generally his own pets, set upon them. Both the quarry and the dogs were transported to wheresoever the Prince happened to be. By the age of nine, when he succeeded to the throne, Louis was hunting three times a week and was considered proficient enough to pursue wild boar, although this did not prevent him from continuing to chase hare in his bedroom with his '*petits chiens*'. His deep attachment to dogs showed in his ability to remember all their names, his constant desire to discuss little else, and the mortification he felt whenever an accident befell any of them.

Even before they received pets of their own, royal children were given toy dogs and cats to habituate them to their presence. Louis played with china dogs and, on his fifth birthday, was given some glass ones by the

François Boucher: **Louis-Philippe-Joseph, duc de Montpensier,** *1749. This shows the Duc d'Orléans, Philippe Egalité, at the age of two. He was beheaded in 1793.*

wife of his physician, Jean Héroard. He still enjoyed playing with these two years later, despite the fact that he was now actively following the hunt, and appears only to have desisted at the age of eleven, when dancing and music became great passions. Toys were normally removed when children officially reached maturity which, in the case of boys, involved the symbolic process of breeching, or changing from frocks to breeches. It was only at this point that children were deemed capable of reason. Catherine the Great (Catherine II, 1729–96, Empress from 1762) recorded in her memoirs how her toys were theoretically confiscated when she was seven but that in reality this was 'a mere question of etiquette, as no-one interfered with me in my games'. Possibly the rule was more rigorously enforced under her descendant, Tsar Alexander III (1845–94, Emperor from 1881), who kept his childhood collection of miniature glass and china animals, which he referred to as his 'treasures', in a secret drawer in his desk until his death. In 1856, at the age of eleven, he had sketched for them an imaginary city which he named Mopsopolis, Pug-City, inhabited by the eponymous dogs.

Another favourite royal game was harnessing pet dogs to miniature carriages which were then pulled along the galleries of palaces. In 1608 Louis attached his dogs, Pataut and Lion, to the carriage that his mother's favourite, Concini, had given him. In April 1715, Madame (Duchesse d'Orléans, 1652–1722, second wife of Louis XIV's brother Philippe and always addressed as Madame) wrote to the Raugravine Louisa, her half-sister, describing how

> after dinner my grandson, the duc de Chartres, came to see me, and I arranged for him a spectacle suitable to his years. It was a triumphal car drawn by a big cat, in which was seated a little lady dog called Andrienne. A pigeon acted as a coachman, two others were pages and a dog served as footman and sat up behind. His name is Picart, and when the lady alights from the carriage, Picart lets down the step. The cat's name is Castille. Picart allows himself to be saddled and has a doll put on his back, and he will do everything that the domestic horses do.[3]

Napoleon's sister Caroline Murat gave a similar carriage to his son the King of Rome, but it was pulled by sheep, trained by Franconi, the famous circus trainer. The carriage arrived in Vienna in November 1815, much to the joy of the boy and the despair of his tutor, Count Dietrichstein, who noted how 'this apparition revived, as if by magic, all those memories of Paris and the imperial splendour of the Court which had been somewhat dimmed since 25 October [when most of his French attendants had been dismissed]. The Prince's playmate, Emile, joined in, and from that day on the excessive and often frenzied gaiety of the two children, as well as their insufferable chatter, grew to such a pitch that it was quite impossible to keep them quiet.'⁴ Pets were sometimes given in order to deflect a child from baleful influences. When he was five years old, in 1816, the King of Rome was taught by his favourite uncle Archduke Francis 'to be not only rude but indecent', according to Leopoldine, his aunt; their brother, Archduke Rainer, gave the boy a basset hound as an alternative companion and soon superseded his brother as the prince's favourite.

Parental neglect or absence was an important factor in building up the symbiotic relationship subsisting between child and pet. However much Louis loved his father, Henri IV was dead before the Prince's tenth birthday and his mother, Marie de Medici, never once kissed him, a view corroborated by the Grande Mademoiselle (daughter of Gaston d'Orléans and cousin of Louis XIV), who wrote: 'My grandmother loved me deeply and showed me, so I have been told, much more tenderness than ever she had shown her own children.' Although Louis was brought up with Henri's ten bastard children, and thus was far from deprived of playmates of his own age, he early grew to dislike them and already by the age of four refused to eat with them. His first friends were the dogs of the *gardes du corps.* When he started to acquire his own pets at the age of four he organised them into a household, appointing his favourite, Cavalon, *'premier chien'.* He was given a miniature black greyhound in 1605 by his cousin, the Duc de Longueville, which he

Detail of the spaniel from the painting by Ferdinand Elle. Louis XIII greatly preferred the company of his dogs to that of his wife.

named Charbon, but also had a *chien d'Ostreland* called Isabelle which slept on his bed at night. This was the dog he had with him while sitting for his portrait by Martin in 1606 and which 'he caressed, kissed, called his sweetheart, for he adored dogs. The *femme de chambre* Mademoiselle Mercier said to him "Monsieur, those bearing arms should not have dogs with them [a reference to the Prince's martial attire for the portrait]", at which he quipped, "but they are good at nipping enemies' legs."' In all he had ten pet dogs as a child.[5]

Not only were dogs uncritical of physical failings, but they exhibited a gentleness and tenderness often lacking in the human species. At Renaissance courts authority had been preferred to force, but the use of corporal punishment gradually spread from Protestant Germany across Europe and by the mid-sixteenth century had become common practice. Lady Jane Grey bewailed the fact that

> When I am in presence either of father or mother, whether I speak, keep silence, sit, stand or go, eat, drink, be merry or sad, be sewing, playing, dancing, or doing anything else, I must do it, as it were, in such weight, measure, and number, even so perfectly as God made the world, else I am so sharply taunted, so cruelly threatened, yea presently sometimes with pinches, nips and bobs, and some ways I will not name for the honour I bear them, so without measure misordered that I think myself in Hell.[6]

Louis was regularly whipped from the age of three with the approval of both his parents – though not of his physician Héroard, who warned that it was undermining the boy's health. Henri IV wrote to his son's nurse, Madame de Montglat, in 1607 insisting 'it is my wish and my command that he be whipped every time he is stubborn or misbehaves, knowing full well from personal experience that nothing in the world is as efficacious'. On his birthday that same year Louis was taken to vespers at the Cordeliers to hear a Te Deum sung in his honour but, seeing one of the Franciscans holding a large whip to keep the dogs out, he took fright and went outside to hide in the elm grove from which nobody could persuade him to emerge. Lest it be thought that children of this period were psychologically inured to corporal punishment, it is interesting to note that when Louis became a father he never applied the whip to his own children, the future Louis XIV and Philippe, Duc d'Orléans.

On the frequent occasions when Louis was bitten, his parents normally took the side of the dog: once in 1608 the Prince went into the garden at Fontainebleau to await his father and in order to 'raise his hat to Soldat, one of the King's dogs, which jumped up at him, taking him by surprise and reducing him to tears. The King upbraided him for being scared, and told him he must be afraid of nothing.' Soldat appears to have found Louis' attentions singularly overwhelming for it bit him again less than a month after when they were playing together and, later that year, 'the dog barking at him, he pretended to bite it; the King upbraided him thinking he was beating the dog. He cried at having displeased the King, the King got angry and led him by the hand to his bedroom.' When his mother's dog, Brigantin, bit Louis on the eyebrow in 1610 she showed no pity, he having accidentally trodden on the dog's paw. Louis stormed out, protesting that Marie de Medici cared more about her dog than she did him. He was probably right.

At European courts, education began in earnest once breeching had taken place and a tutor had been appointed to oversee the prince's upbringing. Hunting manuals and fairytales formed a significant part of the curriculum. The Dauphin, Louis, had mastered Jacques de Fouilloux's *La Vénerie*, written in 1561, by the age of nine. He also greatly admired Conrad Gesner's magisterial *Historiae Animalium*, 1551–8, which Héroard lent him regularly. Fairytales confirmed the hierarchy of the animal kingdom by distinguishing between noble and ignoble creatures in the same manner as medieval bestiaries had done previously and were thus instrumental in reconciling a love for animals with a passion for the chase. From the sixteenth to the twentieth centuries children at all European courts learned the fables of Aesop, and subsequently La Fontaine, by heart. In a letter to his sister Wilhelmina, Margravine of Bayreuth, written in 1748, Frederick the Great (Frederick II, 1712–86, King from 1740) expressed his admiration for the great fabulist: 'Animals often help us to explain our sentiments more naturally and candidly. La Fontaine, author of such pretty fables, was well aware of this; hence the creatures whom he endowed with his eloquence teach man a moral which sadly few put into practice.'[7]

Breeching, with its severance of a prince from female influence and affection, caused many a prince – and his governess – considerable grief and could lead to animosity between the redundant governess and the new tutor, whose position was a source of great potential influence over his charge. Louis was given a tutor in 1609, Monsieur de Souvré, who squabbled with Madame de Montglat, the child's beloved governess, over the child. Souvré attempted to diminish the Dauphin's affection for his dogs as part of forcing him into adulthood. Héroard recorded how Louis 'had a dog called Pataut, the eldest of them all, which he wanted to bring to St Germain and which he loved and had always loved. Monsieur de Souvré said to him, "Sir, you have too many dogs, you must get rid of those that are worthless and particularly those that are too old, like Pataut." "Pataut, monsieur de Souvré, oh! No, I want to look after the old,"' replied the boy. Louis was devoted to his father and saw him relatively often. He paid him a unique compliment when he confided to Madame de Montglat that he liked him even 'more than Pataut'. Nonetheless, on the rare occasion when the Dauphin laughed, Héroard recorded that it was normally prompted by an incident relating to his dogs as, for instance, when he persuaded a courtier to play the bagpipes to Pataut. He also suffered from an appalling stutter, as did his contemporary and future brother-in-law, Charles I, another great dog lover.

Most royal children were raised in relative isolation and tutored privately until the twentieth century. The principal reason for this was the necessity for protecting them against disease and plague. Despite such precautions, the incidence of infant mortality remained extremely high and the death of siblings deprived many princes of potential playmates. The stringent precautions taken to prevent their contracting disease were particularly severe in the case of a sole heir. Henry VIII's only son, the future Edward VI, was brought up at Hampton Court where the walls and floors were washed three times a day. His mother, Jane Seymour, having died in childbirth, and his father being an infrequent visitor, he understandably formed a close tie with his nurse, Mother Jack, ruptured at the age of six when he was breeched. Prince Edward was relatively fortunate: his father arranged for fourteen well-born children to share his education and an exclusive palace school was thus founded. Despite these benefits, it was reported that he laughed out loud only once in his life.

Many royal children were sickly or crippled. The offspring of Louis XIV appear to have been particularly disadvantaged: his illegitimate son, the Duc de Maine, fell victim to infantile paralysis at the age of three and his grandson the Duc de Bourgogne was a hunchback. Queen Christina of Sweden's mother, Maria Eleonora, tried to kill her daughter at birth because she was so ugly and hirsute. Nor did their contemporaries show much tact in these matters: Madame, the Duchesse d'Orléans, always referred to the Duc de Maine in her letters as 'the Cripple'. All were devoted to their pets, creatures indifferent to their physical and mental disabilities which, by seriously handicapping their chances of forging important marriage alliances, diminished their standing at court. Similarly, Kaiser William II's withered arm was long kept secret and he later confessed that the endless corrective exercises he had endured in his youth meant his 'life was often a perfect torment'. Reza, Shah of Persia from 1925 to 1941, was very disappointed in his sickly, fragile child, Muhammad Reza, and largely abandoned him into the hands of a guardian. When the last Shah was deposed in 1979 he dispensed with his most loyal officers but not his dogs, which accompanied him on the only available aeroplane leaving the country – an order of priorities that seriously undermined any chances of a Pahlavi restoration.

The last Tsar's son, Alexis, was not only his sole heir but a victim of haemophilia. The Romanovs allowed none of their children to mix other than with their siblings or immediate relations; they never attended a ball before the age of seventeen and had been to no parties other than those hosted by their aunt, the Grand Duchess Olga. In the case of the Tsarevich his isolation was exacerbated by his physical vulnerability and, although adored by both his parents, he was particularly attached to his pets. His spaniel Joy was his constant companion until their extermination. He also had a cat, Kotka. In 1916 he reported to the Tsarina how 'I took my cat into the garden but she was very timid and ran on to the balcony. She is now asleep on the sofa and Joy is under the table.'[8] The cat was with him during the war, on one occasion getting lost, as Nicholas wrote to Alexandra: it 'hid under those big logs of timber; we put on our coats and went out to look for it. Nagorny [the Tsarevich's personal bodyguard] at once discovered the cat with the aid of an electric lamp, but it took us a long time to make the brute come out – it would not listen. At last he caught it by the hind legs and pulled it through the narrow space.'[9] Unlike the Tsarevich, his sisters had no pets, either because it was discouraged or because their parents were preoccupied with their ailing son. In 1914, when Tatiana, then aged seventeen, finally acquired a pet, she apologised to her mother:

Mama darling mine, Forgive me about the little dog. To say the truth, when he asked should I like to have it if he gave it to me, I at once said yes. You remember, I always wanted to have one, and only afterwards when we came home I thought that suddenly you might not like me having one. But I really was so pleased at the idea that I forgot about everything. Please, darling angel, forgive me. Tell Papa about it. I hope he won't have anything against it. Good night, beloved Mama. God bless and keep you. 1000 kisses from your devoted daughter and loving, Tatiana. Say, darling, you are not angry.

This was doubtless Ortino, mentioned again in 1915.[10] Tatiana's sister Olga was given a cat in 1916.

The relationship between monarch and heir is necessarily strained. As Queen Elizabeth I explained to Mary Queen of Scots when declining to give her official recognition as heir apparent in 1560: 'Think you that I could love my own winding-sheet? Princes cannot like their own children, those that should succeed unto them.'[11] The Duke of Windsor, when Prince of Wales, rarely saw his parents, noting philosophically that 'for better or worse, Royalty is excluded from the more settled forms of domesticity. While affection was certainly not lacking in my upbringing, the mere circumstances of my father's position interposed an impalpable barrier that inhibited the closer continuing intimacy of conventional family life.' He recalled how his early years at Sandringham 'were spent almost entirely under the care of nurses', one of whom would pinch him and twist his arm before he paid his daily visit to his parents at teatime, and the 'sobbing and bawling this treatment invariably evoked understandably puzzled, worried, and finally annoyed them' and led to his being peremptorily dismissed from their presence.[12] He regretted never being alone with his parents, who constantly had either an equerry or lady-in-waiting in attendance, and also that 'except when we were taken to parties for the children of our parents' friends, or the members of the Household brought their sons and daughters to one of the Royal estates, we almost never saw our contemporaries [and] . . . were thus deprived of the company of other children'.[13] His lot was at least preferable to that of the son of the Maharajah of Rewah, who explained to the Viceroy of India, Lord Hardinge, that he kept the boy in a palace miles away, 'because all sons wished to poison their fathers and that his son was thus removed from temptation'.[14]

Princesses fared no better and, like their brothers, found an emotional outlet in keeping pets. James I's daughter, Elizabeth of Bohemia, had so many during her lonely childhood at Coombe Abbey in the care of Lord and Lady Harington that Sir Dudley Carleton, ambassador at The Hague, wrote: 'Of little dogs and monkeys, she hath no great want, having sixteen or seventeen in her own train.' At one time she had no fewer than twenty dogs and later became notorious for favouring her dogs above her children. Her daughter, Sophia, Electress of Hanover, remembered her preferring 'the sight of her monkeys and dogs to that of her children' who, in consequence, were raised in Leyden while Elizabeth remained in The Hague.[15] Frederick the Great's sister, Wilhelmina, alleged 'punches and kicks were my daily bread' – administered by her father. Unlike her brother, she was at least allowed pets, a practice clearly frowned upon at the militaristic Prussian court where Crown Prince Frederick (1831–8, reigned 1888) was later flogged for giving a servant twenty groschen for bringing him his dog from Potsdam (some twenty miles).[16] When her brother was

Detail of the Duke of Windsor's cairn terrier Slipper. The Duke's father, George V, had also been devoted to dogs, most of which he named Bob.

imprisoned at Kustrin, Wilhelmina wrote him clandestine letters, the discovery of which by the King would have had serious and unpleasant repercussions. She recalled how in 1726 she was nearly caught in the act when her father made an unexpected appearance and attempted to open the cabinet behind which, on hearing him approach, she had just had time to thrust her secret letters, though not the inkwell which she held behind her back. He was distracted by her mother:

> She had a very beautiful little Bolognese dog, and I had one too; both these animals were in the bedroom. 'Resolve our differences,' she said to the King, 'my daughter says her dog is more beautiful than mine, and I

maintain the opposite.' He started laughing, and asked me if I were very attached to mine? 'With all my heart,' I answered, for 'he is very lively and has a very good nature.' My reply pleased him, he embraced me several times, making me overturn my ink-well. The black liquid spilt all over my dress, and began to pour all over the floor. I dared not move, for fear the King notice. The situation was saved by his leaving . . .[17]

ROYAL MOTHERS

The principal function of royal women was to produce healthy sons. Few had met their husbands before they wed, or cast eyes on them other than in highly flattering portraits, and most married extremely young, often before reaching puberty. Even when the children they eventually bore were lucky enough to survive infancy, mothers had little, if any, say in their education or upbringing and rarely formed close ties. Royal wives spent their lives in exile from their native country, which was, in many cases, at war with their adoptive land. Linguistic difficulties had to be overcome, established favourites or mistresses tolerated, etiquette strictly adhered to and fidelity rigorously observed. The slightest deviation from these rules of conduct frequently resulted in the spread of unsubstantiated gossip which not only worsened a woman's lot but brought the whole monarchy into disrepute. Frederick the Great's sister, Wilhelmina, was told when her marriage was announced in 1731: 'Great princesses are born to be sacrificed to the good of the state.'[18] Those who did not turn to pets for the disinterested affection lacking elsewhere were rare indeed.

The first ordeals royal wives had to endure were pregnancy and childbirth. Riding and hunting were actively discouraged, particularly in the case of those women, like Marie Antoinette (her mother was already warning her in 1770 that riding was 'dangerous and bad for bearing children, which is your vocation'), who failed to conceive for many years after marriage. At the Spanish court, where etiquette was particularly strict, Pepys was aghast to hear that women 'found to be with child do never stir out of their beds or chambers till they are brought to bed – so ceremonious are they in that point also . . . that the Court there hath no dancings, nor visits at night to see the King or Queene, but is always just like a

Cloyster, nobody stirring in it'.[19] Madame, the Duchesse d'Orléans, was equally shocked after receiving a letter from her stepdaughter, Marie-Louise, Queen of Spain, in 1679, which left her convinced it was

> the most horrible country in the world. Their manners are the most stupid and annoying that can be imagined. Poor child, I pity her with all my heart for having to spend her life in such a country. The little dogs that she took with her are her only consolation. Already such severe rules of behaviour have been imposed upon her that she is not allowed to speak to her old groom. She may only make a sign to him with her hand or nod to him as she passes. The French servants could not accustom themselves to being shut up at first, and they all wanted to return to France.[20]

Not only was childbirth witnessed by a large number of court officials lest the royal infant be swapped at birth, but the risk of death remained high until the twentieth century. In 1716 Madame told the Princess of Wales that her daughter, the Duchesse de Lorraine, 'always makes her farewells when she is approaching her lying-in time, because she always expects to die'.[21] Her granddaughter, Louise-Adelaide, tried to avoid the issue by taking the veil, long a respectable alternative to marriage.

The duty of a royal mother was to bear children, not to raise them. This did not leave them immune to maternal sentiment, and the death of a child in infancy often caused great heartache. When Madame's elder son, the Duc de Valois, died in 1676, she was

> overwhelmed by the unexpected blow. . . . My trouble is that I don't know in the least how to deal with children, and have had no experience in such matters, so that I am forced to believe what they tell me here. But let us change the subject, because the more I think about it the more distracted I become. I have no one to console me because Monsieur left on Thursday with the King to join the army. . . . Unless God accords his special protection to the baby I am carrying at present, I shall have a very poor idea of its chances of life and health, because it is impossible that it should not be affected by all my troubles.[22]

The death of one child left Madame in a state of heightened anxiety for her remaining son, Philippe, the future Regent, then two years old: 'I wish he were three or four years older and past the dangers of early infancy. The doctors know nothing about the care children need, and will listen to nothing that they are told. Already they have dispatched a heap of children into the other world.'[23]

The army that Louis XIV and Monsieur, the Duc d'Orléans, had left to join was at war in her native Palatinate. Madame, like many another royal wife – notably Marie Antoinette and the Tsarina Alexandra – paid dearly for her nationality. As her marriage to the Duc d'Orléans deteriorated, it was used to alienate her children against her. In 1696 she wrote to her aunt, the Electress of Hanover, complaining how, compared to her husband,

> the children and I have scarcely the necessities of life . . . Day by day he stirs up my own children against me, and, for fear my son should notice how little care is taken of him, he allows him to indulge in all sorts of debauchery and even encourages him in it. . . . Thank God, Monsieur does not entangle my daughter in any of his debaucheries, nor has she the slightest inclination towards gallantry, but Monsieur will not leave her in my charge. He always takes her from me and forces her to associate with such riff-raff that it is indeed a miracle that she is not depraved. Moreover, he fills her mind with such a hatred of Germans that she can hardly bear to be with me because I am a German.[24]

In consequence, Madame became 'very sad at not being able to open my heart to those I love. This miserable situation is one reason why I lead such a quiet life. As I cannot live intimately with my son, anything else is galling to me, and I prefer to be left alone.'[25]

Royal babies continued to be wrested from their mothers throughout the eighteenth century. Catherine the Great's son Paul was born in 1754, nine years after her marriage to the Grand Duke Peter. She described in her memoirs how he was taken from her at birth and how she

> had news of him only furtively, for to ask for news would have seemed to express doubt about the care the Empress was giving him and would have been ill-received. She had taken him to her room and the moment he cried, she rushed and literally smothered him with her attentions.
>
> He was kept in an excessively hot room, swaddled in flannel, laid in a cot lined with silver fox, covered with a satin, wadded quilt over which

was another counterpane of pink velvet lined with silver fox. Later on, I often saw him lying like that, bathed in sweat from head to foot so that when he grew up the slightest whiff of air brought about colds and sickness. In addition he was surrounded by a great number of old matrons who with their half-baked remedies, resulting from ignorance, inflicted upon him much more physical and moral harm than good.[26]

Six days after the birth of her daughter Anna in 1758, the celebrations began:

I was told that some of them were magnificent. I did not see any. I was lying in my bed all forlorn, without a soul to keep me company except Mme Vladislavov, for as soon as my confinement was over, not only did the Empress – just as she did the time before – take the child to her rooms, but also, on the pretext that I needed rest, I was abandoned like a miserable creature and no one set foot in my apartments, nor sent to ask how I was.[27]

Not surprisingly she referred to childbirth as the *lit de misère*.

Royal virgins were largely ignorant of sexual matters before they married. Queen Victoria repeatedly reverted to the subject in her letters to her daughter Victoria after she had become Crown Princess of Prussia in 1858, even revealing that her own relationship with Prince Albert was not unadulterated domestic bliss: 'That despising our poor degraded sex – (for what else is it as we poor creatures are born for man's pleasure and amusement, and destined to go through endless sufferings and trials?) is a little in all men's natures; dear Papa even is not quite exempt though he would not admit it.'[28] She described pregnancy as 'an unhappy condition', 'our being like a cow or a dog at such moments; when our poor nature becomes so very animal and unecstatic'[29] – tactless observations given that her daughter had not yet conceived. Crown Princess Victoria gave birth to her first child, the future Kaiser, in 1859, after an extremely difficult labour which left him not just with a withered arm but probable brain damage. In 1861, when Queen Victoria's second daughter, Princess Alice, became engaged to the Grand Duke of Hesse, the Queen wrote to Victoria explaining that Alice 'has the greatest horror of having children, and would rather have none – just as I was as a girl and when I first married

Sir Edwin Landseer: **Princess Victoria with Eos,** *1841. Ruskin said of Landseer: 'It was not by a study of Raphael that he attained his eminent success, but by a healthy love of Scotch Terriers.'*

— so I am very anxious she should know as little about the inevitable miseries as possible; so don't forget, dear'.[30]

Mothers had no say in the upbringing of their sons even when, like Queen Victoria, they were the sovereign and anxious to prevent their children suffering the same loneliness as they had themselves experienced in their youth. In 1858 Queen Victoria described her own childhood to her daughter, the Princess Royal, 'I had led a very unhappy life as a child – had no scope for my very violent feelings of affection – had no brothers and sisters to live with – never had a father – from my unfortunate circumstances was not on a comfortable or at all intimate or confidential footing with my mother – much as I love her now – and did not know what a happy domestic life was!' Later that year she was devastated to be parted from her second son, Prince Alfred, then aged fifteen. She complained to her daughter: 'I have been shamefully deceived about Affie; it was promised me that the last year before he went to sea, he should be with us, instead of which he was taken away and I saw but very little of him, and now he is to go away for many months and I shall not see him God knows! when, and Papa is most cruel upon the subject. I assure you, it is much better to have no children than to have them only to give them up! It is too wretched.' Less than a month later she wrote again:

Dearest Affie is gone; and it will be ten months probably before we shall see his dear face which shed sunshine over the whole house, from his amiable, happy, merry temper; again he was much upset at leaving and sobbed bitterly. . . . Still, sad as it is to part from dear Affie, it is nothing to parting with a daughter; she is gone, as your own child, for ever; she belongs to another, and that is so dreadful a feeling for a mother who has watched over every little trifle as well as every serious moment of the life of her daughter, and has with one small act to abdicate all her rights to another, and to a man!

Her favourite pets were the only living creatures from which the Queen was never forcibly parted and on which she could lavish her undiluted affection. In 1893, at the age of seventy-four, Victoria travelled to the South of France where Xavier Paoli, the detective responsible for her security, was struck by the way in which her 'maternal solicitude was also extended to animals . . . as was proved by the constant cares which she bestowed upon Spot, the fox-terrier, Roy, the collie, and Marco, the toy poodle'.[31]

Elisabeth of Bavaria was sixteen when she married the Austrian Emperor Franz Joseph in 1854. Desperately homesick for her native Bavaria, where she had enjoyed a relatively carefree childhood, she was to some extent mollified by having her pet dogs and parrots brought to her in Vienna, and endeavoured to remain as aloof as possible both from the court and, more specifically, her mother-in-law, the Archduchess Sophia, who strongly disapproved of her affection for animals. When Elisabeth became pregnant, Sophia told Franz Joseph: 'If a woman is always looking at animals, especially during the earlier months, the children may grow up to resemble them. She had better either look in her looking-glass or at you. That would have my complete approval.'[32] A daughter, Sophia, was born in 1855, to be followed by Gisela the following year, Rudolf in 1858 and Maria Valeria a decade later. Elisabeth's niece, Countess Larisch, was struck by her 'stunted maternal instinct. In the course of years, the Archduchess Sophia had succeeded in estranging Gisela and Rudolf from their own mother. Consequently, when Valeria was born in 1868, the Empress guarded her with jealous zeal, brooking no interference in her education.'[33]

The event that was crucial to Elisabeth's decision was the breeching of Archduke Rudolf in 1865 at the age of seven, when his *aja* (governess), Baroness Caroline von Welden, to whom he was devoted, was replaced by a tutor, Major-General Ludwig von Gondrecourt, whose belief in his charge needing tough handling took such extreme forms that the Baroness personally begged the Emperor to intervene. Among the methods he employed was the firing without warning of blank cartridges in his room to test the boy's reactions. Franz Joseph ignored the Empress's pleas, remembering his own affection for his *aja* and putting it all down to an excess of affection. When the Empress heard of the scare tactics to which Rudolf had been subjected, involving being left behind a locked gate at the imperial game reserve, the Lainzer Tiergarten, and told that a wild boar was approaching, causing the complete collapse of the boy's nerves, she issued an ultimatum to the Emperor. He was made to decide between herself and Gondrecourt:

> I wish full and unlimited powers shall be accorded to me in all matters concerning the children, the choice of their household, of their place of residence, and complete control over their upbringing; in short I alone must decide everything about them until they attain their majority. Furthermore I wish that all matters concerning my personal affairs, such for example as the choice of my household, my place of residence, all changes in domestic arrangements etc., etc., shall be left for me alone to decide.[34]

Gondrecourt was replaced by General Joseph Latour von Thurnburg, for whom Rudolf felt an affection until his dying day, entrusting him in his will with the care of his pet dog, Blak.

Elisabeth subrogated her feelings into her dogs, and when she became 'the wandering Empress' in the 1870s, travelling throughout Europe in order to escape what she called the '*corvée*' of court life, she confessed to missing them 'more than her children',[35] although she often took a brace with her. Her preference was for enormous breeds and the kennels at

Schönbrunn were filled with Newfoundlands, St Bernards and Great Danes looked after by the 'dog-boy', as the Keeper of the Imperial Dogs was familiarly known. When she returned from a trip to England in 1882, 'the touching welcome he [Franz Joseph] always gave her on her return to Vienna seems to have moved her less than the boisterous welcome of her favourite dog'.[36] When her Irish wolfhound, Shadow, died, Elisabeth locked herself away for days. The death of her children nevertheless devastated her. Sophia died of measles at the age of two in Buda and it was ten years before Elisabeth could be persuaded to return to the city. When Rudolf committed suicide at Mayerling in 1889 she almost lost her mind. Lord Ormathwaite, Master of Ceremonies to King Edward VII and King George V, remembered seeing her at Cap Martin in 1891 with her sister, Countess Trani, rambling about dogs and horses: 'Never shall I forget her expression. . . . One saw her soul laid bare through her eyes, and if I ever saw a soul in pain it was upon this occasion. My eyes filled with tears and I felt miserable for a long time afterwards . . .'[37]

ROYAL MARRIAGE

Notwithstanding his earlier description of royal assassination as being one of 'the risks of the profession', Franz Joseph was inconsolable when Elisabeth was murdered in 1898 and resisted pressure to take a second wife. By the standards of royal marriage, theirs had not been unsuccessful. Her wanderings across Europe were prompted less by a desire to avoid Franz Joseph than to shirk her irksome duties at court. As with Marie Antoinette before her, the determination to withdraw from public life and enjoy some measure of privacy led – albeit with less damaging consequences – to unsubstantiated allegations of sexual infidelity which further compounded their demoralisation.

For kings and princes, adultery was not merely a birthright and a pleasure, it was virtually compulsory. Lord Hervey, describing the relationship between George II and the Countess of Suffolk, claimed the King 'seemed to look upon a mistress rather as a necessary appurtenance to his grandeur as a prince than an addition to his pleasures as a man, and thus only pretended to distinguish what it was evident he overlooked and affected to caress what it was manifest he did not love'.[38] Mistresses served to bolster the royal image of virility and potency and were particularly important in cases where the royal wife was slow to conceive or infertile. The reputation of Louis XVI, who was dilatory in producing heirs, took no mistresses, and showed uxorious indulgence to his seemingly frivolous wife, suffered irretrievably.

Both Queen Caroline, George II's consort, and the Empress Elisabeth all but encouraged the extramarital liaisons of their husbands, the former in order to be spared the interminable boredom of the King's company, and the latter to fill the vacuum created by her prolonged absences abroad. Many royal wives viewed these peccadilloes less favourably, especially when mistresses were overbearing and tactless. The life of Marie de Medici was poisoned by the mistress of Henri IV, Henriette d'Entragues, Marquise de Verneuil, who referred to the new Queen as 'the fat banker' and, armed with a signed promise of marriage from the King, did her utmost to prevent her children from being reared alongside his legitimate offspring whom she audaciously referred to as 'bastards'. The scandalised Queen was not beyond raising her fist to the King and the court resounded with the noise of their rows.[39]

When kings married infertile wives and either would not, or could not, divorce them, illegitimate children were a necessary affirmation of virility. Those who failed to procreate were susceptible to charges of effeminacy which were highly damaging to the monarchy. Henri IV's predecessor, Henri III, was regularly lampooned as a homosexual transvestite surrounded by '*mignons*' at a time when France was rent by civil war. L'Estoile noted in 1578 how 'such and other forms of behaviour, truly unworthy of the great and magnanimous King he was, gradually made this prince detested'.[40] Irrespective of their sexual predilections, men in the line of succession fulfilled their conjugal obligations for *raisons d'état*. One of the few exceptions was Frederick the Great, who, in 1732, a year before his wedding to Elizabeth Christina (daughter of the Duke of Brunswick-Wolfenbuttel, 1715–97, Queen from 1740), wrote to his sister Wilhelmina: 'I do not like the princess; on the contrary, she rather repels me, and our marriage is meaningless, as both friendship and union are out of the question.'[41] Frederick never revised his opinion and, although they cohabited at Rheinsberg for seven years, he abandoned her for the Neues

Palais in Potsdam and Sans-Souci the moment his father died in 1740 and she never once saw either palace. Of women generally, he later said: 'I have only one, and that is too much for me.'[42]

After four years of wedlock it was only with great difficulty that Louis XIII was persuaded by his favourite, the Duc de Luynes, to consummate his marriage to Anne of Austria, 'resisting to the utmost, until the tears welled up in his eyes'.[43] Whether his reluctance was due to recollections of his parents' stormy relationship or of his father's indelicate assertion that 'the grandeur of Spain was the product of the lance of flesh'[44] is necessarily highly speculative. Their eldest son, the future Louis XIV, was born in 1638, twenty-two years after their wedding, and Philippe, Duc d'Orléans, in 1640. Monsieur, as the latter was known, married Henrietta, daughter of Charles I, in 1661 and when her brother Charles II announced his marriage to the Portuguese infanta he wrote to her: 'yett I hope I shall intertaine her at least better the first night than he did you.'[45] Henrietta had to compete with a number of favourites, including the Chevalier de Lorraine, who tried to effect a separation in 1670 and behaved so badly that Louis XIV finally lost patience and had him imprisoned. Notwithstanding their mutual disregard, two daughters issued from the marriage, to be followed by a further three children in the course of Monsieur's second marriage to Charlotte, daughter of the Elector Palatine.

From the lengthy correspondence that Madame kept up with various German relations, there emerges a clear picture of life with the Duc d'Orléans. In 1683, she ruminated: 'When other enemies hate you and do you an injury, there is always the consolation that some day you can pay them back, but against this one I am not allowed to seek vengeance, and even if it were permitted I should not want to do it, since no misfortune comes to him that I do not share. Indeed, if he is in trouble it falls to my lot alone to soothe him. Everything bad that happens to him I share, but of anything good I have no part.' In 1696 she complained:

> Monsieur has had all the silver which came from the Palatinate melted
> and sold and has given the money to his minions. Every day new
> favourites are brought to him and he sells and pawns all his jewels in
> order to make them presents, and, as God is my witness, if Monsieur

were to die today I should be dependent tomorrow on the favour of the King and would find myself without daily bread. Monsieur says publicly, and does not try to hide it from either his daughter or me, that he is getting old and has no time to lose, and that he does not intend to save anything, but will use everything in order to amuse himself to the end . . . and he acts as he talks . . . in order to take my mind off these sorry thoughts I hunt as often as possible.

After his death, Madame revealed:

All my life, since my earliest youth, I have considered myself so ugly that I have never been tempted to use much ornamentation. Jewels and dress only attract attention to the wearer. It was a good thing that I felt like this because the late Monsieur, who was extremely fond of dressing up, would have had hundreds of quarrels with me as to which of us should wear the most beautiful diamonds. I never used to dress up without his choosing my entire outfit. He himself used to put the rouge on my cheeks.

Time did little to modify her low opinion of her deceased husband, and nearly a decade later she wrote: 'I cannot imagine how people can remarry. I can understand one motive for doing so, and that would be if one were dying of hunger and saw a chance by so doing of procuring a loaf of bread.'[46] Solitude, and the companionship of her eight dogs, two parrots and a canary, were a desirable alternative.

The heterosexual concupiscence of monarchs like Louis XIV and Charles II was little compensation to their wives. When, in 1673, one of Maria Theresa's Spanish servants was repatriated because of the war, she had to plead with the King's mistress, Madame de Montespan, before the decision was revoked: 'the Queen was thrilled and said she would never forget her debt', recorded the sardonic Madame de Sévigné.[47] By dying in 1683, Maria Theresa was at least spared the humiliating spectacle of the elevation of Louis' illegitimate children which so appalled Saint-Simon. Pepys noted how Charles II, who imitated Louis XIV in almost every respect, drove Catherine to distraction with his infidelities. As early as 1663, a year after their marriage, he heard how 'the Queene is much grieved of late at the King's neglecting her, he having not supped once with her this Quarter of the Year, and almost every night with my Lady Castlemayne'.[48]

Queens with no power sought a refuge in piety and pets. For those with little inclination for the cloistered life, languishing unloved in *mariages blancs*, extreme measures were called for. Catherine the Great overcame her antipathy towards her husband Peter III by having him murdered in 1762. She maintained that 'If this Prince had tried in any way to make himself acceptable when I first came to Russia, or in the early years of our union, I would have opened my heart to him. When I saw that I was the one among his whole entourage to whom he paid the least attention merely because I was his wife, it was natural that I did not find this situation pleasant or to my taste; it was not only boring but also offended and hurt me.'[49] Catherine had coped with the ennui of life at the Russian court by taking lovers. The putative father of her son, Paul, was Peter's gentleman-in-waiting, Sergei Vasilyevich Saltykov, who aban-

Detail of the black spaniel from the 1756 painting by R. Mathieu. Catherine the Great even designed her gardens from the perspective of her dog.

doned her before the birth in 1754. By the end of the year she was consoling herself in the arms of the twenty-three-year-old secretary to the British ambassador in St Petersburg, Stanislaw Poniatowski. Catherine revealed in her memoirs how their affair was exposed at Oranienbaum in 1756:

After dinner, I took the remaining company, which was not very large, to see the bedrooms belonging to the Grand Duke and myself. As we reached my recess, a small dog I had then came running to welcome us and barked ferociously at Count Horn [on an official visit to convey the news of the death of his mother, Catherine's grandmother], but when he caught sight of Count Poniatowski I thought he was going to go mad with joy. The room being very small, no one noticed this except Leon Naryshkine [privy to the secret], his sister-in-law and myself; but Count Horn was not deluded, and while I crossed the rooms to come back to the hall, he pulled Count Poniatowski by the coat and said to him: 'My friend, there can be nothing more treacherous than a small dog; the first thing I used to do with a woman I loved was to be sure and give her one, and it was through them that I learned if someone was more favoured than myself. It is an infallible test. As you see, the dog wanted to eat me up, as he did not know me, but he went mad with joy on seeing you again, for it is clear that this is not the first time you have met.' Count Poniatowski laughed the matter off and told him not to be silly, but was unable to dissuade him. Count Horn merely replied, 'you have nothing to fear. I am the soul of discretion.'[50]

Notwithstanding Poniatowski's return to Poland, suspicions had indeed been aroused at court and, by 1759, Catherine's every move was watched. Peter tried to prevent her going to the theatre and, on one occasion, attempted to countermand her carriages: 'I said that in that case I would walk and that I could not imagine why he wanted me to die of boredom in my room with no one but my dog and my parrot for company.' She threatened to ask the Empress's permission to return to her mother.[51]

ROYAL MISTRESSES

Given the sobriquet 'Messalina of the North' on account of her promiscuity, Catherine the Great nonetheless treated her jilted lovers with greater indulgence than any ruler of modern times; Poniatowski owed the throne of Poland to her patronage. The sexual incontinence to which most kings were prone was generally accepted as proof of virility and their natural prerogative. Mistresses came and went, little lamented. The great majority of royal wives at least enjoyed security of tenure. Mistresses, on the other hand, were disposable commodities relinquished once their looks faded, despite all their Herculean labours to retain royal favour. They had to eliminate ambitious rivals, please and amuse their jaded and often dull lovers while steering their way through the labyrinth of court factions each vying to gain access to the royal ear, the only route to power under monarchical governments. Few were successful: Madame de Pompadour destroyed her health in the process; Wallis Simpson got the husband but lost the throne.

The first hurdle facing an aspiring mistress was to attract royal attention and, for those without an entrée at court, the most auspicious occasion was the hunt, not least because it was the abiding passion of the vast majority of kings. A mastery of the language of the hunt was as essential as fluency in anodyne conversation, for monarchs specialised in uncontroversial topics. Henri IV's letters to the Marquise de Verneuil constantly revert to the subject of the hunt, and Louis XIII spoke of little else, as Madame de Motteville heard from Mademoiselle de Hautefort: 'he never talked to her of anything but dogs, birds, and hunting; and I have known her, with all her virtue, when telling me this history, laugh at him because he dared not come near her when conversing with her.'[52]

Given that animals constituted the principal topic of conversation, mistresses were well advised to acquire them. One of the favourites of Louis XIV, the Duchesse de la Vallière, received her spaniel by way of valediction, as Madame, the Duchesse d'Orléans, related:

> It was at the instigation of the Montespan that the King treated la Vallière so badly. Her heart was broken by it . . . [but] she stayed, through penitence, with the Montespan. The latter, who had more spirit, used to mock at her publicly and treated her very badly, and made the King act in the same way. The King had to cross la Vallière's room when he wished to visit Montespan. He had a beautiful spaniel called Malice, and at the instigation of Montespan he took this little dog and threw it at the duchesse de Vallière, saying, 'Here you are, Madam, this will be company enough for you.' It was all the harder to bear since he was not going to remain with her but was going to visit Montespan. Nevertheless she endured all this patiently. She had as many virtues as Montespan had vices.[53]

Madame loathed both Madame de Montespan and Madame de Maintenon, Louis' morganatic wife, whom she held responsible for the King's decision in 1692 that Madame's son Philippe marry Louis' illegitimate daughter by Montespan. It was therefore with enormous satisfaction that she wrote to the Electress of Hanover in 1701, describing the appearance of Louis' erstwhile mistresses: 'Since I have never been beautiful, I have not lost much. Moreover, I see round me women whom I used to know as beauties, and they are now uglier than I am. No one living would recognise Madame de la Vallière now, and Madame de Montespan has a skin like a piece of paper that children have played with, folding and unfolding it. Her whole face is covered with tiny lines very close together. Her beautiful hair is white as snow and her complexion is red.'[54]

That doyenne of royal mistresses, Madame de Pompadour, who retained her ascendancy over the priapic Louis XV for more than twenty years, confided in her *femme de chambre*, Madame de Hausset, the secrets of her success and the errors of her predecessors:

My life is that of the Christian, a perpetual battle: it was not the same for those who managed to earn the good graces of Louis XIV. Madame de la Vallière allowed herself to be duped by Madame de Montespan; but it was her own fault, or rather, the product of her good nature. Initially, she had no inkling because she could not believe in her friend's treachery. Madame de Montespan was dislodged by Madame de Fontange and supplanted by Madame de Maintenon; but her haughtiness and her capriciousness had alienated the King. Moreover, she had no rivals to match mine: but, by the same token, their baseness is my security and, in general, I have little to fear other than infidelities and the difficulty in finding opportunities to ensure they are but transitory. The King likes variety but is also a creature of habit; he fears scandals and detests intrigue. The little maréchale [de Mirepoix, *dame du palais* of Queen Marie Leszczyńska] told me one day: it is your staircase that the King loves; he has grown accustomed to going up and down it. But if he found another woman to whom he could talk about hunting and business, it would all be the same to him after three days.[55]

Madame de Hausset enjoyed the full confidence of Madame de Pompadour, who paid her the ultimate compliment when she revealed 'the King and I think of you as a cat or dog', and therefore had no objection to her remaining in the room during their *têtes-à-têtes*.[56] Pompadour's genuine love of animals was reflected in her taste in art. After the death of her only daughter, Alexandrine, in 1754, her pets increasingly assumed the role of surrogate children. Unlike children or courtiers, however, they never criticised her often disastrous interventions in government policy, nor referred to her as 'Mother Whore', as did the Dauphin. They remained faithful while the King grew ever more debauched and were oblivious to her waning charms. They kept her company during the interminable hours spent shut in her apartments lest Louis make an impromptu visit, and never oppressed her with the relation of tedious anecdotes of the hunt in which she had to feign an unflagging interest.

Louis XIII *by Ferdinand Elle. Elle was Louis XIII's court painter and one of the founder members of the Académie Royale in 1648.*

ABOVE *In this portrait of Elizabeth Charlotte of the Palatine, attributed to J. B. Ruel, the sitter poses with a Bolognese, the breed she later maintained she disliked.*

TOP LEFT *Benjamin von Block: Emperor Joseph I (1678–1711) at the age of six in party clothes with a cocker spaniel. Painted in 1684, the year the artist was ennobled.*

LEFT *Portrait of Anne of Denmark by Paul van Somer, showing the Queen in hunting costume at Oatlands with five black and white miniature greyhounds bearing AR (Anna Regina) on their collars and a liveried black page in attendance.*

Juan Bautista Martínez del Mazo: Queen Mariana of Spain (1635–1696) in mourning for her husband Philip IV, who died in 1665. Her dwarf, Nicolasito, who also features in Las Meninas, *can be seen in the background.*

LEFT *Sir Anthony Van Dyck,*
Charles I, Henrietta Maria
and their two eldest children,
1632. Known as the 'Great
Piece', it was the largest royal
portrait group painted in
England to that date.

BELOW LEFT *Portrait by*
Jean Ranc of Ferdinand VI
with a greyhound wearing a
green collar. The Infante, eldest
son of Philip V and Marie-
Louise of Savoy, was born in
1713 and would have been
around twelve when the
picture was painted.

BELOW *Portrait by Titian*
of Federico Gonzaga, Duke of
Mantua (1500–40),
c. 1529. The Duke owned
more than a hundred dogs in
the course of his life.

ABOVE *Eugene Boudin: Empress Eugenie on the beach at Trouville with her Maltese, Linda.*

RIGHT **Très Riches Heures du Duc de Berry.** *This illustration by Pol de Limbourg for the month of January shows the Duke dining while the* **chiens-goûteurs** *on the table taste the dishes for poison.*

Daniel Mytens: The King departing for the Chase. *Mytens, the leading court painter throughout the 162*

...d early 1630s, was totally eclipsed when Van Dyck arrived in England in 1632.

Portrait by Jean-Marc Nattier of Princess Marie Adelaide, daughter of Louis XV, with a papillon. Nattier won recognition at court in 1740 with the series of portraits he undertook of the younger sisters of Louis XV's mistress, the Comtesse de Mailly.

LIFE AT COURT

When Madame de Pompadour died in 1764 her body was removed from the palace at Versailles with customary haste. Louis XV, watching the funeral cortège pass below the balcony, shed a few tears and returned to the chase. Dufort de Cheverny, *introducteur des ambassadeurs* at that court, asked himself

a hundred times how a king endowed with the most gracious and honest qualities, could seem so indifferent to the death of those around him; I have only been able to come up with one solution. A king has before his eyes a continually moving picture; everyone in his service works in four-monthly sessions; it is a sort of magic lantern. On the other hand, none of those who serves him dies without leaving vacant a place which must be filled. Thus, while he makes one man happy, the continual change means that the memory of him who he has lost is readily effaced.[57]

Madame de Hausset was equally struck by the coldness in the hearts of kings: 'Nothing moves a prince as much as the news that one of his equals is dying. Nobody talks of anything else; but, as soon as they are dead, the subject is closed for ever.'[58]

The cynicism that characterised monarchs was the inevitable consequence of their upbringing and experience. Simultaneously indulged and deprived in their childhoods, often scarred by violent political upheaval, they were surrounded by fawning courtiers whose capacities and sincerity they were not necessarily intelligent enough to judge. Bishop Burnet lamented that 'princes are so little sensible of merit and great services, that they sacrifice their best servants, not only when their affairs seem to require it, but to gratify the humour of a mistress, or the passion of a rising favourite'.[59] Madame de Motteville opined that

the most serious lessons given to kings make no good impression on their minds; for a turn to ridicule is usually given them, which drives away the virtuous thoughts to which they might otherwise have given birth. Princes seldom meet with persons who speak to them strongly; and those who do so are the ones most frequently treated as ridiculous by the courtiers. This is why, their reason being weakened by the care taken to disguise from them the truth, sovereigns do not apply themselves to distinguish the true from the false; and letting their mind go to laziness and lightly passing over good and over evil, they are nearly always carried whithersoever their ministers are pleased to lead them.[60]

With regard to etiquette, no European court could equal that of China, where the Manchu emperors were so punctilious that the omission of the most minute point established by the court of ceremonies was considered a criminal offence. Nonetheless, Western monarchs – and particularly those at the French and Spanish courts – were stifled by etiquette from which they could only get a brief respite in the saddle. Even Louis XIV, who, at Versailles, had transformed the rituals of protocol into an arm of political control, progressively retreated into the privy quarters of the palace and, in 1684, began work on an inner set of apartments comprising a *Cabinet du Billiard où des Chiens* where he sought relaxation in feeding his pets from his own hand.[61]

The memorialist Primi Visconti described the princesses of the blood at the French court as 'more enslaved than women kept in harems; every move is watched and no man has access to them who is not a spy of the King's'.[62] Madame de Maintenon was of the same view: 'There is no convent in existence with rules of austerity to equal those to which court etiquette subjects the great.'[63] Madame, the Duchesse d'Orléans, considered Versailles as 'more boring . . . than any other place in the world'.[64] In 1666, Pepys heard 'the King . . . speak most in contempt of the ceremoniousnesse of the King of Spain, that he doth nothing but under some ridiculous form or other; and will not piss but another must hold the chamber-pot'.[65] When the Duc d'Anjou became King Philip V of Spain in 1700, he was not so much as allowed to smell a flower or open a letter lest they contain poison.[66]

Charles II might have balked at etiquette once restored to the throne, but he had early learned the art of royal monosyllabism from his experiences at the French court. After his escape from England in 1650, he made his way to Compiègne where his mother, Henrietta Maria, was hoping to engineer his marriage to the Grande Mademoiselle, daughter of Gaston, Duc d'Orléans (1608–60), and the richest of the royal heiresses. She was not impressed by her prospective bridegroom:

I found him good-looking. Perhaps he would win me this time. The King [of France] talked to him of dogs, of horses, of the Prince of Orange, and of hunting in his country. He replied in French. Then the Queen asked him about the state of affairs in England. He did not answer. He was questioned several times upon the seriousness of events in his country; he excused himself from answering by saying that he could not speak our tongue, but I assure you that from that moment I resolved not to carry through this marriage project. I suddenly acquired a most unfavourable opinion of him, because a man of his age should have had some intimate knowledge of the state of affairs in his kingdom![67]

In a letter to Pepys of 1681, John Evelyn lambasted the court circle of the King as 'illustrious persons who have leisure and inclinations to cultivate their minds beyond a farce, a horse, a whore and a dog, which, with very little more, are the confines of knowledge and discourse of most of our fine gentlemen and beaux'.[68]

Madame de Motteville analysed

of what nature is that climate called the Court; its corruption, and how fortunate should they esteem themselves who are not fated to live there. The air is never sweet or serene for any one. Even those who, apparently in perfect prosperity, are adored as gods, are the ones most threatened by tempests. The thunder growls incessantly for great and small; and those whom their compatriots regard with envy know no calm. It is a windy, gloomy region, filled with perpetual storms. Men live there little, and during the time that fortune keeps them there, they are always ill of that contagious malady, ambition, which kills their peace, gnaws their heart, sends fumes to their head and often deprives them of their reason. This disease gives them a continual disgust for better things. They are ignorant of the value of equity, justice, kindliness. The sweetness of life, of innocent pleasures, of all that the sages of antiquity counted as good, seem to them ridiculous; they are incapable of knowing virtue and following its precepts, unless chance may happen to remove them from this region. Then, if they can by absence be cured of their malady, they become wise, they become enlightened; and no man can be so good a Christian or so truly a philosopher as a disillusioned courtier.[69]

The essence of court life changed little over the centuries. The Duke of Windsor stated the case for the Crown when he explained: 'the ceremonious façade that provides the public with a romantic illusion of the higher satisfactions of kingship actually disguises an occupation of considerable drudgery'.[70] Both favourites and servants of the Crown were of questionable loyalty whereas pets were pillars of the royal establishment, unswerving in their attachment. Frederick II, King of Denmark between 1559 and 1588, and father of James I's Queen, Anne, went so far as to create an order of chivalry in recognition of his dog, Wilpret's, unique constancy. That great dog lover, Alexander Pope, wrote to his friend Cromwell in 1709 expressing his admiration for the gesture: 'A Modern Instance of Gratitude to a Dog (tho' we have but such few) is that the Chief Order of Denmark (now call'd the Order of the Elephant) was instituted in memory of the fidelity of a Dog nam'd Wild-Brat, by one of their Kings who had been deserted by his Subjects, & gave (his Order) this Motto, or to this effect, which still remains; Wild-Brat was faithful.'[71]

To offset the tedium and cope with the strain of office, many monarchs fondled their pets during council meetings. Henri III would sit bolt upright while receiving ambassadors so as not to disturb the three or more tiny dogs which he kept in a basket suspended by a ribbon from his neck.[72] Charles II was one of the worst culprits and invited some of the most scathing criticism. In 1667 Pepys decried 'the silliness of the King, playing with his dog all the while, or his codpiece, and not minding the business, and what he said was mighty weak'.[73] His dogs were the only creatures in which he truly trusted for, as Bishop Burnet commented after Charles's death:

> He had a very ill opinion both of men and women; and did not think that there was either sincerity or chastity in the world out of principle, but that some had either the one or the other out of humour or vanity. He thought that nobody did serve him out of love: and so he was quits with the world, and loved others as little as he thought they loved him. He hated business, and could not be easily brought to mind any: but when it was necessary, and he was set to it, he would stay as long as his ministers had work for him. The ruin of his reign, and of all his affairs, was occasioned chiefly by his delivering himself up at his first coming over to a mad range of pleasure.[74]

Alabaster portrait of Frederick II of Denmark,
inscribed with the motto 'Wilpret is True'.

John Evelyn was of much the same opinion and it was left to the solitary voice of the poet-courtier Rochester to express delight that:

> His very dog at Council Board,
> Sits grave and wise as any Lord.

Charles II was not exceptional. After the death of his favourite dog, Pompe, in 1703, Charles XII of Sweden (1682–1718) transferred his affections to the feline race and, rather than disturb his cat as it lay asleep on his papers, would write around it, leaving blank the space which it occupied. Similarly, Catherine the Great's letters to Grimm often bore the imprint of a paw mark. Louis XV so relished the company of his cat during council meetings that he named it Collègue.

Even kings who despised etiquette and eschewed it at their courts were loth to be parted from their pets. Peter the Great (1672–1725) was virtually devoid of family feeling: he dispatched both his half-sisters, Sophia and Maria, as well as his first wife, Eudoxia, to nunneries and almost certainly had his son Alexis murdered. Yet he could refuse his dog, Finette, nothing and the diminutive greyhound never left his side. Peter had issued an edict forbidding the presentation of petitions on pain of death. When a court official was accused of corruption and sentenced to the knout, neither his friends nor the Tsar's second wife, Catherine, dared intervene despite their belief in his innocence. Catherine had recourse to the stratagem of attaching an appeal to Finette's collar. Peter granted clemency.[75]

Frederick the Great was no less devoted to his English greyhound, Biche, than Peter was to Finette, and allowed it to sit on his lap while he discussed state affairs. It certainly received far greater affection than any other mortal in the course of his life. He justified his attitude in a letter to Wilhelmina of 1748: 'Biche has good sense and understanding, and I see every day people who behave less rationally than her. If this dog has guessed my feelings towards her, at least she returns them graciously and I love her for that all the more.'[76]

Statue of Frederick the Great with two greyhounds, by Johann Gottfried Schadow. Having failed to secure an official commission to model the late King, Schadow cast this statue at his own expense in 1821–2.

The Purpose of Pets

Pets were kept at court for functional as well as psychological reasons. As Elizabeth I said, 'Princes are set as it were upon stages, in the sight and view of all the world.' Exotic animals contributed to the magnificence of the court and 'noble' breeds were items of prestige, frequently employed in the hunt which, until modern times, was not simply the sport of kings *par excellence* but the incarnation of royal splendour. Cats, and certain breeds of dog, were a means of controlling the spread of vermin. Until La Bouche became an established department of the household, *chiens-goûteurs* tasted all the food at the royal table to ensure against poisoning. Dogs acted as sentinels in the bedchamber, in the military camp and when monarchs were travelling. At the ancient court of China, they were trained to hold candles in their mouths to illuminate the royal path, and the poodles fashionable at Versailles in the late eighteenth century were adept at holding their mistresses' trains in their jaws to prevent their tripping.

From the Renaissance until the nineteenth century, when they were transferred to zoological gardens, the most exotic animals at European courts were kept in royal menageries. In India and parts of Africa, it was not unknown for wild animals to be allowed to roam within the palaces themselves well into the twentieth century. The Grand Duke Alexander recalled how, in the 1930s, he was asked by Zaudita-the-Divine, aunt of Ras Tafari (Haile Selassie), to be guest of honour at a state dinner:

> I was invited to inspect the trained wild animals of Her Imperial
> Majesty and we mixed for a while with a score of lions, tigers and pan-
> thers walking at large in a spacious hall. My secretary tried to escape
> this additional sign of Monarchical Hospitality but was told by
> Zaudita that a man of his wide knowledge of the world would miss a
> great deal by not seeing the results of the training methods practised
> in Abyssinia. I could see his lips move in fervent prayer and when I
> asked him to pat the head of a particularly beautiful panther he turned
> livid and swallowed a couple of pills.[77]

In ancient Abyssinia dogs were so highly venerated that the inhabitants used to elect one as their king, keeping it in great state, surrounded by a numerous train of officers and guards.[78] If European dogs achieved no such ascendancy they nonetheless filled an important role as symbols of royal splendour. Borso, the first Duke of Ferrara, travelled to Rome in 1471, the year of his death, accompanied by five hundred gentlemen whose valets wore cloth of gold and his grooms silver brocade. His one hundred and fifty mules were caparisoned in white, red and green, and there were eighty pages, each of whom led four greyhounds on leashes, as well as bands of Orientals leading several tame leopards. So impressive were these displays of wealth and magnificence that European rulers elsewhere were eager to imitate Italian courtly examples.

Pomp and ostentation could also be used as a smokescreen. When Louis XI was dying in 1483, Philippe de Commynes described how

he sent men off in all directions outside the kingdom. To promote the marriage with England he promptly paid King Edward and the other Englishmen what he had granted them. In Spain it was friendship and fair words with presents for all. Everywhere he had horses or mules bought, whatever the cost, or at least in those countries where he wanted them to think he was well, though not in this kingdom. At great expense he sent for dogs from every quarter; mastiffs from Spain, small greyhound bitches, greyhounds and spaniels from Brittany, small shaggy dogs from Valencia, all of which he bought more dearly than people usually like to sell them. He sent especially to Sicily for a mule from a certain officer of that country and paid him double its value. In Naples he bought horses and strange animals from all over the place, such as a kind of small wolf, called a jackal from Barbary, which was no larger than a small fox. To Denmark he sent for two kinds of animals, one called an elk which has the body of a stag, is as large as a wild ox and has thick short horns. The other was a reindeer, which is like a fallow deer in body and colour and has much larger antlers, for I have seen a reindeer with fifty-four points. For six each of these animals he paid the merchants four thousand five hundred German florins. When all these animals were brought to him he did not count the cost nor, in the majority of cases, did he even speak to those who had brought them. And so, in short, he did many similar things so that he was more feared by his neighbours and subjects than he had ever been, for that was his intention and he did it for that reason.[79]

In the East dogs and cats had significant ceremonial duties to perform. In ancient Japan there were special detachments of the infantry of the imperial guard called *hayabito* who wore dog masks and whose orders were to bark like dogs not only when the emperor started out on a journey but also at curves in the road and river crossings. They were also present at certain court ceremonies and there remain very old stone images at Yamato and Nava of men with dog-heads. The *hayabito*, in the form of statues, guarded dead emperors in the *misasagi* or burial grounds.[80] In Siam cats guarded the palaces and temples and, when a member of the royal family died, one of his cats was buried with him; small holes were pierced in the tomb and when – and if – it escaped, the royal soul was deemed to have passed into the animal which was thereupon conducted to the temple with all due honours. At coronations a cat was carried by the court chamberlain in procession to the throne-room.

When the Dowager Empress of China died in 1908, her favourite Pekingese was led before the coffin by the chief eunuch to the Eastern Tombs:

> Li Lien-ying, old and weary, preceded the Imperial bier to the region
> of the tombs, carrying the Empress's favourite dog, Moo-tan [peony],
> a yellow and white Pekingese with a white spot on its forehead. Thus
> was observed a precedent set nine hundred years before, for on the
> death of the Emperor T'ai Tsung of the Sung Dynasty [in 997], his
> little dog, T'ao Hua [peach flower] had followed the Son of Heaven to
> his last resting place and had died of grief at the portal of the
> Imperial tomb. The next Emperor, Chen Tsung, had issued a decree,
> ordering the little dog's body to be wrapped in the cloth of an
> Imperial umbrella and buried alongside its master. Tzu-hsi's dog is also
> supposed to have died of grief, but some say that Moo-tan was smug-
> gled away during the internment and sold by one of the eunuchs.[81]

Despite their credentials as the most highly qualified vermin controllers, cats were eschewed at most European courts between the thirteenth and seventeenth centuries as a result of their unfortunate association with first plague and, later, witchcraft. Many monarchs found the spectacle of their dogs slaughtering rats and mice wholesale extremely gratifying. Shortly before his death in 1483, when he was too weak to move from his bedchamber,

Louis XI regularly summoned his best rat- and mice-catching dogs and watched them at work.[82] Louis XIII witnessed a combat between cats and rats at the Louvre in 1614.[83] Eventually, the position of rat-catcher became a respected office at court and, under the Hanovers, incumbents like Robert Smith, in the service of George II's daughter, Princess Amelia, wore a special uniform of scarlet and yellow worsted, on which were depicted figures of mice devouring wheatsheaves.[84] Rat-catching was a highly reputable and lucrative business at a time when vermin posed a very real threat to human life. To possess a pet adept at killing rats and mice was a universal aspiration. In 1814, the Prince Regent's daughter, Princess Charlotte, had three tricolour toy spaniels which she bred with Bull-Dog Billy, the most famous rat-catcher in England. On one occasion Billy had killed a hundred rats in Cock Pit, Duck Lane, Westminster, in five and a half minutes. Billy's proud owner was paid £10 for his dog's stud services. In 1884 Victoria had a rough-coated Chinese pug shown in England by John Strugnell which had its own business card bearing the legend 'Ratcatcher to HM Queen Victoria', and so efficiently did it attend to its office that it was called Strugnell's King Dick.

In the course of the nineteenth century dachshunds (badger-hounds), acquired a reputation for being supremely able rat-catchers. One of the first specimens of the breed to reach England was Däckel, a gift to Queen Victoria in 1845 from her relations in Coburg, and the forebear of five generations of royal dachshunds. In 1849 Däckel won its laurels when it pounced upon an enormous rat at Windsor in the presence of the Queen, who remarked: 'the rat made an awful noise, though he was killed right out pretty quickly.' At the Tsarist court, the obligation to keep dachshunds was not always welcomed. The Grand Duke Alexander had 'bitter memories of the strict regulations which made myself and my cousins wear plain uniforms, limited our choice of household pets to German dachshunds and Persian cats, and forced us to sleep on narrow, iron bunks'.[85]

The practice of using *chiens-goûteurs* to taste food for poisoning appears to have originated at the Burgundian court, and the small puppies that can be seen on the banqueting table in the *Très Riches Heures* of the Duc de Berry, a work produced between 1413 and 1416, reflect assassination fears rather than primitive eating habits. However vigilant the *officiers de la Bouche* might

Portrait of Däckel by Sir Edwin Landseer. Däckel arrived from Germany in 1845 and died aged fifteen in 1859. The dachshund was an ace rat-catcher.

be, none could guarantee that the royal fare had not been tampered with. No means existed for analysing poison and the inefficacy of antidotes was proven by the number of deaths among the prisoners on whom they were tested. Ignorance of the causes of disease inevitably led to melodramatic conjecture when people in apparently good health unexpectedly died. In 1670, when Henrietta d'Orléans lay dying in agony, she alleged she had been poisoned but balked at the suggestion made by her husband, Monsieur, the prime suspect, that some of the chicory water she had recently been drinking be tested on her dog. Her favourite *femme de chambre*, Madame des Bordes, who had prepared the mixture, regarded the allegations as foundless and sipped the drink herself without suffering any ill effects.[86] Although Monsieur was exculpated, the suspicion of his guilt lingered on for years. In 1689, when Monsieur appointed d'Effiat, his Master of the Horse, to the position of governor of their son, Madame was less shocked by the fact that he was known to be a practising homosexual – someone who liked to storm the *'château de derrière'*, as she put it – than by his rumoured involvement in the death of Henrietta.[87] Between 1670 and 1682 the so-called Affair of the Poisons, involving as it did the most illustrious names at the French court, kept the whole of France spellbound. The most famous case was that of the Marquise de Brinvilliers, who, in 1676, was tried for the murder of her father and two brothers and for attempting to poison her husband. She was executed and burned, leading Madame de Sévigné to observe, 'we are all inhaling her now ... and will develop toxic humours as a consequence.'[88] The obsession with poisoning did not die out until well into the eighteenth century. Even in the nineteenth century, when the employment of *chiens-goûteurs* had fallen into desuetude, monarchs reverted to such time-honoured methods when deprived of loyal court officials whose duty it was to remove the sources of culinary anxiety, notably when they were in exile or prison. Napoleon, who often reverted to the subject of the Brinvilliers affair on St Helena, would have been well advised to modify his low opinion of dogs, if only for practical reasons. Carlota, ex-Empress of Mexico, whose mind had become deranged as a result of the shooting of Maximilian at Queretaro in 1867, refused under any circumstances to be parted from her cat, which sampled all the food which, in her paranoia, she believed to be poisoned.

Another important function of dogs was to guard their royal owners and alert them to intruders. Until the nineteenth century, other than in periods of civil unrest, public access to palaces was relatively easy, and even the gentlemen of the bedchamber were not always able to prevent strangers gaining entry to the monarch's privy quarters. Dogs, with their more acute hearing, were a sensible security measure. Edward VI's life was saved by his dog in January 1549. Seymour, Lord High Admiral and brother of both Protector Somerset and the King's mother, Jane Seymour, was planning to marry Princess Elizabeth and seize power. Intending to kidnap Edward, he stole into the palace but on unlocking the door leading from the antechamber to the King's bedroom, the King's dog started barking furiously. Although Seymour promptly shot it dead, a Yeoman of the Guard had heard the noise and rushed to Edward's assistance. The King was mortified by the death of his pet and refused to listen to Seymour's lame excuses. He was sent to the Tower and executed two months later.

During the French Wars of Religion in the sixteenth century, fears of assassination were so rife that the court assumed the appearance of an entrenched camp. In a letter of 1576, Henri de Navarre, later King Henri IV, described the situation: 'The court is the strangest you have ever seen. All of us are virtually always poised to cut each other's throats. We carry daggers, chain-mail shirts and even breast-plates under our cloaks . . . the King is no less at risk than I am.' The King, Henri III, was evidently fully aware of his vulnerability for he created the famous Forty-Five, a unit of bodyguards later immortalised by Alexandre Dumas. They were to remain in permanent service in the royal antechamber. In 1589 he recruited a further four gentlemen whose duty was to keep a vigil eye on the King throughout the day, never allowing him out of their sight.[89] Henri III, a devotee of small dogs, had three particular favourites in 1589: Liline, Titi and Mimi, which slept at night on his bed and had been trained to bark at the slightest irregularity. When a stranger entered the royal presence at Saint-Cloud on 1 August 1589, the King, foolishly reassured by the monk's habit his assassin, Clément, was wearing, chose to ignore Liline's querulous barking and was stabbed to death.[90]

Unwelcome intruders were not necessarily assassins. At the court of the young Louis XV, during the regency of the Duc d'Orléans, the Princesse de Conti became so incensed by the endless unannounced nocturnal visits paid to her by her jealous husband that

> she had recourse to a singular stratagem. She trained an enormous mastiff to sleep on her bed and ward off unwanted callers by biting them. One night, in order to lure the prince – who slept in the apartment directly under hers – to her quarters, she made so much noise that he promptly arrived, hoping to catch her in the act of adultery. The Prince de Conti, beside himself, searched under the bed and in every corner of the room, wielding his sword. The princesse, who had rehearsed her *coup*, unleashed the dog which then tore his hand to shreds. A violent quarrel ensued between husband and wife, who wanted to save the life of the dog. The prince ended up stroking the dog and the wife declared that the mastiff only slept with her every night to protect her against intruders.[91]

EXILE AND PRISON

Royal exiles and prisoners were even more dependent on their pets to perform sentry duties, act as *officiers de santé* and fill the void created by the restrictions of their confinement. Mary Stuart acquired her life-long love of dogs at the Valois court where she arrived in 1548, at the age of five. Betrothed to the Dauphin Francis, her junior by a year, and at a loss to speak a word of French, the twenty-two lapdogs with which they constantly played must have proved a welcome diversion. The Dauphin ascended the throne in 1559 but died the following year. Mary Stuart returned to Scotland with some of the Maltese dogs so fashionable at the French court; blue velvet collars feature in her palace inventories. They had a daily ration of two loaves of bread and the special servants who attended to their needs were periodically dispatched to France, presumably to procure new specimens.[92]

From 1568, when she fled her rebellious subjects and threw herself on the mercy of Elizabeth I, until her execution nineteen years later, Mary Stuart remained a captive, the conditions of her detention progressively deteriorating. She never saw her son James again and the gifts she sent were intercepted. Meanwhile, he was ably brainwashed by George Buchanan into believing that his mother was a cold-hearted killer, responsible for his father's death. As a woman who had passionately enjoyed the chase, she felt the lack of exercise and fresh air keenly, becoming ill and prematurely aged. By her death she was completely lame. She sought consolation in embroidery, the devotion of a handful of remaining servants and in her religious faith. In the last decade of her life she received several secret visits from a Jesuit priest, Samérie. She was not, however, entirely cut off from the outside world and, in about 1574, received some Maltese dogs from France, one of which was included in a miniature painted of her in 1578, possibly commissioned by her gaoler, Bess

Detail from the engraving by Perrissin showing the Maltese dogs so coveted by Mary, Queen of Scots.

of Hardwick.[93] These dogs, or at least one of them, accompanied Mary Stuart to her last prison, Fotheringhay Castle, in 1586. It was with her when she was executed on 8 February 1587: 'Then one of the executioners pulling off her garters espied her little dog, which was crept under her clothes, which could not be gotten forth but by force. It afterwards would not depart from the dead corpse, but came and laid between her head and shoulders, which being imbrued with her blood was carried away and washed, as all things else were, that had any blood, was either burned or clean washed.'[94] Possibly it was with his grandmother in mind that Charles I took his spaniel Rogue with him to Carisbrooke Castle in 1648, refusing to be parted from it when he was beheaded the following year.

Exile was paradise compared to the hell of imprisonment, particularly when the victim was fabulously rich. La Grande Mademoiselle, Anne-Marie-Louise d'Orléans, exiled to St Fargeau for her part in the Fronde des Princes, as the revolt against Cardinal Mazarin between 1650 and 1653 was known, was nonetheless cast into despondency: 'fear and vexation took possession of me. I wept bitterly. To be exiled from court; to have only a dwelling as ugly as this; to realise that this was the best of my châteaux!'[95] Hunting, and her dogs, became her chief consolation and occupation. What should have been a joyful reconciliation with her father, Gaston, Louis XIV's uncle, at Blois in 1657 was marred by the fact that he was

> exceedingly ill at ease, and did not know what to say; if it had not been for my dogs, one of them called Queen, the other Madame Mouse, both of them greyhounds, no one would have said anything. Monsieur began to pet them. Everything he did with the intention of pleasing me made me feel wretched; I felt like weeping. Nothing remarkable happened at Blois while I was there except that Madame Mouse fell into the moat and dislocated her leg. As I was returning from a walk I heard her yelping, and ran to her; the doctor tried his best to heal her leg, but couldn't, and to help things along they put her in a manure-pile in one of the courtyards. Monsieur went out at midnight to see how she was. This was considered by the hoi-polloi a wonderful proof of my father's tenderness: as for myself I should have preferred marks of affection and kindness that were more essential.[96]

Like Mary Stuart earlier, Marie Antoinette had loved dogs since childhood. It was a taste she shared with her many siblings and her mother, Maria Theresa, who together decorated the Porcelain Room at Schönbrunn with paintings of dogs and cats depicted in imaginary Japanese settings. Although the painting by Martin van Meytens II (1695–1770) of the Emperor and Empress with their eleven surviving children was clearly intended to show dynastic solidity, the two small dogs playing skittishly in the foreground suggest the relative domesticity and informality that prevailed at the Hapsburg, as opposed to the French Bourbon, court. In 1776 Johannes Zoffany undertook a series of family portraits at the behest of the Archduke Leopold, including one of the latter with a small dog and another showing his sister Maria Christina with a spaniel on her lap. So pleased was the Empress with the results that the artist was made a Baron of the Holy Roman Empire. Although Zoffany did not travel to France to paint the French Queen, Marie Antoinette's admiration for artists adept at the portrayal of animals was evident from her patronage of the painter Anne Vallayer-Coster (1744–1818), one of France's most accomplished *animaliers*, to whom she gave lodgings at the Louvre in 1781.

Marie Antoinette married the future Louis XVI in 1770, and her *lecteur*, the Abbé de Vermond, entered the nuptial chamber after the wedding night to find the Dauphine rolling on the floor with a puppy. She soon applied to the Austrian ambassador, Mercy-Argenteau, to have her pug, Mops, brought to Versailles from Vienna, where French nuptial protocol insisted it remain, and he lost no time in informing the Empress how Marie Antoinette's passion for dogs and general frivolity was causing consternation at the Bourbon court. (In 1810, when Napoleon married Marie-Louise, the daughter of the Austrian Emperor, he was determined to observe the 1770 protocol in every detail and she too had to forsake her pet dog when she left Vienna.) Maria-Theresa issued a sharp reprimand to her daughter in 1771: 'a shameless complaisance for people who have subjugated you by treating you like a child, in arranging rides with you, playing with children and dogs, etc. Such are the ties which attach you to them in preference to your master, and which in the long run will make you an object of ridicule, neither loved nor esteemed.'[97] As usual, Marie Antoinette paid lip-service to her mother while continuing to do precisely as she pleased, viewing the elaborate etiquette at Versailles with ill-concealed contempt. By walking on the terraces with her pets she distracted the spaniels of the Swiss Guard, which were specially trained to scent intruders.

Through no fault of her own, Marie Antoinette's marriage remained unconsummated for seven years. His doctors' advice that exercise and a healthy diet would cure his sexual problems could not have fallen on more receptive ears, and Louis XVI spent every disposable moment of his time hunting, before retiring early to bed while his vivacious wife amused herself at the gaming tables with a coterie of conspicuous favourites. It was largely as a result of pressure from Marie Antoinette's brother, Joseph, that Louis was finally persuaded to undergo the minor surgery that his phimosis necessitated and, in 1778, their first child, Madame Royale, was born. By this time the image of both the King and Queen was irredeemably tarnished.

Of all Marie Antoinette's favourites the Swede, Axel Fersen, whom she met at a ball in Paris in 1774, proved the most devoted and steadfast when the revolution broke out in 1789. They shared a common bond in their love of dogs and Fersen's pet, Odin, accompanied him in all his peregrinations across Europe as unofficial ambassador of King Gustavus III. In 1784, when he returned to Sweden for a year, he told his secretary to contact the breeder, de Boye, in order to obtain 'not a small dog . . . tell him it is for the Queen of France'.[98] Fersen returned to France in 1785, the same year as Marie Antoinette's younger son, Louis, was born. If he did indeed bring a large Swedish dog back with him, it would have been allowed nowhere near the infant, for reasons that the Queen explained to the Governess of the Children of France, the Duchesse de Tourzel, in her letter of appointment of 1789: 'any noise to which he is not accustomed frightens him; for example, he is afraid of dogs, because he has heard them bark near him. I have never forced him to see them, because I believe that as his reason develops, his fears will subside.'

The small dog that Marie Antoinette kept at the Tuileries was a gift from another favourite, the Princesse de Lamballe, who had procured it in England and brought it back to France with her when she returned in 1792 at the Queen's request. Whatever her maternal misgivings, Marie Antoinette urgently needed a dog to alert her to dangerous intruders. The Duchesse de Tourzel, ostensibly unaware of Marie Antoinette's predilection for animals, chafed: 'Will anyone credit that a Queen of France was reduced to having a little dog sleep in her room, to warn her if the slightest noise was heard in it?' By naming the dog Thisbée after the heroine of clas-

sical mythology who killed herself rather than live without her Pyramus, Marie Antoinette may have intended to flatter Fersen who, even after the abortive flight to Varennes of 1791, had not abandoned hope of rescuing the royal family from captivity. Gustavus III had heard of his succession to the Swedish throne during a performance of *Pyramus and Thisbé* in 1772. Alternatively, the naming of the dog may provide a clue to its breed; Buffon, in his *Histoire Naturelle*, referred to a strain of spaniel – now identified as almost certainly the cocker – as the *Pyrame*. Fersen and Marie Antoinette had met for the last time at the Tuileries in February 1792. Later in the year he was to realise that the dangers attendant upon assisting the King and

Detail of a cocker spaniel from the painting by Block. Buffon in his **Histoire Naturelle** *referred to the cocker as the Pyrame.*

Queen were not confined to France; he wrote to Marie Antoinette from Brussels in August lamenting: 'To cap all my vexations I have lost my two dogs; they were poisoned this morning and died simultaneously. Their loss has deeply grieved me, they were very precious.'[99] Thisbée almost certainly accompanied the Queen when the royal family was transferred to the Temple after the revolutionary *journée* of 10 August, and in all probability remained there after she was incarcerated at the Conciergerie in August 1793. Madame Royale's spaniel, Mignon, may well have been one and the same dog, the name alone changed in order to remove any sentimental reference to Fersen, whom the Queen's daughter heartily despised.

In their reaction against the Terror, contemporary historians gave highly romanticised accounts of Thisbée's forlorn efforts to reach Marie Antoinette at the Conciergerie, culminating in the dog's eventual suicide. The dog that did provide a small measure of comfort to the Queen in the last remaining months of her life was almost certainly inherited from an earlier victim of the guillotine. The revolutionary prisons ran amok with such dogs, and the gaoler's wife, Madame Richard, had taken pity on Marie Antoinette and done all in her power to improve her dismal lot. Monseigneur de Salamon, a friend of the Richards from *ancien régime* days, was imprisoned in the Queen's cell after her death. He managed to persuade Richard to allow the door to be opened at daybreak:

> On the first morning that I benefited from this measure a pug dog came into the room as the door opened, and after jumping on my bed and exploring it all over, ran out again. This was the Queen's pug, which Richard had obtained possession of, and treated with the greatest care. The dog's object in coming in like that was to smell his mistress's mattresses. I saw him behave in this way every morning at the same hour, for three whole months, and in spite of all my efforts I was never able to catch him.[100]

Madame Royale was released from the Temple in December 1795. Fersen, who saw her with Mignon in Vienna early the following year, described the dog as 'a sort of red-and-white spaniel. It had belonged to her brother and was his companion in misfortune; when he died the dog was forgotten but its unerring instinct led it to Madame's apartment where it squatted outside the door until allowed in. Madame, who was ignorant of her brother's death, recognised the dog and kept it, believing it had got lost.'[101] This was the story he heard but it did not tally with the facts, as he himself was aware: 'The dog which Madame said she was allowed to take with her and had belonged to her brother is undoubtedly a mistake, he had an aversion to them and they terrified him.'[102] Furthermore, she had not seen Louis since his isolation from the rest of his family in 1793 and could only have recognised the dog if she had known it previously. The eyewitness, François Hüe, *officier de la Chambre du Roi*, who had attended the royal family from the time they were first incarcerated in the Temple, described the dog in 1795 as having been *'for a long time* the sole witness of her [Madame Royale's] misery'.[103] The beatification of her mother demanded that no act of kindness, not even the toleration of a pet dog on the part of the revolutionary guards, should detract from the image of total privation and sacrifice.

Mignon remained Madame Royale's constant companion during the years of exile she spent with her uncle, Louis XVIII, until 1801, when it fell to its death from the balcony of the Poniatowski Palace in Warsaw. Louis wrote to the poet Jacques Delille asking him to compose an epitaph, but the reply failed to materialise, having been seized by the French police. Delille subsequently rectified the situation by including an elegy to Mignon in a poem, 'Malheur et Pitié', which reveals he was fully versed in the legend of the spaniel's origins:

> Be then the subject and the honour of my Canto,
> Oh You! who by consoling your royal mistress
> Until your last breath, proved your tenderness,
> Who beguiled her woes, enlivened her prison;
> Of a brother's last farewells, sole and tragic gift;
> Alas! That fate, which had robbed her of a father,
> To crown her misery, separated her brother,
> Left alone to face a hostile destiny,
> For her he forwent his last friend.
> Words fail me! The startling whims of tyrants!
> They who dragged her parents to their doom,
> Surrounded her with death, cast her down with adversity,
> Yet allowed her the animal, her companion in chains.[104]

In the course of their three-hundred-year ascendancy, no European dynasty was as subject to violence as the Romanovs. The internecine struggles that were such a regular feature of the Russian court resulted in the murder of so many princes that, by the early nineteenth century, Talleyrand was prompted to observe they would be well advised to find a more plausible excuse than apoplexy to account for their frequent demise. Under these circumstances, the dynasty's devotion to dogs was scarcely surprising. When Catherine the Great became Empress in 1762 she immediately forced Peter III to abdicate and, 'like a child who is sent to bed', according to Frederick the Great, he was dispatched to Ropsha, some twenty miles from St Petersburg. Catherine wrote to inform Poniatowski, 'the only things he asked me for were his mistress, his dog, his negro and his violin; but for fear of the scandal and increasing the agitation of his guards I only sent him the last three.' He was killed by her lover Orlov later in the year.[105]

By the mid-nineteenth century the greatest danger the Tsars had to face was assassination at the hands of increasingly organised groups of revolutionaries and nihilists both at home and abroad. They never travelled other than in the company of large dogs. Princess Felix Salm-Salm recalled being joined by Alexander II as she walked on the promenade at Ems in Germany in 1870: 'after half an hour, which passed in a very pleasant and interesting conversation, His Majesty left, quite alone and unattended as he had come, except by a large mastiff, which followed him everywhere like his shadow.'[106] The dog died in 1881 when a bomb was thrown into the royal carriage. As the constant companions of their royal masters, pets were as vulnerable to assassination as their owners. Kamchatka, the sheepdog of Alexander III, was crushed to death by falling debris when the imperial train was blown up by revolutionaries at Borki in 1888. The Tsar himself received serious injuries which helped see him to an early grave in 1894, before he had reached the age of fifty. The last Tsar and Tsarina also had a greyhound, Lofki, which they took to Paris with them in 1901.[107]

Alexander III's youngest daughter, the Grand Duchess Olga, married the homosexual Prince Peter of Oldenburg in 1901. Not only did their fifteen-year marriage remain entirely celibate but he 'loathed pets about the house'[108] and refused to allow her any. Her brother, Nicholas II, finally bought her a palace of her own in Sergeivskaya Street which she adored because she could 'have her pets take possession of the sofas and armchairs and every morning she could be seen walking the streets of St Petersburg accompanied by her borzoi, a poodle and a big husky'.[109] This pleasure proved to be short-lived for, in 1917, Olga had to flee the city and seek refuge at Al-Todor, the estate of Grand Duke Alexander near Yalta where she was later joined by her faithful maid, Minka, who, of all the dogs – and possessions – had only managed to bring the diminutive poodle.[110]

During their captivity at Tobolsk and Ekaterinburg the royal family found much solace in their chin Jimmy and spaniel Joy. The former was a gift from Ania Vyrubova, the close friend of the Tsarina who, as the person responsible for introducing her to Rasputin, had inadvertently done her much harm. Anastasia wrote to their benefactor in December 1917: 'The little dog you gave is always with us and is very nice.' Joy, the Tsarevich's spaniel, was a more established member of the household. The dog had accompanied him to the front in 1915, although the Tsarina nursed doubts as to its ability to enhance the royal image at this crucial moment in the war. Alexandra wrote to Nicholas:

> How charming Alexei's photos are, the one standing ought to be sold as postcards – both might be really – please, be done with Baby, also for the public and then we can send them to the soldiers. If in the south, then cross and medal without coats and in caps and if at the Headquarters or on the way there, near a wood, overcoat and fur cap. Fredericks asked my opinion, whether to permit that cinema of Baby and Joy can be allowed to be shown in public; not having seen it, I cannot judge, so leave it to you to decide. Baby told Mr Gilliard, that it was silly to see him '*faisant des pirouettes*' and that the dog looked cleverer than he.[111]

The Tsarevich's assessment of his dog's intelligence was astute: in December 1917 Alexei wrote to Petrov, his Russian-language tutor, relating how: 'Joy is getting fatter every day as he keeps eating rubbish from the refuse pit. Everyone chases him away with sticks. He has a lot of friends in the town and is always running away.'[112] Consequently, the dog alone survived the immolation of the royal family in the cellar of the Ipatiev House the following year. Joy was rescued by Letyomin, a Red Guard who, having had no involvement in the murder of the imperial family, assumed he would have nothing to fear from the advancing White Russians. Repenting of his naivety at the eleventh hour, Letyomin abandoned Joy, the dog so famously attached to Alexei that it provided potentially important clues to his whereabouts. Paul Chauchavadve heard how his uncle, Paul Rodzianko, who entered Ekaterinburg with the Whites, 'saw the Tsarevich's spaniel running in circles. Recognising him, he called him by name. The spaniel came, wagging his tail uncertainly, stumbling a little, finally bumping his nose into Rodzianko's leg. He was totally blind. Eventually my uncle brought him to England, where Joy lived on for a number of years on the Rodzianko farm near Windsor.' Despite the loss of its sight, caused presumably by the shock of the events that took place on that July evening, the little blind dog of the Tsarevich lived on well into the Twenties in close proximity of the castle to which its ill-fated master had thought himself to be on the point of being spirited.[113]

On the night of the 16 July, Jimmy shared their fate, beaten to death with a rifle butt. Yurovsky, one of the assassins, recalled how, despite having been 'warned through Botkin [the Tsarevich's doctor] not to take anything with them, they nevertheless brought a few small things, pillows, handbags etc., and even a small dog'[114] when they descended into the basement of the Ipatiev House naively expecting to hear of their imminent release. Another of the Guards, Mikhail Medvedev, later told his son that 'when they loaded the corpses on to the lorry, he was in charge of the loading – the corpse of a tiny dog fell out of the sleeve of the outfit of one of the grand duchesses.'[115] Jimmy's body was not found until a year later, 25 June 1919, at the bottom of the Four Brothers' Mine where the imperial family had originally been buried. The burial team having returned to Ekaterinburg and blabbed, the decision had been reached to reinter the bodies elsewhere, dousing them in acid to remove all possible trace. The corpse of the chin, suspiciously well preserved after a year in a mine shaft, added to the enigma of the whereabouts of the Romanovs and became one of the key elements in the endless investigations, both official and unofficial, which the absence of their skeletons inevitably sparked.[116]

HUMAN DEATH

In the absence of canine or feline autobiographies, the degree of bereavement felt by pets when their royal owners died is necessarily hard to gauge. Colourful tales of animal suicide were popular from the mid-eighteenth century when the newly fashionable emotional ideals of 'sentiment' and 'feeling' were extended to creatures and occasionally, as in the case of Marie Antoinette, they served a hagiographic function. Eye-witness accounts were often highly subjective, more revealing of the sentimentality of the narrator than of the grief of the pet. When Louis, the Duc de Bourgogne, died in 1712, Madame described how 'Monsieur le Dauphin's little dog made me cry. The poor creature went to the gallery of the chapel to look for his master where he had seen him kneeling for the last time.'[117] Confusion and grief are not synonymous. Nonetheless, some dogs clearly did merit the devotion lavished upon them by their owners and showed the loyalty which, in the eyes of their cynical and misanthropic masters, was their principal appeal. Had the story of Mary Stuart's dog been fictional, the author would doubtless have felt compelled to invent a more heart-rending *dénouement*. The grief of Edward VII's dog, Caesar, was witnessed by too many courtiers to warrant scepticism.

Many rulers turned to their pets in their last hours. As Gian Galeazzo Sforza lay on his death-bed in 1494 at his great palace in Pavia, his last request was for his greyhounds to be brought to his bedside. Louis XI of France asked for both his favourite dog and his hunting-horn to be buried with him. In an engraving by Jean Perrissin and Jacques Tortorel forming part of a collection commissioned to commemorate events that had taken place in France since 1559, Henri II, father-in-law of Mary Stuart, was depicted on his death-bed with two Maltese dogs. The last words uttered by Frederick the Great in 1786 were for his greyhound; noticing the dog shivering on the floor he ordered a servant to 'throw a quilt over her'. He had specifically stipulated that he should be interred among his dogs on the terrace at Sans-Souci, the palace named in celebration of the state he was fast approaching, but such a grave was considered unworthy of him and he was buried in the Garrison Church in Potsdam.

Sir James Reid, who was at Victoria's bedside in 1901, described how: 'In the forenoon the Queen suddenly asked for her favourite little dog Turi [a Pomeranian], but unfortunately he was out for exercise and not to be found. However, when he returned he was taken and put on the Queen's bed, who patted him and seemed pleased to have him beside her.'[118] According to the Baroness de Stoeckl, wife of the Russian diplomat, Victoria's great-grandson, the Duke of Kent, had intimations of mortality when he left his house, Coppins, in August 1942:

How handsome he looks in his Air Force uniform, and again I perceive that heavenly look which I have noticed for the last three days. He kisses me. I still insist for his presence at my fête. He smiles, but does not answer that question. We go around to the front door. He kisses his wife; they have already taken leave of each other privately. He stoops and strokes 'Muff' his Chow, turns to the butler Bysouth: 'What will you do with him when I am gone?' Strange question, as he was so often leaving.[119]

His brother, the Duke of Windsor, died in 1972 with his pug, Black Diamond, on his bed and the words 'Mama! Mama!' on his lips.[120] The dog expired very soon afterwards of the same cancer that had killed its master.

Many were careful to make provision for their pets in their wills. Madame de Pompadour bequeathed her spaniel, Mimi, her parrot and monkey to the Comte de Buffon who, although a partisan of the Queen, had impeccable credentials as the greatest natural historian of the day. Her wishes were not respected, however, and her brother, the Marquis de Marigny, 'unpleasant as he was over every aspect of her immense estate, presented to the duchesse de Choiseul the little dog which she had requested as a memento of her friend, though not before he had taken the extraordinary precaution of removing its collar, because it was made of solid silver'.[121] Pompadour's contemporary, Madame du Deffand, erstwhile mistress of the French Regent, Philippe II, Duc d'Orléans, left her dog, Tonton, to her old friend Horace Walpole. On its arrival at Strawberry Hill in 1781 the dog caused havoc:

> I brought him this morning to take possession of his new villa; but his inauguration has not been at all pacific. As he has already found out that he may be as despotic as at Saint-Joseph's [the convent where Madame du Deffand died], he began with exiling my beautiful little cat. . . . He then flew at one of my dogs, who returned it, by biting his foot till it bled; but was severely beaten for it. I immediately rang for Margaret [his housekeeper] to dress his foot; but in the midst of my tribulations could not keep my countenance; for she cried: 'Poor little thing, he does not understand my language!' – I hope she will not recollect too that he is a papist![122]

When Queen Mary Henrietta, wife of Leopold II of Belgium, died in 1902, she left her *griffon bruxellois*, Whin, a legacy of £2,000 and a personal servant to cope with its needs for the rest of its life. Mary Henrietta was the mother of Stephanie, who had married the Hapsburg Crown Prince Rudolf in 1881. In the first of his two wills, drawn up in 1878, Rudolf stipulated that his former tutor, 'Latour, in memory of me, is to look well after my dog, Blak, who was my faithful hunting companion; Bombelles [Comptroller of the Crown Prince's Household] is to keep and

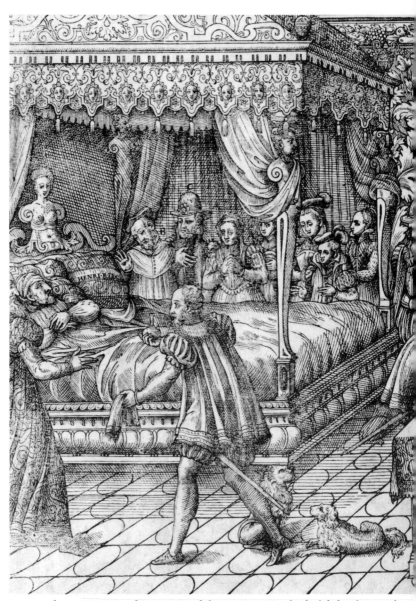

Engraving by Jean Perrissin and Jacques Tortorel showing Henri II on his death-bed with two Maltese

TOVRNELLES

chiens de Lyon. *Perrissin, a native of Lyon, had ample opportunity to observe the eponymous breed.*

care for Kastor and Schlifferl; one of them is good and faithful and the other can smile wisely. My eagle-owls and *Schweisshunds*, as well as the dachshunds are to go to poor huntsmen.'[123] In his last will, written two years before his suicide at Mayerling in 1889, Rudolf bequeathed 'all my dogs, whether hounds kept for sporting purposes or dogs kept as pets, to my huntsmen and loaders, and also the staff in the Wienerwald and in the Danubian preserves'.[124] That neither Bombelles nor Latour, apparently Rudolf's most trusted friends, nor Stephanie herself – a great animal lover – were considered worthy to look after his beloved dogs, reveals the depths of disillusionment and depression into which he had sunk.

ANTHROPOMORPHISM

The suggestion that canine and feline autobiographies did not exist is not entirely accurate – ghost-writers were at hand to oblige. The first dog to describe his life at court was Souillard, the greyhound who briefly belonged to Louis XI before entering the household of the *Grand Sénéschal*, Jacques de Brézé, husband of the illegitimate daughter of Charles VII and Agnès Sorel. 'The Sayings of the Good Dog Souillard' were written in the 1480s:

> To King Louis of France, whom hunting made so happy,
> Was I given as a pedigree puppy,
> And presented by him to the Sénéschal Gaston,
> Who to the Grand Sénéschal then passed me on.
> Thus I served all three, who treated me so well;
> In hunting the stag I had no close rival.
> Now I am old and live in comfort and ease,
> For the love I bear the King, do nothing to displease
> The Master to whom I belong and am so dear
> That he gives me bread and meat as daily fare.
> Snugly in his room beside the fire I sleep,
> With straw and a beautiful bed kept spotless and neat.[125]

Relais, the greyhound of Louis XII, followed suit twenty years later with an autobiography ghosted by the King himself and intended as an example to his descendants, that they might behave as well as he or even, if possible, better.

Although the Phrygian slave Aesŏp created the genre in about the seventh century BC, it was La Fontaine who transformed the fable into a literary style much admired and emulated at court and in the salons. To counter any hostile reaction that might have arisen from their thinly veiled criticism of the privileged and the powerful, La Fontaine shrewdly dedicated the first volume of his fables to the Dauphin, the second to Louis XIV's mistress, Madame de Montespan, and the third to the Duc de Bourgogne. They were an instant bestseller. In his own lifetime he exercised enormous influence over Madame Antoinette Deshoulières, considered by Voltaire the greatest poetess of her generation, whose cat Grisette corresponded with Tata, the cat of the Marquise de Montglas, and Dom Gris, that of the Duchesse de Béthune. In England, Marquise, the dog owned in the 1720s by the Countess of Suffolk, George II's mistress, took to corresponding with Lord Chesterfield. Horace Walpole himself resisted pressure to lend his literary abilities to writing fables, arguing that he had too much respect for animals. Frederick the Great had no such reservations and, in 1762, composed 'The Two Dogs and The Man', a murderous fable in which two ravenous mastiffs engage in a savage contest over a morsel of food only to be separated by a stranger who, 'without rhyme or reason', savagely beats the dogs with a stick. The King who 'stole Silesia', in Bismarck's words, and precipitated Europe into a quarter of a century of bloodshed because, as he admitted in a celebrated letter of 1741, 'the satisfaction of seeing my name in the papers and later in history has seduced me', then piously concluded with the lines:

> We dogs go into battle
> For a few bones; you, for territory.
>
> Amongst dogs genuine need breeds enmities
> Between you it is but pride and a hundred vanities.[126]

Frederick's greyhounds, and Biche in particular, were unique at the Prussian court in being privy to the King's thoughts. Their discretion was guaranteed, a consideration of abiding importance to a man who declared: 'If I thought that my shirt or my skin knew anything of my intentions, I would tear them off.' In response to a long letter from his sister

Wilhelmina's spaniel, Folichon, written in May 1748, Biche momentarily forgot herself, exposing the emotional man concealed behind the austere mask. These lines warrant being quoted in full as they not only reveal the affective vacuum in the lives of monarchs but are the fullest expression of royal anthropomorphism available. They were written seventeen years after Wilhelmina had left Berlin:

Admit, my dear Biche, that the human race is truly deranged and does itself little justice. They pride themselves on being uniquely capable of good sense and rational thought when generally but equipped with the shadow of these faculties. Do you not share my admiration for this bunch of philosophers who subject us to in-depth study while remaining utterly ignorant of what they are themselves? How many theories they have formed about us! Some declare us automatons, others as demons expelled from Paradise, and others still as creatures endowed with an instinct which they are nonetheless unable to define. We both know, my dear Biche, what we are and merely laugh at such errors, themselves the very products of human vanity. Looks apart, are we not like men in all respects? Are our passions any different? Love, jealousy, anger, greed are as much our tyrants as they are theirs and, if there is any difference between us, it is this: we possess fewer vices and many more virtues. Men are fickle, inconstant, selfish, ambitious; faults of which we are free. We, on the other hand, are faithful, constant, affectionate and grateful, qualities all but unknown in their society. We are the most faithful of friends. We love our masters unequivocally, irrespective of whether they be grand or humble. Far from despising us, men should follow our example.

Forgive this long discussion; it is a preamble leading to a more interesting topic. You, adorable Biche, lead me to make all these reflections; the love I bear you is their mainspring. Yes, too adorable bitch, I love and adore you. Your wit, your charm, your thousand glittering qualities, have subjugated me. Alas! I cannot recall without bursting into tears how you pawed me so tenderly when I took my fatal leave of you. In strong contrast to the *soi-disant* rational race, you exhibited sincere feelings and said to me: I love you, my dear Folichon. Hence, since our separation, I have but languished. Thin and gaunt, I have spent my time sitting melancholically at the feet of my mistress. I hear her lament the cruelty of being parted from a cherished brother and speak endlessly of the happy times she spent with him in Berlin, without being able to join in the conversation. Alarmed by my unhappiness, and in order to cheer me up, she gathered together a harem of all the most beautiful bitches in these provinces, but to no avail; I spurned them all. Finally she sought to lift my spirits with the lure of wealth. Would you believe, adorable Biche, that material gain, of so little consequence to us, managed to succeed where caresses and the most seductive pleasures had failed? Casting my eyes on the opulent gifts from my mistress, I resolved immediately to make you an offering. At least, I thought to myself beautiful Biche will think about me every time she sleeps on this sofa; she will drink my health in this bowl, and possibly shed a few tears over my absence. I instantly began to leap and cavort about begging my mistress, who understands my language perfectly, to fulfil my wishes. I dictated this letter to her. The friendship she feels towards me convinced her the effort was worth making. Accept, therefore, most beloved Biche, this small gift which, by bringing me into contact with you, gives me pleasure; asleep on this sofa, think occasionally of your tender Folichon, who will never cease to love and to cherish you nor to wag her tail a hundred times a day in celebration of your honour and glory. Folichon.

Biche replied from Potsdam later that month:

I am unaccustomed to such gallantry; I have always observed the strict chastity of the ladies of my country and preferred the idea of romantic heroism to a brief adventure which might spoil my figure; but I forgive in Folichon what I would never accept from a low-bred dog [*chien roturier*]. The great affection which my master feels for his mistress has convinced me that one dog alone can I accept as a lover. Yes, Folichon, not only do I receive your gifts gladly but I also accept your kind paw, and I give my heart all the more willingly for knowing that a morning dedicated to philosophy is what suits me best. I was most surprised to see that my master, who read me your letter, is entirely of your opinion; he is almost as rational as we are and has a good mind; but what I object to in your letter is that, in humbling the *amour-propre* of the human race, so consumed with pride and vanity you have made no exception of your mistress. Yes, Folichon, say what you please, I have met her, this adorable mistress, and you will never persuade me that she is not a member of a race far superior to ours; her virtues are divine, so much kindness, constancy, humanity and charity, that I swear to you she outstrips me. You know how so few ideas are shared; you, my master and myself, we belong to the same race and it is only on account of his laziness and in order to avoid coursing on all fours that my master does not call himself a greyhound. Slanderers say he is an Epicurean; for Epicurean read cynic, and for cynic read dog. But your mistress is quite different. What kindness she showed both me and my master! What wit she displays in conversation! And an indescribable grace, an air of dignity tempered by affability, which make her appear totally adorable to me! I beg you, let me be placed at her feet, but my master first of all. He speaks to me of nothing but her; I had great difficulty consoling him this winter. He received a letter which reduced him to mortal anguish; all my little caresses, all my acts of tenderness fell on deaf ears; I wore myself out trying to cheer him up but he was dead to the world and I feared I was in disgrace. Finally, dear Folichon, happy days returned; gaiety dissipated fear and, at the moment, we live very tranquilly. Your gallantry has rescued me from the state of lethargy into which I had fallen; I realise I have a heart meant for love. God! where would we be without passions? Life would amount to no more than perpetual death; we would vegetate on Earth like plants, which live without pleasure and die without pain. Now that I love, I perceive the Universe differently; the air I breathe is sweeter, the sun shines more brightly and all Nature is more animated. But, charming Folichon, are our pleasures to remain mere wishful-thinking, shall we not turn the desire of our hearts and our most cherished wishes into reality? Are we to remain as mad as men? They subsist on desires, they nourish their minds on fancies and while they waste their time on frivolous projects, death creeps up on them unawares, snatching away both themselves and their ambitions. Let us be wiser; let us not chase after shadows but seize the object itself. I offer you these jewels as proof of my word and as an assurance that I shall always remain, Your faithful Biche.[127]

64

One of the more bizarre ways in which the royal desire to humanise animals manifested itself was in the arrangement of canine marriages. The same phenomenon recurs across the centuries. In the early seventeenth century Marie de Medici asked the Duchesse d'Angoulême to procure a husband of the same breed for her spaniel Mignonette, and her son, Louis, who could not abide his bitches having litters outside wedlock any more than he could his father's mistresses, would marry them in time to salvage their reputations.[128] Earlier this century, Axel Munthe, physician to Queen Victoria of Sweden (1862–1930, wife of Gustavus V), found for his dog, Lisa, 'a husband, a miniature dachshund like herself, of equally distinguished stock, who travelled, with a lackey and an escort, all the way from the Royal Palace in Rome to Materita, where they were to be married'.[129] It was a rare instance of a commoner marrying into royalty, reflecting the high esteem in which Munthe was held.

The grandest wedding of them all which took place in the 1920s at a cost of £22,000, was that of the golden retriever Bobby and Roshanara, the favourite dog of the Maharajah of Junagadh. Most of the Indian princes and social élite were invited, the Viceroy Lord Irwin alone declining. The groom, met at the station by the nawab on a caparisoned elephant accompanied by two hundred and fifty dogs dressed in jewelled brocade, alighted on to a red carpet flanked by a two-legged guard of honour. A military band played the wedding march. Roshanara, who had been elaborately groomed and scented, wore an ornate coat and necklace as she was carried on a silver palanquin to the Durbar Hall. Bobby had gold bracelets on his paws, a gold necklace and an embroidered silk cummerbund. Moslem priests, too intimidated to dare refuse, officiated at the ceremony which the Maharajah witnessed from his throne. The bride and groom then hosted a wedding breakfast for their guests before retiring to their nuptial chamber. The marriage consummated, Bobby retired to kennels while the expectant mother was kept in an air-conditioned room in the palace where, after the delivery, she spent the rest of her life reclining on velvet cushions, while her royal master danced in attendance, indulging her every whim.[130]

Canine autobiographies, correspondence and marriages aside, most princes were capable of distinguishing between the human race and the brute creation, albeit frequently to the detriment of the former. Such was not the case with Christian VII of Denmark or the two penultimate Wittelsbach Kings of Bavaria, Ludwig II and Otto I. Elie-Salomon-François Reverdil succeeded the Lutheran pastor, Ditlev Reventlow, as tutor of the Crown Prince Christian of Denmark (1749–1808, King from 1766) when he retired in 1760. He reckoned that no royal child had ever been subjected to the brutal methods countenanced at the Danish court, although Frederick the Great's upbringing might have furnished another example. When Reventlow arrived to supervise Christian's lessons he

> made him repeat his exercise-book, to which he added his own comments, pinched the prince, bruised his hands, beat him black and blue: the child got confused and jumbled his words. He was scolded and maltreated, one moment for having repeated too mechanically, the next for having made omissions. . . . His bad mood ever worsening the tutor would call for a whip. Although no longer regularly used, the threat remained very real. These sad scenes essentially took place in public for they could be heard the length and breadth of the palace. The crowds of courtiers coming to adore the rising sun saw the object of their homage, a very handsome and affectionate boy, appear with his eyes swollen by tears, scanning the face of his tormentor to know whom amongst them he should address.[131]

By the time he ascended the throne as Christian VII in 1766, he was already suffering from advanced schizophrenia and progressively withdrew into a private world of his own fantasy where his closest companion, the dog Gourmand, was appointed Councillor and voted a salary.[132]

During the last six years of his life, Ludwig II of Bavaria (1845–86, King from 1864), divided his time between his castles at Linderhof and Herrenchiemsee where 'the King's servants had to scratch at the woodwork to announce their presence at the door . . . because the King could tolerate a lackey only if acting the dog that His Majesty believed him to be. . . . His valets had to approach him crouching on their stomachs – no one wearing the royal livery dared look at the King in the face.'[133] After Ludwig's mysterious death in 1886 he was succeeded by his brother Otto, with whom the dynasty's notorious mental instability reached its zenith. Known in his youth as 'Cheerful Otto', he had rapidly declined into madness and spent the thirteen years prior to Ludwig's death incarcerated in a padded cell at the castle of Furstenreid. He remained there for a further seventeen years while his uncle, Prince Luitpold, ruled as regent. Literally barking mad, Otto was convinced he was a dog and moved about his cell on all fours, refusing all food unless presented in a bowl on the floor. The servants who attended him addressed him respectfully as 'your Majesty', to which he would reply by barking at them furiously.

*Portrait by Jean Ranc of the Cardinal Infante Don Luis Antonio de Borbón
(1727–85), son of Philip V and Elizabeth Farnese, hence half-brother of
Ferdinand VI, at the age of eight when he was appointed Archbishop of Toledo.*

CHAPTER TWO

Pet Preferences

T HE MOST IMPORTANT FACTOR determining the choice of a pet was availability and, until the nineteenth century, this was extremely limited. In the sixteenth century Dr Caius could identify no more than sixteen breeds of dog in England and these he categorised according to function rather than appearance. Although several breeds — and principally the spaniel — were not indigenous, the primitive nature of transportation impeded the introduction of new strains. While hunting, the principal pursuit of all monarchs irrespective of gender, inevitably led them to form attachments to favourite hounds, it in no way obviated the need for palace dogs and, from the Renaissance onwards, ruling families cherished the company of domestic animals. Many of the breeds they admired having either changed beyond recognition or become extinct, it is chiefly through portraiture that royal tastes can be established.

ROYAL PET PORTRAITS

Devoted to pets as most princes undoubtedly were, the commissioning of their portraits was an obvious way of expressing their feelings. The life of a pet was necessarily short and a painting was a way of paying tribute to the place they had held in their master's affections. The presence of a dog encouraged royal sitters to relax and provided a subject of conversation on which few were likely to falter. The depiction of a dog could also serve multifarious purposes, from indicating rank and enhancing royal prestige to simply helping in the general composition. Some of the animals in royal portraiture almost certainly belonged to the artists themselves. Portraits including pets not only commanded higher prices but exploiting sentimentality could attract royal patronage, the goal of every ambitious painter. However important in suggesting dynastic solidity or domestic virtue, these animals were never purely symbolic. Unlike their masters, animals were rarely idealised and the most accomplished paintings provide valuable evidence as to which breeds were fashionable at court and how they have changed, sometimes almost out of recognition. They also furnish important insights into life at court.

The first representation of a pet dog in art has been identified by Kenneth Clark as the terrier in Jan van Eyck's *The Arnolfini Marriage*, painted in 1434, in which the dog, unlike the wife, is painted from life.[1] The artist applied the same naturalism in an earlier work, the *Hours of Turin*, depicting four different breeds, including miniature greyhounds in front of William VI, Count of Holland. The Flemish School, and particularly Jan van Eyck and Hans Memling, had a powerful impact on the early Renaissance painters of Italy who strove to achieve ever greater naturalism based on the close observation of nature. The works of Vittore Carpaccio, Pisanello and Piero della Francesca abound with animals. They had no need to have recourse to imagination in their depiction of nature, the menageries and gardens in which Renaissance princes took such pride providing ample material.

At the courts of Burgundy and Renaissance Italy, the relationship between artist and patron was relaxed and informal, with princes frequently paying impromptu visits to the studio. Painters wishing to have prior notice of such visits were well advised to take the precaution of acquiring a pet dog. In 1433, Holland was united with Burgundy, and van Eyck was appointed *valet de chambre* at the court of Philip the Good, subsequently being sent on diplomatic missions to Spain and Portugal. Under Philip's son and successor, Charles the Bold (1467–77), the painter Jean Hennecart (d. 1470) served the Duke in the same capacity. One of his illustrations depicts Philip on his death-bed with a miniature greyhound at his feet. The Burgundian practice of appointing court painters *valets de chambre* was imitated at the French court. During the reign of Louis XI (1461–83) Jean Fouquet filled this dual role as did his successor as *Peintre du Roi*, Jean Bourdichon (1457–1521). When, in 1469, the King instituted the Order of St Michael, Fouquet illustrated the book of the Order's statutes and the frontispiece shows Louis at a session of the Chapter of the Order registering little interest in the proceedings but preoccupied with his favourite greyhound, the aptly named Cherami (Dear Friend), portrayed in the foreground. Both a greyhound and a 'comforter' – as lapdogs were originally known – feature prominently in a far earlier manuscript of c. 1412, where the anonymous illustrator depicts the pioneering feminist and first French woman writer, Christine de Pisan (c. 1364–c. 1430), presenting her works to Isabel of France, consort of Charles VI, known as the Mad (reigned 1380–1422). The miniature, in which the Queen is shown sitting among her gentlewomen in her chamber, is an invaluable pictorial document, throwing light not only on the arrangement of the Queen's privy chamber at the French court in the early fifteenth century but also on the breeds of dog then favoured.

Jean Perréal (c. 1450–c. 1530) served three French kings, Charles VIII, Louis XII and Francis I, as court painter and *valet de chambre* and, like van Eyck more than half a century earlier, was sent on diplomatic missions, travelling to England in 1514 to negotiate a marriage alliance between Louis XII and Mary Tudor. On such occasions pictures featured among the presents customarily exchanged between courts, and the representation of a greyhound was an affirmation of pedigree and nobility. Greyhounds epitomised the chivalric ideal of noble actions and good blood and were constantly described as 'gentil', in the sense of well born and honourable. Skelton, tutor and court poet of Henry VIII, wrote:

> From whens that maistife came
> Let him neuer confounde
> The gentil greyhound.

Perréal always painted directly from life and his naturalism was much admired by that discerning Maecenas, the Duke of Mantua, Federico II Gonzaga (reigned 1519–40, Duke in 1530) who commissioned a portrait when he met the painter on one of his visits to Italy in the entourage of Francis I. Having witnessed at first hand the conspicuous magnificence of the courts of Italy, French kings were determined to lure back to France artists of the same calibre to add lustre to their own courts. Competing for artists became 'an important aspect of the cultural rivalry that existed among European courts in the Renaissance'.[2] Many were doubtless relieved to abandon their war-ravaged homeland and benefit from the generous remuneration offered to them. Benvenuto Cellini and Leonardo da Vinci both succumbed to the temptation, the latter enjoying an annuity of five hundred livres in the three years he spent in France before his death in 1519. Titian, however, declined Francis I's invitation, although the King was to some extent mollified by having his portrait painted by the master in 1538. Unlike so many of the portraits of Francis I, that of Titian included none of the greyhounds that the King was known to prefer.

The fact that the origin of the greyhound remains shrouded in mystery is a testament to the breed's antiquity. Probably of Egyptian origin, the 'grey' may be a corruption of 'grik', the Arab for Greek, and the dogs were later frequently depicted in Hellenic art. They would have reached Rome from Greece; Cleopatra was said to have given miniature specimens to Caesar.[3] Gavin Hamilton excavated the famous Vatican Group of two greyhounds, dating from the second century AD, in the 1770s, appropriately enough from a site known as Monte Cagnolo, or Dog-hill. The Romans introduced the breed throughout the empire, and the game laws introduced by Canute in England in 1016, forbidding ownership of hunting dogs to all but the nobility, almost certainly included greyhounds. Although their popularity at European courts was early established, it was when St Louis brought greyhounds back from the Crusades that they became the subject of Christian iconography and the embodiment of the chivalric ideal. Nonetheless, medieval Books of Hours show them to have been more than simple emblematic beasts and make it clear that they were the everyday companions of their owners. Queen Mary's Psalter proves them to have been popular at the English court by the early fourteenth century.

The greyhounds that feature in so many Renaissance masterpieces were portraits of court pets. Bred with all the professionalism the age could muster, and used principally for hunting, they nevertheless occupied the ducal palaces where they were kept in great luxury. The greyhounds in Piero della Francesco's fresco in the Tempio Malatestiano in Rimini belonged to Sigismondo Pandolfo Malatesta (1432–68), a gift from Pier Francesco di Lorenzo de Medici.[4] Many of the beautiful drawings by Pisanello were of the greyhounds of Borso, Duke of Ferrara (ruled 1450–71), reckoned the finest of their breed in Italy. Leonora, the wife of his successor, Ercole I (ruled 1471–1505), owned a special strain which enjoyed such a high reputation that they were sought after by discerning dog lovers throughout the peninsula.[5] Andrea Mantegna worked at the court of Mantua from 1460 to 1506. His frescoes in the Camera degli Sposi, completed in 1474, portray the large white greyhounds of Ludovico Gonzaga. Two years later Mantegna was given a large amount of land by the Marquis where he 'wished to make a display of his importance by raising an edifice remarkable for its decorative beauty'.[6] Visiting his palace of St Sebastiano at Mantua in 1515, the Venetian ambassadors described the Marquis 'reclining on a couch by the hearth of a richly adorned room, with his best dwarf clad in gold brocade,

Antonio Pisanello: **Head of a Greyhound**. *Pisanello worked for several Italian courts and invented the personal commemorative medal.*

and three superb greyhounds at his feet. Three pages stood by, waving large fans, lest even a hair should fall upon him; a quantity of falcons and hawks in leash were in the room, and the walls were hung with pictures of favourite dogs and horses.'[7] Bernabo Visconti in Milan owned no fewer than five thousand greyhounds fed at the expense of his subjects.

Miniature greyhounds were kept as pets at all the courts of Europe from this period. The French King, Charles IX, had a particular favourite, Courte, celebrated in verse by Ronsard:

> But as soon as she could be
> In her master's company
> And stroked by her King
> Her friends counted for nothing,
> And she would bite them as felon
> Suffering that no-one
> Should approach him whom she loved.[8]

As a result of Henri IV's prohibition of the use of large greyhounds in hunting because of the destruction of game, the miniature strain became increasingly popular from the early seventeenth century. Italian greyhounds were the favourites of Anne of Denmark, James I's Queen, and can be seen in her portrait by Paul van Somer. Her predilection was shared by her son for reasons explained by Alexander Pope in a letter to a friend written in 1709: 'Sir William Trumbull has told me a Story which he heard from one that was present when our King Charls I, being with some of his Court, during his Troubles, and a Discourse arising what Sort of Dogs deservd Pre-eminence, & it being on all hands agreed to belong either to a Spaniell or Greyhound, the King gave his opinion on the Part of the Greyhound, because (said he) it has all the Good-nature of the other, without the fawning. A fine piece of Satire upon his Courtiers, with which I will conclude my Discourse on Dogs.'[9] Charles I even named one of his ships *The Greyhound*. Oliver Cromwell had a greyhound with the sinister name of Coffin-nail.[10] Charles II must have liked them in his youth when he was painted with one by Sir Peter Lely. His mother, Henrietta Maria, certainly did; the greyhounds in Van Dyck's *Family of Charles I* were described as the 'Queenes little doggs'.[11]

Fashionable at Versailles, greyhounds were virtually *de rigueur* at the Bourbon court of Spain in the early eighteenth century. On the recommendation of Hyacinthe Rigaud, under whom he had served an apprenticeship, the French painter Jean Ranc (1674–1735) was sent in 1722 to Madrid where Philip V was anxious to emulate the style of his grandfather's, Louis XIV's, age. Appointed *pintor de camera*, a more prestigious title than *pintor del rey*, Ranc undertook portraits of the royal families of both Spain and Portugal. His picture of the young Ferdinand VI (1713–59, King from 1746) as a child includes a small greyhound. Copies of Ranc's portraits were sent to other European courts, in accordance with the standard practice of the day, and this publicity for a breed contributed to the spread of its popularity. There is a greyhound in one of the earliest works undertaken by Antoine Pesne (1683–1757) after his appointment as First Painter to the Prussian Court of Frederick I in 1711, *Wilhelmina of Prussia and her brother Frederick*, dated 1714, when they were both children. Wary of the frugal regime at the court of Frederick William I, who had succeeded to the throne in 1713, Pesne soon left Prussia and did not return until 1732. He travelled to St Petersburg to paint Peter the Great, another monarch to favour miniature greyhounds, to Dessau, Dresden, Paris and London, undertaking many royal commissions, most of which have disappeared without trace. He became a French academician in 1720. On his return to Prussia he was appointed by Georg Wenceslaus von Knobelsdorff to execute the painted decorations for the Crown Prince at Schloss Rheinsberg and, after Frederick the Great became King in 1740, those at Charlottenburg, Potsdam and Sans-Souci. The only contemporary representation of Frederick's dogs in existence is on the ceiling of Sans-Souci, where they are modelled in stucco, chasing hares in a manner that the notoriously anti-hunting monarch must have despised. Frederick the Great allegedly owned no fewer than thirty-five miniature greyhounds in the course of his life; two can be seen in the posthumous statue of the King by Gottfried Schadow. They were also among the favourite dogs of Ferdinand IV of Naples (ruled 1759–1825), who was painted by Angelica Kauffmann with several gambolling around him.

Although royal dog painting antedated Titian, it was he who introduced the combination of master and dog and whose influence on the genre remained paramount until the nineteenth century. The portrait most crucial to his meteoric rise at the court of the Holy Roman Emperor Charles V was that of the Marquis of Mantua, Federico Gonzaga II, painted with his lapdog c. 1529, which Charles saw when he stayed in Mantua between 1529 and 1530. In 1532 Charles com-missioned Titian to copy the portrait of him with his Irish wolfhound by Jacob Seisenegger (1505–67) which was in his brother Ferdinand's possession. When Charles received Titian's portrait in 1536, he was so impressed that he immediately created the post of Court Painter specifi-cally for him. Apart from being granted the exclusive privilege of painting the Emperor, the artist became Count Palatine, Knight of the Golden Spur and Knight of Caesar. His children were ennobled and he himself received a thou-sand gold scudi for every work commis-sioned. No painter would be granted such honours until Rubens a century later.

Detail of the portrait by Titian of Federico Gonzaga, Duke of Mantua (1500–40), c. 1529. The Duke owned more than a hundred dogs in the course of his life.

Portrait by Titian of Charles V. Charles V likened the artist to Alexander the Great's painter Apelles. The dog's name was probably Sampere, the Catalan for St Peter.

In his portrait of Federico Gonzaga, Titian jettisoned the traditional panoply of majesty to convey an image of relaxed authority and aristocratic confidence, enhanced rather than diminished by the presence of the small dog whose obvious pedigree mirrors that of its master. The dog in the painting was Federico's own favourite pet, one of some hundred he was said to have owned in the course of his life. Lapdogs had previously been represented as exclusively female companions, large hounds being deemed more appropriate as symbols of virility.

The breeds of small dog in many early court paintings are all but impossible to identify. During the Middle Ages only hunting dogs had been subjected to classification and the first reference to toy dogs in English literature did not occur until 1486 when Dame Juliana Berners, Prioress of Sopwell Nunnery in Hertfordshire, described 'smalle ladyes poppees that bere aweye the fleas' in her *Boke of St Albans*. Dr John Caius, physician to the children of Henry VIII and author in 1570 of the first book in England entirely devoted to dogs, *Englishe Dogges*, took a dim view of these breeds:

> small indeed and chiefly sought after for the amusement and pleasure of women. The smaller the kind the more pleasing it is, so that they may carry them in their bosoms, in their beds; and in their arms in their carriages. That kind of dog are altogether useless for any purposes, except that they ease pain of the stomach, being often applied to it, or frequently born in the bosom of the diseased person, by the moderation of their vital heat. Moreover it is believed from their sickness and frequently their death that diseases even are transferred to them, as if the evil passed over to them owing to the intermingling of vital heat.[12]

Termed 'comforters' after their alleged curative powers, toy dogs received a bad press from other English natural historians of the sixteenth century. Their owners were likened to the Sybarites whom Timon of Athens had described going to the bath attended by their dogs. William Harrison, in 1588, was even more damning than Caius, describing them as

> little and prettie, proper and fine, and sought out far and neere to satisfie the nice delicacie of daintie dames, and wanton womens willes; instruments of follie to plaie and dallie withall, in trifling away the treasure of time, to withdraw their minds from more commendable exercises, and to

content their corrupt concupiscences with vaine disport, a sillie poore shift to shun their irkesome idleness. These Sybariticall puppies, the smaller they be . . . the better they be accepted, the more pleasure also they provoke, as meet plaiefellowes for minsing mistresses to beare in their bosoms, to keepe companie withall in their chambers, to succour with sleepe in bed, and nourish with meat at bord, to lie in their laps, and licke their lips as they lie . . . in their wagons and coches.[13]

Shakespeare shared this low opinion of lapdogs; in *Othello* II. iii, Iago says of Cassio, having got him drunk:

> He'll be as full of quarrell and offence
> As my young Mistress' dogge.

Impervious to such criticism, ladies at court and queens themselves continued to obtain these dogs both 'far and neere'. Anne Boleyn found great solace in her little Purkoy, a French toy dog which probably resembled the one in the portrait by François Clouet of Marguerite d'Angoulême, sister of Francis I, copied by an anonymous painter in 1544. It is clear from the Lisle Letters that such dogs were unavailable in England at this date. Anne of Cleves is thought to have introduced the strain of liver-and-white toy spaniel when she married Henry VIII in 1539. The interest she developed in breeding greyhounds subsequent to her divorce from the King later that year may well have originated in early childhood at the court of Cleves, where the Duke's private secretary had been the celebrated natural historian Conrad Heresbach (b. 1496). In 1546 she sent two brace of greyhound to her brother. Hitherto unknown in England, tiny spaniels wearing collars and bells can be seen in Antonis Mor's 1554 marriage portrait of Philip II and Mary Tudor, for which he was awarded a knighthood. The Privy Purse Expenses of the Queen include a payment 'geuene to Sir Bryan Tuke's seruante, bringing a cowple of litle fayre houndes to my Lade's grace, 5s.'.[14] She also paid fifteen shillings for 'a litle Spanyell'.

Pets are a rarity in English royal portraiture of the sixteenth century, although relatively common in portraits of courtiers. Holbein the Younger (c. 1497–1543), the King's Painter from 1536, painted many pets but none belonging to the royal family. When Charles II commissioned the Flemish painter, Remigius van Leemput, to copy Holbein's dynastic portrait of Henry

Portrait by Federico Zuccaro of Elizabeth I with a miniature beagle. It was drawn in 1575, the year she hunted with her miniature beagles on the Earl of Leicester's estate at Kenilworth.

VII, Elizabeth of York, Henry VIII and Jane Seymour, he added a comforter at the feet of the latter, although it had not existed in the original which was destroyed in the Whitehall fire of 1698. Elizabeth I did not share her parents' predilection for toy dogs; her pocket beagles were hunting dogs. Nevertheless, the beagle in Federico Zuccaro's 1575 portrait of the Queen was no simple symbol of fidelity. The painting was almost certainly a companion piece to the drawing of the Earl of Leicester by the same artist but, as it would have been inappropriate to be portrayed alongside her favourite, the dog was included as a private message between them, a reference to the hunting she had enjoyed on his estate at Kenilworth earlier that same year. The small dog

Portrait by Giuseppe Arcimboldo of Maximilian II and his three eldest children. A 'comforter' sits at the Empress's feet. The youngest of the infants in the picture was Rudolf, whose birth assured the survival of the dynasty.

at her feet in the c. 1580 portrait by Marcus Gheeraerts the Elder was almost certainly the painter's pet, brought with him to England in 1567/8 when he, like so many Flemish painters of the period, had to flee religious persecution in the Low Countries. No such inhibitions hampered artists on the

Continent. The group portrait of the Emperor Maximilian II with his wife and three eldest children, painted by Giuseppe Arcimboldo in 1553, shows a comforter in the foreground, clamouring for its mistress's attention. Dynasties had begun to celebrate their solidity by commissioning works devoid of martial allusions. Tudor insecurity precluded such liberties and toy dogs only made their debut in British royal portraiture under the Stuarts.

Whether described as emanating from Lyon, Cuba, Manila or Tenerife, the Maltese dog was popular across Europe from the fifteenth century when it appeared in works by Hans Memling, Albrecht Dürer and Vittore Carpaccio. The latter two kept them as pets. The Swedish naturalist Carl Linnaeus (1707–78), in his *Systema Naturae* of 1758, distinguished two types: the *canis pilosus*, or long-haired Maltese, and the *canis parus melitans*, or miniature Maltese; Joannes Jonstonus added a further type, the lion-dog, in 1755. This was probably the shih tzu, a breed of Tibetan origin, named after the Mongol emperor of the Chinese Yuan dynasty (1260–94), which first appeared in royal portraiture at this period. Johann Zoffany painted *Charlotte, Princess Royal and Prince William*, later Duke of Clarence, with a shih tzu in c. 1770, and

Johann Zoffany: **Charlotte, Princess Royal and Prince William** *with a shih tzu c. 1770. The breed was named after the thirteenth-century Mongol emperor of China.*

another – or possibly the same dog – can by seen in Sir Joshua Reynolds's 1774 portrait of Princess Sophia Matilda of Gloucester, George III's niece. The miniature by Charlotte Jones (1768–1847) of Princess Charlotte of Wales, daughter of George IV, with a lion-dog is undoubtedly indebted to Titian's portrait of Federico Gonzaga. Shih tzus were favoured by many British monarchs until the reign of the present Queen whose father, George VI, had one named Choo-Choo after the train-like noise it made and which the King considered 'the most unsavoury member of our family',[15] presumably because of the breed's tendency to eat its own faeces.

The Maltese retained its popularity at most European courts until the nineteenth century. Titian incorporated Philip II's Maltese dog in his *Venus and the Organ Player*; Mytens painted the Maltese of Henrietta Maria in his painting of *The King departing for the Chase*. Sir William Beechey (1753–1839), who was appointed Portrait Painter to Queen Charlotte in 1793, painted her with

Daniel Mytens: Detail of The King departing for the Chase *showing the Maltese of Henrietta Maria.*

a tiny Maltese in her arms in 1796. The popularity of the breed at the court of Spain in the eighteenth century is attested to in the works of Francisco Goya, *pintor del camera* from 1786. William IV's wife, Queen Adelaide, gave a Maltese, Quiz, to the Duchess of Kent in 1839, painted, on Victoria's instruction, by Edwin Landseer the same year; Queen Victoria's, Chico, was painted by T. M. Joy in 1845, lying on a plush red cushion. The Empress Eugenie also favoured the breed and was painted by Eugene Boudin in 1863, strolling with her dog, Linda, and ladies on the beach at Trouville.

Eugene Boudin: Detail of Empress Eugenie on the beach at Trouville with her Maltese, Linda.

Although they had not fallen into total disfavour at the French court of the eighteenth century, Maltese dogs were a rarity by the 1770s and, when the Comte de Buffon was writing his *Histoire Naturelle*, he was compelled to have recourse to drawings in the King's Print Room in order to illustrate the breed. He described how 'these dogs were very fashionable a few years ago, but at present they are hardly seen. They were so small that ladies carried them in their sleeves. At last they gave them up, doubtless because of the dirtiness that is inseparable from long-haired dogs, for they could not clip them without taking away their principal attraction.'[16] In their place were miniature spaniels, or Bolognese, and papillons, chihuahua–spaniel crosses. The latter, known in England as Spanish dogs after their country of origin, were the favourite breed of Louis XV's daughter, Marie Adelaide (1732–99), and she was portrayed by Jean-Marc Nattier in 1759 with

Detail from a portrait by Jean-Marc Nattier of Princess Marie Adelaide, daughter of Louis XV, with a papillon.

her white papillon sitting on a sheet of music at her feet. The Bolognese first made their appearance at the French court under Louis XIV but had long been popular in Italy, where Titian included them in both his portraits of Eleonora Gonzaga, Duchess of Urbino, painted between 1536 and 1538. Veronese portrayed red-and-white toy spaniels in many of his works, including his fresco of the Barbaro household c. 1561 and *The Family of Darius before Alexander*, where they wear collars with bells and are attended by a dwarf. Dr Caius referred to them in his *Englishe Dogges* of 1576: 'the most part of their Skynnes are white, and if they be marcked with any spottes, they are commonly red'. The attachment of the Medici to the breed died only with the dynasty itself. Cosimo II, Grand Duke from 1590 to 1621, presented his wife, Maria Maddalena, with an ivory statuette of her favourite spaniel lying on an ebony box. It was Cosimo who commissioned the painting of the Medici dogs by Tiberio Titi. Both Anna Maria

Ivory statuette of a Bolognese spaniel on an ebony box edged with ivory presented to Maria Maddalena by her husband, Cosimo II, Grand Duke of Tuscany (1590–1621). One of the earliest figurines of a dog, it was modelled from her own pet.

Lodovica (1667–1743) and her brother, Gian Gastone, last of the Medici, kept them as pets. Anna Maria and her husband, the Elector Palatine, can be seen with a Bolognese in a painting by Gian Francesco Douren. Their existence in the Netherlands from an early date is evident from the portrait by Katharina de Hemessen (c. 1527–66) of an unknown sitter with a Bolognese, again wearing a collar with bells, painted in 1551.

The Bolognese dogs at the court of Louis XIV are clearly visible in the works of Pierre Mignard (1612–95) and Nicolas de Largillière (1656–1746). Pierre Mignard, who succeeded Le Brun as the King's *premier peintre* in 1690, included a black spaniel – the first in French art – in his 1687 portrait of *Monseigneur and his Family*. The dogs introduce a note of domesticity into the painting without detracting from the dignity of the sitters. Largillière also excelled at royal family group portraits and, in *Louis XIV with the Grand Dauphin, the Duc de Bourgogne, the Infant Duc de Bretagne, and their Governess, Madame de Ventadour*, the Bolognese in the foreground

Detail from a portrait of the Grand Dauphin and his family.

serves a compositional and didactic function by completing the circle of the four generations of Bourbons represented on the canvas and indicating the line of succession. The playfully yapping spaniel and the pug which lurks behind the Duc de Bourgogne also act as a counterpoise to the patrician stiffness of the royal family and help convey a message of dynastic and domestic security. In fact, unbeknown to either the sitters or the artist, all three princes were to die by 1712, leaving the continuation of the French Bourbon dynasty in serious doubt. Where the Bolognese in Largillière's portrait bolstered the notion of dynastic strength, the weak and ailing spaniel in Diego Velásquez's 1659 portrait of the Spanish infante Felipe Prosper serves as a metaphor for the condition of either the artist himself, the Prince, or even the Spanish Hapsburgs. All were doomed: Velásquez expired in 1660, the Prince in 1661 and the dynasty in 1700.

The portrait by Nicolas de Largillière of **Louis XIV and his Heirs** *includes a Bolognese and a pug. The Bolognese became a potent symbol of dynastic security.*

Largillière had studied in London in the studio of Sir Peter Lely but returned to France in 1679 after the Popish Plot of the previous year unleashed a period of violent anti-Catholicism. He had fallen heavily under the influence of Sir Anthony Van Dyck (1599–1641) whose paintings of Charles I and his family were masterpieces of invention. Van Dyck had been appointed 'principalle paynter in Ordinary to their Majesties' and knighted in 1632. Although he had trained as an assistant in Rubens's studio in Antwerp, Van Dyck's portraits of the royal family hark back to Titian, nineteen of whose works he had in his own possession, including the *Vendramin Family* of c. 1543–7, in which the boys are shown seated on the altar steps with their toy spaniel. The great Venetian master's 1542 portrait of Clarissa Strozzi, in which the child is depicted with her pet dog but without her parents, was the first of its kind in Western art. Van Dyck's painting of the three eldest children of Charles I, completed in 1635, was heavily indebted to these works. Commissioned for Henrietta Maria's sister, Christina of Savoy, Charles I was incensed by Van Dyck's portrayal of the future Charles II in a frock, the customary wear of princes before they were breeched. Paintings had to advertise the majesty of the Stuart dynasty and, notwithstanding the close personal ties between the courts of Turin and Whitehall, convey a public as well as a private message. Van Dyck did not court disfavour again and repainted the children the same year, this time with Charles breeched. Van Dyck flattered his sitters sometimes out of recognition: when Sophia, Electress of Hanover, met Queen Henrietta Maria, she noted in her memoirs: 'the fine portraits of Van Dyck had given me such an idea of the beauty of all English ladies, that I was surprised to find the Queen (so beautiful in her picture) a little woman with long, lean arms, crooked shoulders, and teeth protruding from her mouth like guns from a fort.'[17] This was precisely the artist's intention: copies of these paintings were sent to other European courts with a view to forging dynastic alliances and had to suggest health and robustness in an age when so many children died in infancy. Charles II was the first Stuart child born in England since the dynasty succeeded the Tudors in 1603. In the 1637 portrait of the five eldest children of Charles I, by placing Charles alongside an enormous mastiff, Van Dyck was able to suggest not simply the precocious height of the royal heir, but his early sense of command, the tamed beast on whose head Charles rests his hand symbolic of an acquiescent and peaceful nation. Notwithstanding the significance of the mastiff as the embodiment of strength, this was a breed universally admired at the period and one, like the King Charles spaniels, much favoured at the English court. The spaniels, authentic pets, gave the royal family an established air, radiating domesticity and security. Charles I needed no large hounds to confirm his virility; his abundance of healthy children was sufficient proof.

The potency of the images created by Van Dyck was not lost on other court painters seeking to bolster fragile dynasties. Pierre Gobert (1662–1744) painted the infant Louis XV with his small pet dog on several occasions for distribution to other countries at a time when the continuation of the French Bourbons hung in the balance. Not yet breeched, Louis wears a frock, but any suspicion of effeminacy is counterbalanced by the Prince's total command over the fierce little dog, snarling menacingly at the pet monkey. Sir Francis Grant's painting of *Queen Victoria with Victoria, Princess Royal, and Albert Edward, Prince of Wales*, commissioned in 1842 by the Queen

Portrait by Pierre Gobert of the infant Louis XV with a dog and a monkey. Gobert was favoured by Louis XIV from 1682 and was considered one of the foremost portrait painters of his day.

herself as a present for Prince Albert, closely imitated Van Dyck's 1632 portrait of *Charles I and his Family*, except that, in lieu of the miniature greyhounds, are the Queen's favourite Skye terrier, Dandie Dinmont, and Albert's greyhound, Eos. Albert Edward, then just one year old, was the first heir apparent to be born since the Prince Regent in 1762. Furthermore, as the first English royal couple to be glorified as husband and wife in the domestic sense, Charles I and Henrietta Maria were an obvious model for Victoria and Albert. If fledgling dynasties needed able propagandists it was no less politic on the part of artists themselves to flatter their sitters. Not only were official portraitists subject to royal whim – Daniel Mytens had been totally eclipsed at the court of Charles I by Van Dyck – but they were vulnerable to forces beyond even royal control: Charles II's crypto-Catholicism was of no avail to Largillière. It was important to achieve universal appeal lest war, revolution or dynastic extinction imperil their careers and require them to seek patronage at alternative courts. Van Dyck himself became so tired of portraiture that he hoped to be commissioned by the French court to decorate the Grande Galerie of the Louvre.

The spaniels in Van Dyck's portraits of Charles I and his family are far larger than their toy counterparts at continental courts and were almost certainly of the springer strain, admired as much for their abilities in the field as for their qualities as pets. A very old breed, of Spanish origin as the name suggests, they first reached England under the Plantagenets. They are mentioned in both Chaucer and the Duke of York's 'Mayster of Game', written between 1406 and 1413. They early enjoyed a greater reputation for being submissive and ingratiating than virtually any other breed. In *A Midsummer Night's Dream* II.i, Helena tells Demetrius:

Detail from portrait of the **Three Eldest Children of Charles I** *by* **Anthony Van Dyck**.

I am your spaniel; and, Demetrius:
The more you beat me, I will fawn on you.
Use me but as your spaniel, spurn me, strike me,
Neglect me, lose me; only give me leave,
Unworthy as I am, to follow you.
What worser place can I beg in your love —
And yet a place of high respect with me —
Than to be used as you use your dog?

With the exception of James I, all the Stuart kings were devoted to spaniels. There were so many at the court of Charles II that the King's Gentleman of the Bedchamber, the Earl of Ailesbury, would use them as metaphors for toadyism, describing a contemporary as being as 'pliant as a spaniel dog'.[18] With the demise of the Crown in 1689, and the accession of William III, both dynasty and dogs were eschewed and the pug, totem of Protestant Holland, succeeded the spaniel as court favourite. By linking the spaniel with Charles I pictorially, Van Dyck was largely, if unintentionally, responsible for its disgrace. Spaniels became part of Stuart mythology. The Maltese dogs of Mary Stuart, first of the house's martyrs, were transmogrified into King Charles spaniels, an eponym never applied to the breed at the time. Every King Charles spaniel across the land was said to have wept at the execution of Charles I. By becoming the 'Cavalier' King Charles, the strain of spaniel favoured by Charles II was inextricably linked with the Civil War and the royalist cause and the Restoration of 1660 was thus metamorphosed into a 'Cavalier' victory. Charles II was said to have given these spaniels the freedom of every inn in the land, although no such statute has ever been traced.

After the rout of the Young Pretender at Culloden in 1746, the Jacobites gradually lost their potency as a threat and the spaniel ceased to be stigmatised by the Hanoverians, for whom ownership of a 'King Charles', Cavalier or otherwise, would have been an unacceptable humiliation. The rehabilitation of the breed at court was a measure of the security of the dynasty and a final act of reconciliation. Just two months after Culloden, the Swiss painter Barthélemey du Pan (1712–63) painted a portrait of the children of Frederick, Prince of Wales, which not only included two spaniels but also depicted Prince George in a jacket of red tartan very similar to that now

P. E. Stroehling's portrait of George III at Windsor was painted in 1807, the year the legitimate line of Stuarts became extinct.

known as 'Royal Stewart'. George Knapton's version of the same subject, painted in 1751, shows a pug and a spaniel. During the reign of George III the breed received a full royal pardon. In 1765 the King spent £525 buying back Van Dyck's *Five Eldest Children of Charles I* for the royal collection and, in the portrait by Johann Zoffany (1733–1810) of *George Prince of Wales and Prince Frederick* painted that same year, not only do the royal children play with a spaniel but Van Dyck's picture of the *Three Eldest Children of Charles I* can be seen hanging on the wall in the background. In his portrait of *Queen Charlotte with Members of Her Family* – and a small spaniel – of 1770, Zoffany's sitters wear Van Dyck costume. Gainsborough's 1781 portrait of Charlotte with her spaniel, Badine, considered by many as the finest of the reign, confirmed his position as unofficial court painter and guaranteed further royal commissions. John Hoppner (c. 1758–1810), Principal Painter of the Prince of Wales from 1793, had painted Princess Amelia with a spaniel in 1785. Spaniels can be seen in many of the portraits of the King and his family painted by the German artist P. E. Stroehling in the early nineteenth century at the request of the Prince Regent who appointed him his Historical Painter in 1810. In his picture of George III at Windsor, not only does the King have a spaniel at his feet, looking up at him lovingly, but the statue of Charles II is clearly visible in the background. This was painted in 1807, the year when the legitimate Stuart line became extinct. It was an appropriate moment to stress the legitimacy of the dynasty: Hanover had been annexed by the Prussians the previous year and Napoleon was busily removing recalcitrant monarchs from their hereditary thrones.

Although official recognition as the 'King Charles' spaniel necessarily had to wait until the founding of the Kennel Club, the breed had clearly long laid claim to the title. Thomas Bewick, in his *General History of Quadrupeds*, published in 1790, referred to the toy spaniel as 'that beautiful little dog, King Charles' dog',[19] and when Edwin Landseer painted the dogs of Mr Vernon in 1832 the portrait was unequivocally titled *Spaniels of the King Charles Breed* or *Cavalier's Pets*. In his painting of Queen Victoria's pets, her spaniel Dash sits regally on a plush velvet stool with two greyhounds behind her like courtiers. Such was the popularity of the breed that by 1841 there were five thousand spaniels kept as parlour pets in London alone. King Charles spaniels received their official baptism in 1902 when Edward VII overrode the Kennel Club, which preferred to have them categorised as English toy spaniels, to insist on the maintenance of their royal title; the Cavalier King Charles was not officially recognised as a breed until 1945.

Notwithstanding the many references to his spaniels in contemporary memoirs, his dogs rarely feature in the portraits of Charles II. One of the few to include them was painted by his court painter Hendrik Danckerts (c. 1625–c. 1679) and shows the King being presented with a pineapple by Rose, the Royal Gardener. The two dogs are toy spaniels of a strain indistinguishable from those depicted in continental art of the period. Early in his reign, when Charles appealed for the return of a dog he had lost, he rather illogically stressed that 'the dog was not

Detail of spaniel from Danckerts' painting of Charles II being presented with a pineapple.

born nor bred in England and would never forsake his master', as if it might run into linguistic difficulties without him to act as interpreter. His spaniels were almost certainly Bolognese, with no ties of kinship to those preferred by his father and most probably obtained in France where he spent much of his exile. When Charles sailed back to England aboard the *Naseby* in 1660, Pepys, who accompanied him, noted the presence of a dog 'that the King loved (which shit in the boat, which made us laugh and me think that a King and all that belong to him are but just as others are)'.[20] Jean Nocret's portrait of Charles's sister, Henriette, Duchesse d'Orléans, shows her with a toy spaniel on her lap. It was perhaps her liking for them which led the Duc d'Orléans' second wife, Charlotte, daughter of the Elector Palatine, to repudiate them in favour of a larger strain: 'a pretty little dog is all very well for amusement, but not to console oneself with. I do not like Boulognes [sic],

Detail of the Bologna spaniel from Ruel's painting of Charlotte of the Palatinate. It reveals that she liked the strain well enough in her youth.

because they are too delicate. I much prefer French spaniels. I have usually four of them at my heels and at night they sleep beside me.'[21]

Pugs had been considered partisans of the House of Nassau-Orange since William the Silent (1533–84, Stadholder from 1572), first of the hereditary Stadholders of the United Provinces of the Netherlands, took up arms against the Spanish. In his 'Actions of the Low Countries', written in 1618, Sir Roger Williams described how, in c. 1573,

> the Prince of Orange being retired into the camp, Julian Romero, with earnest persuasions, procured licence of the Duke d'Alva to hasard a camisado or night attack, upon the Prince. At midnight Julian sallied out of the trenches with a thousand armed men, mostly pikes, who forced all the guards that they found in their way into the place of arms before the Prince's tent, and killed two of his secretaries. The Prince himself escaped very narrowly, for I have often heard him say that he thought but for a dog he should have been taken or slain. The attack was made with such resolution that the guards took no alarm until their fellows were running to the place of arms with their enemies at their heels, when this dog, hearing a great noise, fell to scratching and crying, and awakened him before any of his men; and though the Prince slept armed, with a lackey always holding one of his horses ready bridled and saddled, yet at the going out of his tent with much ado he recovered his horse before the enemy arrived. Nevertheless one of his equerries was slain, taking horse presently after him, as were divers of his servants. The Prince, to show his gratitude, until his dying day, kept one of that dog's race, and so did many of his friends and followers. These animals were not remarkable for their beauty, being little white dogs, with crooked noses, called camuses [flat-nosed].[22]

Pugs long remained the national dog of the Netherlands and, as late as 1780, William Beckford noted their ubiquity in Utrecht, where he saw 'scarce an avenue but swarmed with female josses; little squat pug-dogs waddling at their sides, the attributes, I suppose, of these fair divinities'.[23]

William III brought pugs with him to England in 1688 and they rapidly became the most fashionable pet of the aristocracy in the first half of the eighteenth century and as important an accessory as the black page. George II was portrayed by Charles Phillips (1708–42) in the library at

Portrait of George II painted by Charles Phillips in 1737, showing the King with two pugs in the library of St James's Palace.

St James's Palace with two pugs at his feet. In a poem written in 1728, John Gay describes how:

> Poor pug was caught, to town conveyed,
> There sold. How envied was his doom,
> Made captive in a lady's room.

They retained their popularity at court until the close of the nineteenth century. In a painting undertaken in 1800 by the Belgian artist Albrecht de Vriendt, George III can be seen playing cards with a pug at his feet. Victoria, in the course of her long reign, owned no fewer than thirty-six, many of which were painted by Charles Burton Barber in the 1870s and 1880s.

They fell out of favour with the British monarchy in the twentieth century but recovered quasi-royal status in the 1950s when adopted as the preferred breed of the Duke and Duchess of Windsor, who owned nine altogether. Their cult of the pug was taken to extremes: not only did their mansion contain innumerable Meissen figurines and artefacts, but the Duke applied his prodigious talent for *gros point* to the embroidery of their portraits on to cushions. The Duke had thitherto shown a preference for cairns, as had his father George V, and had continued to acquire them until and beyond the abdication, when Charles Bedaux presented him with Preezie. The repudiation of the cairn by the Duchess was a conscious act of defiance, not lost on the Queen Mother, who has allegedly detested pugs ever since. The antagonism

Photograph of the Duke and Duchess of Windsor with a pug, by Dorothy Wilding. The fixation of the childless Windsors with the breed began in the 1950s.

between the two women was long-standing. In retaliation for the Prince of Wales's and Mrs Simpson's 'secret' pseudonym, 'Cookie', for the Duchess of York, as she was then styled, the latter changed the name of her corgi, Rozavel Golden Eagle, to 'Dookie' – a sardonic reference to Wallis's American pronunciation of 'Dukie', as Wallis somewhat indecorously called George. Wallis, who appears to have exhibited no liking for pets before she met Edward in 1932, had to bide her time before she could repay in kind. Opportunity presented itself in 1955 when the crisis provoked by Princess Margaret's desire to marry a divorced commoner was at its height: the Duchess of Windsor named one of her pugs Peter Townsend.

From their first appearance in Europe towards the end of the sixteenth century, pugs had rapidly ingratiated themselves at continental courts and such was their popularity that, from 1738, when Pope Clement XII forbade membership of masonic orders, the breed was adopted as a symbol by many highborn Catholics forming themselves into quasi-masonic lodges. These were styled Orders of Mopses (after the German for pug) and, unlike the freemasons, admitted women. To prove their affiliation, members carried snuffboxes, the finest made of hard-paste porcelain with jewelled gold and silver mounts and adorned with images of pugs. These, together with figurines of the dog, were produced at the Meissen porcelain factory where the *modellmeister* from 1733 was the Elector of Saxony's court sculptor, J. J. Kandler (1706–75). The Chinese had been manufacturing models of animals for centuries before Meissen discovered the secret behind hard-paste porcelain in 1710, but such was the influence of Kandler that they were soon using his models as prototypes for the pugs and greyhounds that they exported to Europe.

Although Kandler sculpted models of all the breeds fashionable in Saxony at the time – principally pugs, Bolognese, Great Danes and dachshunds – he was less a pioneer than a reflection of the new rococo taste for individual pet portraits. Previously dogs had featured in art as accessories in the unfolding of a story or were represented alongside their illustrious owners. Official *peintres d'animaux*, like A. F. Desportes (1661–1743), had specialised in hunting – as opposed to domestic – scenes. One of the first artists to explore this new genre was Francisco Michans at the court of Philip V of Spain, who portrayed Fidel, the French poodle of the infante Don Fernando (1713–59, King from 1746), with the lion-clip favoured

Portrait by Francisco Michans of the poodle Fidel, belonging to the infante Don Fernando. It was probably a posthumous tribute to the prince's favourite dog.

at the time, standing immobile beside what is in all probability the dog's own sarcophagus. Canine fidelity was a theme also celebrated by Kandler's counterpart at the French court, Jean-Jacques Bachelier (1724–1806), Directeur of the Manufacture de Sèvres from 1756 to 1793, and protégé of Louis XV's mistress, Madame de Pompadour. His double portrait of her spaniel, Mimi, and poodle, Iñes, was exhibited at the Salon of 1759. She had thirteen of his paintings altogether. Madame de Pompadour also patronised Christophe Huet (1700–59) who entitled his portraits of Mimi and Inès *La Constance* and *La Fidélité* respectively. She commissioned both Guérin and Boucher to paint her with Mimi.[24]

On her death in 1764, Madame de Pompadour bequeathed five works by Jean-Baptiste Oudry (1686–1755), all of animals, to her brother, the Marquis de Marigny. The formative influence on Oudry was not Desportes but Nicolas de Largillière, under whom he had served a five-year apprenticeship from around 1705. In 1724 he made contact with Louis Fagon, *Intendant des Finances*, and Henri-Camille, Marquis de Beringhen, *Premier Ecuyer du Roi*, and thus one of the most important courtiers involved in the organisation of the Royal Hunt. Oudry soon began to attract the King's attention, and in 1726 he was commissioned to paint Louis XV's Italian greyhounds, Misse and Turlù. The same year, he was given lodgings at the Tuileries Palace and presented a command exhibition at Versailles. Confirmation that Desportes had been eclipsed came with the commission to paint the series of nine Royal Hunts of Louis XV in 1733. Oudry drew from life, and the models for the animals in these canvases were provided by the menagerie at Versailles.

Oudry was not confined to painting the Royal Hunt, however, and he completed a set of 275 drawings for an illustrated edition of the fables of La Fontaine in 1734, besides designing eight tapestries depicting Ovid's *Metamorphoses* for Beauvais. The most noted of all his later works was the *Bitchhound Nursing her Pups*, exhibited in the Salon of 1753, a revolutionary work which 'pin-pointed the moment when that all-embracing empathy between man and dog was first recorded so fully and so tenderly in a canine environment'.[25] The degree of maternal sentiment exuded by the bitch was unparalleled in contemporary depictions of women with their young. Oudry pioneered the pictorial humanisation of the dog and heavily influenced all French artists of the genre from Carle van Loo and Boucher, his pupil, through to Fragonard, Nattier and Greuze. After the hiatus of the Revolution and Empire, a school of *animaliers* emerged, led by Antoine-Louis Barye (1796–1875) and specialising in animals divested of their owners.

Individual portraits of pets first appeared in England as a result of continental influence. One of the earliest models of a dog was William Hogarth's pug Trump, sculpted in the 1740s by the French Huguenot immigrant Roubiliac, and subsequently used as a model by the Chelsea Porcelain manufacture. Roubiliac made a significant contribution to the formation of English rococo. The eccentric cross-dressing sculptor, Anne Seymour Damer (1748–1828 – it was to her that Horace Walpole bequeathed Strawberry Hill in 1797) specialised in sentimentalised models of miniature dogs. So devoted was she to her own dog that, on her death in 1828, she insisted on being buried with its ashes. Thomas Gainsborough's mastery as an animal artist was most ably demonstrated in his 1771 portrait of Tristram and Fox, his own *Pomeranian with her Puppy*, a

Model of Hogarth's pug Trump, by Louis-François Roubiliac. The figure was used as a source for the white glazed figures produced by the Chelsea Porcelain Manufactory.

breed only recently introduced from Germany but which was rapidly becoming a favourite in court and aristocratic circles. The greatest animal painter of them all was unquestionably George Stubbs (1724–1806), whose portraits of dogs combined extraordinary anatomical precision with profound insight into the inner psychology of the animal. His *White Poodle on a Punt*, painted in the 1780s, clearly conveyed the anxiety of the dog, stranded without its master. By the 1790s Stubbs finally attracted royal notice and he painted no fewer than eighteen oils for the Prince of Wales in the short number of years that remained of his life. As with Gainsborough, the Pomeranian, Fino, may have been his own pet. It figures in both *Fino and Tiny*, and in *The Prince of Wales' Phaeton*, commissioned in 1793. The future George IV did not keep pets, only their portraits.

George IV's brother and successor, William IV, was a great patron of animal art. He inherited the dog portraitist Henry Bernard Chalon from Frederica, Duchess of York, whose passion for all dogs had been celebrated in a portrait by Stroehling in 1811 which includes a running dog, a gun dog, a Maltese and a Portuguese water dog. From 1831, William also employed an official Animal Painter, R. B. Davies, the son of the huntsman of George III who had trained under Beechey. Both artists later enjoyed the patronage of Victoria and Albert.

QUEEN VICTORIA

No reigning monarch ever exhibited greater devotion to – and catholicism in her choice of – pets than Queen Victoria in the course of her sixty-four years on the throne. The breeding programme that she and Prince Albert introduced extended to all the dogs in their possession and was emulated by her aristocratic subjects. Her sentimentality towards animals was the single most important factor in transforming the British into a nation renowned for their kindness to animals, a reputation they had never previously enjoyed. On several occasions the Queen personally intervened to ensure the successful passage of legislation drawn up to improve the animal lot. Her dogs became symbols of her prestige as ruler of the mightiest empire of the nineteenth century and specimens of her favourite breeds were coveted by princes across the globe.

Both Victoria and Albert loved animals and in the 1840s owned no fewer than thirty-three; the number would rise to eighty-eight by the end of the reign. They were far too numerous to be kept in the royal palaces, and the architect Henry Ashton was called in to design kennels to accommodate the surplus. Maynard, the first kennel-master, was dismissed in 1848 when he was discovered to be an embezzler. He was replaced by the Scot, John Macdonald, who retained the post until his death from consumption in 1860, when Joseph Hill succeeded him. Friedrich Keyl's painting of the kennels in 1850 shows Macdonald's daughter, Annie, fondly attending a wide variety of dogs. Victoria's kennels were a new departure in as much that they did not exclusively house hunting dogs. All the royal dogs, regardless of size, were considered as pets, and regularly visited by the Queen when in residence at Windsor.

The kennels were high on the list of priorities for visitors to Windsor, and Baroness Bunsen, wife of the Prussian ambassador to England from 1841 until 1854, reported how, 'if the Ladies in Waiting were agreeable, one could walk or drive with them, to go and see the Queen's dogs in their establishment'.[26] In a letter to her granddaughter in 1854 she described her expedition:

> I had a nice walk in the park between 11 and 12, and got Grandpapa to go with me, as far as the place where the Queen's dogs live. There is a pretty cottage with a garden, where a nice Highland woman lives, with

her five children; and she let us pass in through a succession of yards, where the different dogs were put either together or separate, according as they liked each other's company. There were beautiful dogs of all kinds, but the curiosities were, a pug all black, which I thought handsomer than the common ones, just as, if I *must* see a Negro, I would rather he was quite black than only dingy. Then there was a Chinese dog with a sky-blue tongue, and his coat all chocolate brown, from nose to tail, and to the very ends of his paws – with a droll, sly countenance – and a Cashmere dog, as big as a young lion, and with just such legs and paws – very goodnatured to those he knows, but terrible to meet as an enemy:– also an Esquimaux dog, who was one bush of hair, with sly fox-eyes and sharp nose peeping out – who must find himself much too warm in this country. The dogs were pleased to be noticed, and I should have liked to have sat down amongst them, and tried to draw them – the places were as sweet and clean as your chicken-yard.

Friedrich Keyl's painting of Queen Victoria's kennels at Windsor, 1850. Here she housed 'beautiful dogs of all kinds'.

A visit to the kennels was considered one of the high points of a state visit and Victoria noted in her diary on 17 April 1855 how she, Napoleon III and the Empress Eugenie 'walked by the Kennel, where we looked at the dogs'.[27] Victoria continued to visit the kennels until the end of her reign; in 1897 *Country Life* described how the aged Queen 'drives up in her ponychaise to the "Queen's door" – an entrance to the Spitz Court which faces the "Apron Piece" – and stops in her carriage to look at the dogs. The animals which she wishes to see are then brought out one by one, or in couples, and are either handed up into the carriage to be petted, or are let loose in groups so that the Queen may see them at play together. Her Majesty seldom comes to Windsor without making the kennels her first visit, and it is her custom to make it also her last before leaving for Balmoral or the Isle of Wight.'

Whether sufficiently privileged to reside in the royal palaces or relegated to the kennel in the Home Park at Windsor, all Victoria's pets had their portraits commissioned, normally on their arrival at court but sometimes posthumously, a practice facilitated towards the end of the nineteenth century when artists had photographs at their disposal. The portraits were hung either at the kennel or in one of the royal residences, depending as much on artistic preference as on the degree of attachment to the pet in question. Of the three individual dog portraits painted of Albert's favourite greyhound, Eos, by Edwin Landseer and George Morley in 1841, and Thomas Musgrove Joy in 1843, only Landseer's was hung in Windsor Castle. Virtually all of the animal portraits at Windsor were gifts exchanged between Victoria and Albert and their immediate family. When the royal couple particularly admired a painting commissioned as a gift outside their household, they occasionally had copies made. Sir Francis Grant painted *Victoria, Princess Royal, and Albert Edward, Prince of Wales* in 1842 as a present for the Duchess of Kent, and Victoria asked Thomas Musgrove Joy to copy it for Albert the following year. Although the portraits are virtually identical, the Queen clearly objected to Grant's use of Van Dyck costume, and the royal infants in Joy's work wear contemporary clothes. Although the dog in both pictures is a Skye terrier, begging in exactly the same fashion, Grant's is a portrait of Islay and Joy's of Dandie Dinmont.

The favourite painter of Victoria and Albert was Sir Edwin Landseer who personally instructed them both in the art of etching. When he died the Queen had in her possession no fewer than thirty-nine oils, sixteen chalk drawings, two frescoes and innumerable sketches. He was far more highly paid than any other animal artist working for the court, receiving an average of £200 per painting as early as 1840 and an impressive £840 for his *Windsor Castle in Modern Times: Queen Victoria, Prince Albert, and Victoria Princess Royal*, 1840–3, which shows Eos and three Skye terriers, Cairnach, Islay and Dandie Dinmont, the latter given pride of place on the sofa.[28] Landseer received a knighthood in 1850 and, on his death in 1873, a state funeral in St Paul's Cathedral. He owed his pre-eminence to the consummate skill with which he humanised animals. His canvases frequently contain historical references: in the 1841 portrait of Eos, the representation of the standard trappings of nineteenth-century nobility – top hat, white gloves and cane – recalls Titian's revolutionary picture of Federico Gonzaga, albeit with the important distinction that here they are illustrative of the pedigree of the dog, not the prince. Many of the portraits he undertook of the royal children in the 1840s, where he depicts them fearlessly petting the large dogs belonging to their parents, are clear references to Van Dyck. His 1841 portrait of the infant Princess Victoria with Eos, where the greyhound guards the cradle and nuzzles its head between the infant's feet, is a neo-Gothic piece, in which he reworks the ancient legend of the Welsh Prince Llewellyn and his deer-hound, Gellert. According to this tale, Llewellyn left Gellert to watch over his infant and, returning to find the cradle empty apart from some bloodstained clothes, immediately killed his dog which he wrongly held responsible for the death, little realising that it had in fact saved him from a wolf. Landseer, or his royal patrons, must have liked the theme, for he returned to it in 1843 when he painted *Princess Alice Asleep*, only, on this occasion, the Queen's favourite Skye terrier, Dandie Dinmont, somewhat improbably guards the cradle.

Nonetheless, Landseer enjoyed no royal monopoly, not least because a tendency towards depression and alcoholism made him progressively unreliable, and portraits were commissioned from a wide variety of artists, including the great Winterhalter, whose 1849 portrait *Albert, Prince of Wales and Prince Alfred*, was one of the very few of his works to include a dog. On the strength of his recommendation by Landseer, Friedrich Wilhelm Keyl, a native of Frankfurt, was commissioned in 1847 to paint the favourite royal dachshund, *Waldina and her Puppies*, where the artist makes no secret of his debt to Oudry's *Bitchhound*, itself the inspiration for *Bloodhound and Pups*, painted by Landseer's brother, Charles (1799–1879), in 1839. Keyl remained friendly with Edwin Landseer until his death and occasionally acted as his assistant. For Landseer's *Queen Victoria at Osborne*, completed in 1867, Keyl sketched the collie, Sharp, which lies obediently at John Brown's feet. It was probably Prince Albert who suggested the idea of making up the album of small watercolour paintings, 'Portraits of Dogs etc.', which occupied Keyl from 1847 to his death in 1871. The vacuum left by the death of Keyl and Landseer was filled by the latter's warm admirer, Charles Burton Barber, who continued to hold sway until his own death in 1894. One of the last animal portraitists to work for Victoria was Maud Earl, who emigrated to the United States in 1917, conscious that World War I was dealing a death blow to royal and aristocratic patronage of the arts.

The animal paintings commissioned by Victoria and Albert provide the clearest evidence for their pet preferences and their evolution over the course of her long reign. That Victoria's love of greyhounds antedated the

Friedrich Wilhelm Keyl: **Waldina and her Puppies,** *1847. Keyl was introduced to Victoria by Landseer and worked at court for over twenty years.*

arrival of Eos with Albert in 1840 is indicated by George Morley's portraits of Nero and Hector in 1836 and 1837, and Landseer's painting of *Queen Victoria on Horseback* completed in 1838. After Albert's premature death in 1861, Landseer's noble portrait of Eos was kept in the Prince's dressing room at Buckingham Palace, which the Queen

Edwin Landseer: detail from **Queen Victoria at Osborne,** *1867.*

maintained as a shrine. In 1895, when Marie Mallet, Victoria's maid of honour from 1887 to 1891, presented her young son Victor to the Queen, the boy endeared himself by lavishing praise on the painting: 'the Queen was enchanted, no courtier could have spoken better,' commented the proud mother.[29] Victoria's admiration for greyhounds appears to have dwindled over the years despite the breeding programme established with Eos. When she was given Giddy by Lord Lurgan in 1873, both the bitch and its portrait by Charles Burton Barber were dispatched to the kennels.

Skye terriers were the favourite pets of the Queen in the 1840s. Scotty, aptly named after its country of origin, was the first, soon followed by Islay, Dandie Dinmont and Cairnach, all of which were painted by Landseer and other court artists, often on more than one occasion. As was habitually the case with Victoria, a whole dynasty of Skye terriers was named after Cairnach; Otto Weber (1832–88) painted a dog by that name in 1875, sitting with Dot in the Queen's room at the kennels. Boz, the Skye terrier painted by Keyl in 1861 and Landseer in 1867, had been the pet of the Duchess of Kent and was inherited by Victoria on her mother's death.

There is little evidence to suggest that Victoria preferred small breeds and Albert larger ones. The painting by T. M. Joy of four dogs in 1845 which includes the German boar-hound, Vulcan, a present from Coburg in 1845, Nelson the Newfoundland and Hotspur the bloodhound, was commissioned by Albert as a present for the Queen, as was the portrait of the St Bernard, Maurice, by John William Bottomley in 1859. Large dogs were often sent by foreign princes and, however gratefully received, their size alone was sufficient to ensure their instant removal to the kennels.

Dogs were loved indiscriminately by Victoria and Albert and even the paintings can be misleading. Charles Burton Barber's 1877 painting of *A Family of Pugs* may have sufficiently pleased the Queen to earn a place at Osborne, but the dogs themselves were kept at the kennels which provide the backdrop.

One breed Victoria unquestionably favoured above most was the dachshund. The earliest was Waldmann, sent from Germany in 1840 and painted by both Landseer and George Morley the following year. Däckel, another gift from their native Germany, arrived in 1845 and was soon sitting for Landseer; both portrait and dog resided at Windsor Castle. As with other breeds, dynasties were soon firmly established, with puppies confusingly receiving the same names as their forebears – rather as princes themselves. Dacko, a descendant of Däckel born in the kennels in 1859, was painted by Keyl in 1871. Waldmann, the subject of a posthumous painting by Charles Burton Barber in 1881, was purchased by the Queen in Baden in 1872, a year after the death of her beloved Dacko, and was not necessarily related to the earlier dog of that name. There was another dachshund, Waldie, modelled by the sculptor Boehm in 1869 lying beside John Brown. Victoria was given yet another Waldmann by her daughter, Princess Christian of Schleswig-Holstein, in 1895. All the dachshund portraits appear to have hung in various royal palaces.

By the mid-1860s dachshunds were suffering competition from collies, a breed Victoria had first encountered in the Highlands and which came to embody her passion for all things Scottish. She kept the portrait of one of her early favourites, Sharp (1864–79), painted by Charles Burton Barber in 1872, in her dressing room at Osborne. Sharp was also modelled by Boehm, once with John Brown and on two separate occasions, between 1869 and 1872, with the Queen. Although she owned five collies named Noble, it was Noble IV, a gift in 1872, which she particularly cherished. Barber painted the dog on at least eight occasions; his 1877 group portrait of *Queen Victoria with Princess Beatrice and a Group of Dogs at Windsor*, shows Waldmann with three collies, Sharp, Noble IV and Fern, painted entirely from photographs. Noble was sculpted by Boehm in 1884 so realistically that visitors to Osborne persist in stroking it to this day.[30] In the 1870s both Victoria and the Prince of Wales were given specimens of a new strain of collie by the breeder H. W. Charles of Wellerbourne whose dogs were entirely white. One of the Queen's, Snowball, was painted by Barber in 1879 together with a brace of Pomeranians, Janey and Marco. The Snowball in the 1895 portrait by Maud Earl must necessarily be a later addition to the family, sharing its predecessor's name in time-honoured Victorian fashion. Barber also painted Nanny, another of the Queen's white collies, in 1885, with Spot, a smooth-haired fox-terrier.

By the 1880s fox-terriers and Pomeranians were rapidly threatening the hegemony of the collies. Spot had been painted by Barber in 1883 with another fox-terrier of the Queen's, Wat, and two royal collies attended by John Brown who had died earlier in the year. Spot was the subject of two further portraits by Barber in 1885 and 1887. Victoria purchased her first Pomeranian in Florence in 1888 and christened it Marco, lest it forget its country of origin. She grew so attached to this dog that it accompanied her wherever she travelled and was portrayed by Reuben Cole in 1890 and by Barber in 1892 standing on the Queen's breakfast table at Windsor.

Photograph of Queen Victoria's dog Snowball. The white strain of collie was first bred in the 1870s.

EDWARD AND ALEXANDRA

Both Edward and Alexandra had loved animals since childhood and, after their marriage in 1863, they began to accumulate pets of all breeds as enthusiastically as did the Queen, who gave them as a wedding present a Minton dinner service decorated with pictures after Landseer of their favourite dogs. Victoria also commissioned many portraits of their pets, the best painted by Charles Burton Barber, which she gave to them as presents. Fozzy, the Pomeranian that accompanied the Prince of Wales to India in 1875, was painted in 1877, and Beaty, a gift from the Tsar, in 1889. Rover and Puggy, the favourite collie and pug of the Princess of Wales, were painted by Barber in 1878. Boehm modelled Tom, Edward's favourite poodle, in 1870. Alexandra's confession, 'I like people, but I love animals', was borne out by her behaviour. She not only collected strays but allowed a great many animals to roam wild at Sandringham House. Her bookplates, which she designed herself, were decorated with pictures of 'her favourite books, her favourite music, her favourite dogs, a picture of Windsor, a picture of the Palace at Copenhagen, and a little strip of music, the first bars of her favourite song . . .'[31]

The estate at Sandringham was purchased in 1870 and the kennels were built in 1879 on similar lines to those in the Home Park, Windsor, closed by King Edward in 1903. All his mother's dogs, of which there remained over seventy, were transferred to the kennels at Sandringham which comprised some fifteen houses, each with a yard and every five having a grass plot in front. There was a large paddock where the dogs exercised and separate kennels for sick dogs and puppies. In 1897 they were under the supervision of W. Brunsdon, who wore livery whenever in attendance on the Prince. In January that year, *Country Life* described it as consisting of

> a dark green coat and waistcoat, with gold buttons, bearing a suitable
> design, whilst round his hat is a gold cord and tassel, the whole giving
> an idea of serviceableness and decided smartness, especially when seen
> at one of the hunting parties, when it stands out in quiet contrast to the
> blue blouses and black hats with scarlet bands of the innumerable beat-
> ers. In cases of slight sickness amongst the dogs under his charge,
> Brunsdon administers whatever remedy he may think fit to use, and he
> is acknowledged to be very successful in his treatment; but in cases of

serious illness Mr. Sewell is sent for from London, and then takes all responsibility upon himself. Brunsdon's house is in the kennel enclosure; the back of it . . . facing the kennels and yards, so that should any disturbance arise at night, he has only a few steps to go to set matters right.

Alexandra emulated Victoria in paying regular visits to the kennels, as Baroness de Stoeckl recorded: 'On Sunday afternoons the kennels had to be visited, the Queen and Empress covered in huge white aprons, baskets filled with pieces of bread, followed by the guests and Court; the latter bored at having to do the same thing every Sunday. The dogs seemed to smell that bread much before they could possibly see it. They started barking, the noise unbelievable, throwing themselves against the bars of their kennels. A few were let out, others were too fierce, jumping all over their Majesties.'[32] In a painting by Thomas Blinks and Fred Morgan completed in 1902, *Queen Alexandra with Her Grandchildren and Her Favourite Pets* – which includes a schipperke for the first time – the Queen is shown feeding the dogs herself from a basket while a kennel helper is releasing a collie from the kennels in the background.

Frances Fairman: **Haru and Togo,** *1902. Togo was a gift to Queen Alexandra from the Empress of Japan.*

Photograph of the favourite dogs of the Princess of Wales in 1897 with Plumpy the chow and two chins.

Alexandra commissioned many portraits of her dogs and was particularly anxious to have her favourite Japanese spaniels, or chins, immortalised. Luke Fildes had painted the Princess of Wales with one of these dogs in 1893 but, when Alexandra became patron of the Ladies' Kennel Association in 1894, she was keen to promote many of its female artist members. Both Mrs Gertrude Massey and Miss Frances Fairman painted her Japanese spaniels and the latter also undertook a portrait of Togo, a gift from the Mikado in 1902, which appropriately shows chrysanthemum petals strewn across the floor. The most celebrated of all Edward's pets was portrayed by both Fairman and Maud Earl, who described how she 'painted the picture of Caesar at Buckingham Palace. The work was under the direct and constant supervision of King Edward and Queen Alexandra. I was given a room between the private apartments of the monarch and his consort.'[33] Entitled *Caesar: I belong to the King*, the engravings made subsequently by the Berlin Photographic Company shot both dog and picture to fame. The greatest honour bestowed on the royal favourite was to be modelled by Fabergé in chalcedony with cabochon-ruby eyes, replete with brown enamelled gold collar and bell and bearing the famous inscription 'I belong to the King'. Edward judged it a good likeness and presented it to the Queen in 1908. They had first visited Fabergé's showroom in 1894 when in Russia for the funeral of Alexander III and the marriage of his successor, Nicholas II, to Alexandra of Hesse. From the moment he established a showroom in London in 1903 the King and Queen became avid collectors of his animal miniatures which they displayed in two large glass cabinets in the drawing room at Sandringham, illuminated each night by specially installed electric lights.

Fabergé models of Edward and Alexandra's pets. The King and Queen were enthusiastic patrons of the Russian jeweller.

CAESAR

Caesar was bred by the Duchess of Newcastle and presented to the King by Lord Dudley in 1902. So instantly and strongly was Edward attached to the dog that it was a case of *aut Caesar aut nullus* from the outset and it escorted him everywhere until the King's death in 1910. Edward's assistant private secretary, Sir Frederick Ponsonby, who accompanied the King on all his trips to the Continent, was aboard the royal yacht, *Victoria and Albert*, in 1902 when the King was convalescing after a serious illness. Ponsonby was summoned to the royal presence to find Edward sitting in bed smoking a cigar. When Queen Alexandra came in, Ponsonby described how 'I felt I ought to make myself scarce, and when Caesar, the King's terrier, was brought in I discreetly left'.

Caesar was a cross that all servants of the Crown had to bear: Charles Hardinge, assistant under-secretary at the Foreign Office, who travelled with Edward VII on his royal tour in 1903, recalled in his memoirs how 'the King had a delightful rough-haired terrier named Caesar that never left him. Whenever I went into the King's cabin this dog always went for my trousers and worried them, much to the King's delight. I used not to take the slightest notice and went on talking all the time to the King, which I think amused His Majesty still more.'[34]

Xavier Paoli, the special commissary attached to the Paris Detective Service, and the man responsible for the King's personal safety in France, left an invaluable record of the internal arrangements of Edward's household as it functioned on the Continent:

> The two footmen who accompanied the King when travelling also had settled duties. One of them, Hoepfner, was a German who owed his brilliant career to his fine carriage. . . When King Edward noticed his gigantic height and the correctness of his bearing, he took him into his service in his turn. Hoepfner waited on the sovereign at table and opened the door of the royal apartments, whereas the other footman, a British subject called Wellard, was charged exclusively with the care of His Majesty's clothes, boots and dog, an absorbing duty when we reflect that the King travelled with 70 pieces of luggage, including a countless number of Gladstone bags, and that he took with him some 40 suits of clothes and over 20 pairs of boots and shoes.

Photograph of Edward VII and Caesar. The most celebrated of all the King's dogs, Caesar was a cross the entire court had to bear.

There was also the dog.

Caesar was a person of importance. This long-haired, rough-coated, white fox-terrier, with the black ears, was not exactly distinguished for the aristocratic elegance that marks Queen Alexandra's dogs, whose acquaintance I have also had the opportunity of making. Caesar had rather what we Frenchmen call *la beauté du diable*. He had a strong personality and a quick intelligence. He was very independent in his ways, a little mischievous and playful and deeply attached to his royal master, who pampered him as one would a child. When the King was travelling, Caesar went with him everywhere and did not leave him day or night, for he slept in an easy-chair to the right of his bed. He was present at all the King's meals and willingly accepted any bits of meat or sugar which the guests offered him. I succeeded in winning his good graces and we became first-rate friends. On the other hand, once he was out of doors, he cut all his acquaintances. Whether on the beach at Biarritz or in the Rue de la Paix in Paris, he was always seen at the King's heels, proudly displaying a collar that bore the legend 'I am Caesar, the King's dog [sic]'. And it was as though he knew it. When Wellard, the second footman, had brushed the King's clothes and cleaned the King's boots, he proceeded to groom Caesar; for the high favour which the terrier enjoyed compelled him to be always scrupulously clean. Every morning, he was washed and cleaned with care. I will not go so far as to swear that he liked it. Nevertheless he submitted to it with resignation.[35]

The privileged few who were invited by the King to be his guests on his annual jaunt to Biarritz found it unbearably tedious, not least because of Caesar. Violet, the daughter of Edward's mistress, Alice Keppel, was in the royal party of 1906. She later admitted in an unpublished memoir, 'Triple Violette', how she detested the dog which had sat on her knee as they drove to a picnic and, despite its regular ablutions, allegedly stank.[36] The King himself considered Caesar to be one of the major obstacles to the Entente Cordiale.

The lover of Violet Keppel (later Trefusis), Vita Sackville-West, was one of the millions who attended the funeral of Edward VII in 1910 and recalled how 'everyone cried when they saw the King's little dog following the coffin'.[37] On Alexandra's instructions, Caesar was placed immediately behind the gun carriage, trotting alongside the late King's charger, led by

Photograph of Edward VII's funeral procession. The sight of Caesar following the coffin reduced spectators to tears.

Maclean, the royal gillie and gun-loader, and accompanied by the members of the royal family, nine kings, scores of princes and high dignitaries from virtually every country in the world. John Wheeler-Bennett recorded how the German 'Emperor marched with the new King, George V, and his only surviving uncle, the Duke of Connaught, all resplendent in the uniform of British field-marshals. Although what impressed me most deeply at the time was the sight of Caesar, the late King's wire-haired terrier, being led by a royal groom behind the charger with boots reversed in the stirrups . . .'[38] The Kaiser, himself a great dog lover, was among the few diarists never to mention Caesar, despite having met the dog on many occasions, but then his memoirs equally omitted any reference to his own dachshunds.

Caesar was inconsolable when Edward died and spent days whining pitifully outside the King's bedroom door, refusing to eat. Eventually Alexandra was able to coax him back to normal by lavishing attention on him and taking him into her own room. The dog's reputation remained undiminished. *Silent Sorrow*, the painting by Maud Earl in which Caesar is seen leaning his head on his master's chair, was reproduced in the *London Illustrated News* on 21 May 1910, and a book, *Where's Master?*, was published the same year.[39] Baroness de

Stoeckl was at Sandringham after Edward's death and recalled how on 'the last day of our visit, during luncheon, several dogs came into the room, a fox terrier amongst them. The Princess [Victoria] whispered to me *"C'est le célèbre"*.'[40]

Caesar died after an operation in April 1914 with Alexandra at his side, stroking his head. He was buried at Marlborough House, in the dog cemetery built by the Queen, and flowers were regularly placed on his grave. Alexandra composed the inscription herself: 'Our beloved Caesar who was the King's Faithful and Constant Companion until Death and My Greatest Comforter in my Loneliness and Sorrow for Four Years after. Died April 18th 1914.' In 1918 Caesar was symbolically reunited with Edward when his recumbent figure was carved at the King's feet on his tomb in St George's Chapel, Windsor.

DOG SHOWS

As neither Caesar nor the Queen's Japanese spaniels were outstanding examples of their breeds they did not feature among the royal dogs participating in various dog shows from 1864 until the death of Alexandra in 1925. The idea of the dog show evolved from dog-fighting and rat-catching contests, called 'matches' or 'leads', at which owners had gathered to compare the skills of their animals, usually in public houses. The invention of the railway greatly facilitated the transportation of animals across the country and, in 1859, the first British dog show was held in the town hall in Newcastle-upon-Tyne. At a similar show in Birmingham a few months later, non-sporting breeds participated for the first time. This was the year that saw the publication of Charles Darwin's *The Origin of Species by Means of Natural Selection*. The discovery of evolution coincided with that of genetics by the Austrian botanist and biologist, Gregor Johann Mendel (1822–84). Ignorance of inheritance characteristics had thitherto meant dogs being classified according to function rather than appearance. Certain breeds might be admired for their noble qualities but comparisons within breeds were unheard of. Pedigree was a philosophical, not a scientific, concept. As a result of the findings of Darwin and Mendel, axioms like *bon chien, chien de race*, which dated back to the Renaissance, became statements of irrefutable fact where before they had been little more than expressions of the

Christian belief in a divinely ordained hierarchy in the natural world. One of the principal objectives of the Kennel Club from its foundation in 1873 was to discourage the breeding of mongrels, and the first volume of their Stud Book refused to list any dogs exhibited before 1859 because of their unverifiable antecedents. Pets mirrored the social status of their owners and purity of breed soon became the preoccupation of the newly launched specialist dog clubs which vied with each other to attract royal patronage.

The International Dog Show, held in London in 1863, was the first to attract royal attention. The Duchess of Manchester entered two Russian borzois, Sultan and Juba, bred by Prince Karl of Prussia (1801–83), and won first prize with the latter. The Prince and Princess of Wales were regular participants in various dog shows from 1864 when they entered two borzois, a Newfoundland, an Indian mastiff, a Russian retriever and a harrier at the second International Show held in Laycock's Yard, Islington. They particularly favoured shows held by the Kennel Club, which enjoyed Edward's patronage from its inception in 1873, and Charles Cruft, who held his first show at the Royal Aquarium in London in 1889. From 1891, when it was held at the Royal Agricultural Hall for the first time, Cruft's Great Dog Show was pre-eminent in the field. Cruft must have had some inkling of the winners for he chose as emblem a medallion of Victoria's collie, Darnley II, lifted from the portrait by Charles Burton Barber, and surmounted by the British crown. The Queen had consented to exhibit not just her collie but three Pomeranians, Gena, Fluffy and Nino, the latter two bred by herself, in the category of 'Open White Dogs', all of which won prizes. The Prince of Wales entered four bassets, which he too had bred himself from the original brace, Babil and Bijou, given to him by the Comtesse de Paris. Royal patronage guaranteed that their favourite breeds – and Charles Cruft – reigned supreme.

Victoria's association with Cruft's came to an abrupt end in 1893 when she attributed an outbreak of canine distemper in her kennels to contact with the other dogs at the show. Nothing daunted, the Prince and Princess of Wales remained eager participants, becoming the arbiters of canine taste by the turn of the century when the newly launched illustrated journals, like *Country Life*, began to run features on their pets and kennels. It was no coincidence that, among the most popular breeds in

Photograph of Alix the borzoi and Queen Alexandra. Alix, a gift to the Queen from the Tsar, enjoyed such celebrity that people would queue for hours simply to catch a glimpse of the elegant champion.

1908, when the Kennel Club registered 535 dogs, were Pomeranians, fox-terriers, Pekingese and collies, all of which could command extremely high prices. A champion collie or fox-terrier might fetch as much as £1,000 and £375 respectively. The priciest dog of them all was the bor-zoi, a breed unknown in Britain before 1863 when both Victoria and

Alexandra received a brace from the Tsar, bred in the kennels of Prince Galitzin. The Grand Duke Nicholas and the Tsar exhibited their own borzois at Cruft's in 1892. Alix, the favourite pet borzoi of Alexandra, which she received from the Tsar in 1895, was exhibited on more occasions than any other of her dogs, winning over a hundred awards in the course of its show life, including the celebrated five-hundred-guinea Dohlpur Cup. Alix's countless admirers would queue for hours at dog shows simply to catch a glimpse of the most famous of all the Queen's pets.[41]

Like Victoria before them, Edward and Alexandra loved all dogs irrespective of nationality and were eager to exhibit breeds thitherto unfamiliar in Britain. Their cosmopolitan example was followed by the country at large and the attempt, in 1869, to establish a National Dog Club met with disaster. In 1876 the judge at the Fakenham Show was nevertheless shaken by the Prince's insistence on entering four Indian dogs, including a brace of Rampur hounds, given to him during his recent tour of the subcontinent. The introduction of the quarantine laws in 1901 put paid to international shows and prevented continental breeders, royal or otherwise, from competing. The *cordon sanitaire* nevertheless proved a boon to British breeders, who concentrated on achieving ever higher standards in dogs popularised by their royal associations. Dogs from aristocratic kennels were *ipso facto* the most coveted: the Duchess of Newcastle specialised in Clumbers, borzois and fox-terriers; Sir Everett Millais in bassets; the Countess of Warwick in Japanese spaniels. Although dog shows and Kennel Clubs had burgeoned across Europe at much the same time, it was to British-bred dogs that foreigners aspired, as the French veterinarian Pierre Megnin observed in 1883: 'we confidently admire everything that comes from abroad and, more especially, from England.'[42] Royal tastes were imitated across the globe and religious principles discarded where prejudicial to ownership of a prized dog; Sir Vincent Caillard, financial representative of England, Holland and Belgium in Constantinople and a confidant of the Sultan, told Marie Mallet that Abdul Hamid II, who had acceded to the Ottoman throne in 1875, liked nothing better than 'giving his favourite collie a daily bath, taming tame ducks on a tiny pond and learning the bicycle'.[43] Irrespective of whether they were Hindu or Moslem, the anglomania of the vast majority of the Indian princes led them to spend astronomical sums on prize pedigree dogs from Cruft's. The grandson of the Maharajah of Kapurthala recalled how 'we would hear the patter of his [the Maharajah's] Pekingese or Pomeranians preceding him and they would come straight into the room because they knew exactly where he was going'.[44] Artists, as well as breeders, were the beneficiaries of this mania for pure-breeds: Reuben Ward Binks, who was patronised by Edward VII and George V, went to India and painted about one hundred of the dogs of the Maharajah Dhiraj of Patiala, including Labradors, springer and cocker spaniels, fox-terriers and chows.[45]

Cruft's closed its doors during the years 1917–21 when food shortages made the very idea of exhibiting toy dogs tasteless. As a result of the war, certain breeds, previously prized as being preferred by the royal family, became tainted by their nationality. Dachshunds, once fêted as the favourite breed of Victoria, were spurned as German dogs, worse still the beloved pets of the Queen's grandson, Britain's arch-foe, the Kaiser. The unprecedented popularity of the German shepherd dog was the result of its rebirth not simply as a French animal but, more specifically, Alsatian. It thus embodied France's bitter struggle to recover Alsace, ceded to Germany after the Franco-Prussian War. The dog was given official recognition as an 'Alsatian' by the Kennel Club in 1919. The Prince of Wales, later Edward VIII, was an early admirer, entering his Alsatian, Claus of Seale, at Cruft's in the 1920s. His grandmother, the Duchess of Teck, had kept the most prestigious kennels in Germany before the war. Ironically, on his visits to the front, the Kaiser had been accompanied not by his dachshunds, with their far from martial gait, but by an 'Alsatian' or Deutsche Schäferhund named Senta. Inevitably, it was the favourite breed of Adolf Hitler, whose passion for Blondie was such that he poisoned it in the bunker in 1945. Give a dog a bad name and hang him.

Royal influence was bound to decline after World War I, not least because so many dynasties disappeared in its wake. Ownership of luxury dogs was frowned upon in the interwar years of economic depression. Alexandra ignored the pressure put on her to cut the cost of her kennels and continued to show dogs, particularly borzois, which had become an even rarer breed since their wholesale slaughter by the Bolsheviks in the Soviet Union. Their personal love of dogs notwithstanding, British monarchs kept a progressively lower profile and rarely exhibited. They also began to eschew 'foreign' breeds, electing to keep such 'British' breeds as Clumbers and Labradors – neither of which was of British origin – and cairns and corgis, both quintessentially national breeds. George VI was the last monarch to enter Cruft's and when, two years later in 1938, Cruft himself died, royal patronage of the show abruptly ceased. HM the Queen has only once attended a dog show, that held by the Welsh Corgi League in 1947. Nonetheless, as a result of her preference for the breed, the number of Pembrokeshire corgi registrations increased from 240 to 4,595 between 1934 and 1951. Mrs Thelma Gray, the breeder of two early royal favourites, Dookie and Jane, commanded prices of over £1,000 for her corgis in the United States.

CATS

In China, the tradition of flower and animal painting dates back to the T'ang Dynasty (AD 618–906). Artists sought to convey the Buddhist belief in the sanctity of all life and considered accuracy of observation as secondary. This did not detract from their skill, and Kenneth Clark rated Chinese cat painting under the Mings (1368–1644) as the greatest in the world.[46] The eunuch Liu Jou Yu, who wrote reminiscences of the last three Ming emperors, recorded:

> there are three or four men, body servants of the Emperor, whose special business is the feeding of those cats which have official rank or are famous. Upon all these cats the Emperors have bestowed their affections one above the other. Awaiting the Emperor's grant of names and official rank, ordinary male cats are called 'old father', the analogue for the female being 'old maid'. The pay given to the eunuchs for the upkeep of each cat is according to its rank. So noisy are the cats that all the Emperor's sons and daughters at childhood are continually brought to sickness, even unto death; and who is there that dares to complain? If there had been some places near the dwelling-house in which the cats could have been confined it would have been a good thing. We have heard that, because their sons and grandsons grew up in the palace under nurses, and loving only one wife, do not realise the importance of the rearing of children and of obtaining sons, the Imperial ancestors bred cats and pigeons.[47]

Wang T'ung-kuei, court historian under the Emperor Chia Ching (reigned 1521–67), described the favourite cat as being

> of faintly blue colour but her two eyebrows were clearly jade-white and she was called Shuang-mei [Frosty Eyebrows]. She surmised the Emperor's intentions very well. Whomever His Majesty summoned and wherever her Imperial master went, she always led. She waited upon the Emperor until he slept and then she lay still like a stump. His Majesty was very fond of her and, when she died, ordered that she should be buried in the North side of the Wan-sui mountains. By her grave was erected a stone tablet inscribed with three characters: 'Ch'ui-lung Chung' [grave of a dragon with two horns].[48]

The Mings were China's first ailurophile dynasty. Dogs were banned from the Ancestral Temple and palaces. When the chief eunuch at the court of the Emperor Wan Li (reigned 1572–1620) discovered that one of his underlings was harbouring a dog in secret, he extorted a thousand silver tails as the price of his silence.[49]

Although the Pekingese reasserted its supremacy at the court of the Manchus after 1644, cats continued to be kept as pets, particularly by royal princesses, who were virtually confined within the palaces, because it was 'a moral crime for a woman to be seen abroad in high society'.[50] The restrictions on their mobility exacerbated the monotony of court life and made the keeping of pets all the more desirable. In 1819 the Abbé Grosier recorded how 'the cat, in China, as in Europe, is the tender object of predilection and the favourite of the gentler sex. . . . Chinese ladies never allow them to leave their apartments where the most delicate of nourishment and the tenderest of care are lavished upon them. These cats are of a pure white, their coat is very long, the hairs fine and silky. Their ears are pendant. They do not catch mice, and leave this ignoble chase to the cats of vulgar race with which, be it noted, China is abundantly supplied.'[51]

The rise to popularity of the cat at seventeenth-century European courts owed much to the decline of falconry as a sport and of the fashion for birds in general as domestic pets. Having ceased to be demonised, cats became much admired for their ability to catch vermin. Unlike dogs, however, they rarely featured in royal art, not least because of the difficulties presented by persuading them to sit for their portraits. Angora cats were highly prized in Italy and plentiful at the court of Louis XV for whom, in 1772, Sèvres manufactured a *vase angora* with a hissing Angora cat forming the knob on the cover. They were also popular pets at the court of his contemporary, Catherine the Great, who was given a kitten by her lover, Potemkin. The Russian for cat is so called after a favourite imperial pet. When Tsar Nicholas II's cousin, the Grand Duke Nikolai Mikhailovich, was seized by the revolutionaries in 1917, he successfully pleaded for his cat to be allowed to accompany him to the Peter and Paul fortress in St Petersburg. Gorky's attempts to save the life of this known reformer and celebrated academic were thwarted by Lenin with the words: 'The Revolution does not need historians' and the Grand Duke met his end with his cat on his lap.[52] Cats of the Persian strain were kept by Victoria who, in 1885, commissioned Charles Burton Barber to paint *Cat and Dogs Belonging to the Queen*, in which the pug, fox-terrier and dachshund demonstrate truly noble self-control in obediently refraining from mounting an attack on their hereditary enemy. This painting is unique in being the only one of her animal paintings to show a cat. The Persians, Flypie and White Heather, were adopted by Edward and Alexandra when Victoria died in 1901.

Cat shows were held annually at the Crystal Palace in London from 1871. Despite their popularity they never attained the same prestige as the dog shows, principally because breeds differed in little other than their coats and were less susceptible to genetic manipulation. Cats did not take kindly to arranged marriages and pure-breeds were thus harder to guarantee, a major handicap in this Darwinian era when hybrid animals were increasingly perceived as being as wicked as the human products of miscegenation. Nor was spaying yet practised. Cats needed a mythology: it was claimed that the Siamese strain was the exclusive property of the King in its native Siam. They were introduced into France by the ambassador to Siam, Auguste Pavie. So successful was this propaganda that imports soared. Abyssinians, first brought from Africa in 1869, were subjected to the same marketing treatment and hailed as the favourites of their emperors. The Burmese cat was introduced as a consequence of colonial expansion, and the Chinese cat when the country was forced to open its doors to European trade in the 1860s. The former are the favourite breed of Princess Michael of Kent.

PET AVERSIONS

The mysterious, enigmatic nature of the cat, which so endeared the animal to the ancient Egyptians and orientals, was precisely what militated against its appeal in the West. The legacy of the cat's demonisation by the Catholic Church in the thirteenth century was the continuation of the popular sport of ritually slaughtering them on saints' days well into the nineteenth century, despite the fact that, by this time, popes themselves kept cats: Micetto, the cat of Leo XII, was inherited by Chateaubriand in 1829. Unlike dogs, cats were elusive and independent, resistant to human domination. They had a 'feminine' quality which rendered male owners susceptible to the charge of weakness and – by extension – impotence. The celibacy of the post-Reformation Catholic clergy, and the prohibition on their hunting, led many to keep cats, rather than dogs, as pets and companions. Cardinal Wolsey had a cat and was accused of having bewitched Henry VIII, that monarch whose desperate need to obtain a divorce from the barren Catherine of Aragon so radically affected the course of British history.[53] According to George Cavendish, who wrote a biography of his former employer, Wolsey, in 1557, it was Pope Clement VII's aversion to the English envoy's greyhound which caused the divorce negotiations to be ruptured: he was said to have been poised to sign the papers when the envoy entered with his dog which, springing up suddenly among the throng of cardinals, knocked over the stool on which the pontiff was resting his gouty foot. Maddened with pain, and cursing the English King, Clement VII threw the papers aside and refused to discuss the subject further.

However, some of the most celebrated clerical cat lovers never kept pets of any description. It was from the incongruous marriage of might and impotence that the myth of Cardinal Richelieu was conceived. Paradis de Moncrif, *lecteur* of Queen Marie Leszczyńska and toady at the court of Louis XV, was the author of the story in which, as the power behind the throne of Louis XIII, Richelieu was cast as a satanic figure who sat and slept surrounded by kittens (he killed them when they reached maturity), essentially familiars, who lent their diabolical aid to maintain this sinister, feline minister in office. Attention was thus skilfully deflected from the King himself who, although the eventual father of the ultra-virile Louis

XIV, produced no heirs during the first twenty-two years of his marriage to Anne of Austria. The association of cats, witchcraft and impotence explains their omission from royal portraiture from the reign of Louis XIV onwards.

Conversely, cats have been endowed with a magical ability to detect the overweening ambitions of dictators, many of whom have consequently been accused of ailurophobia on the flimsiest evidence. No record exists of Napoleon either liking or hating cats, though he clearly disliked dogs indiscriminately, from Fortuné, the pug of the Empress Josephine, to Tom Pipes, the Newfoundland belonging to Admiral Cockburn which became his *bête noire* aboard HMS *Northumberland* and continued to fill the role after they landed on St Helena in 1815. Genuine ailurophobes suffer from an irrational fear of cats. Such was the case with the uncle of the Emperor of Korea, Kojong (reigned 1864–1907), whose chief minister, William Franklin Sands, recorded a couple of incidents in his memoirs. During a palace revolution in 1894 Kojong and the Crown Prince had been saved by a servant girl, Om, who was later rewarded with a title and went on to become the mother of the Emperor's third child. One day Sands was

> on duty in the palace when I heard a most indecorous noise in my courtyard; a heavy running, the scolding of eunuchs and little squeals of some child's laughter. I suspected the baby Prince, the lady Om's son, who was a privileged character. Into the room burst the Emperor's uncle, the 'Fat Prince', panting and perspiring and gasping 'that the child will be the death of me', and after him the baby with a cat in his arms and a flock of disturbed palace eunuchs. I knew the Fat Prince's weakness, an aversion to cats so strong that they made him ill. I had seen him faint once at dinner at the legation because of a small kitten hidden behind a curtain, which he could not see, but felt to be there.[54]

The Dowager Empress of China also suffered from an irrational fear of cats and the eunuchs who reared them had to be extremely circumspect. The American portrait painter, Katharine Carl, who spent many months in Peking in 1903, noticed how the eunuchs kept them ' "sub rosa" and within rigid bounds, on no condition allowing them to come within Her Majesty's ken'.[55]

After A. Sanchez Coello. Archduke Albrecht was fourteen at the time he sat for this portrait in 1573. His dog's collar bears a pilgrim's badge. Coello was a pupil of Mor.

CHAPTER THREE

Creature Comforts

'I N GREAT MATTERS,' wrote the wit, Sébastien Chamfort, 'men
show themselves as they find it appropriate to do so; but, in small
matters, they reveal themselves as they truly are.' Nowhere is this
statement better vindicated than in the attentions lavished upon pets by
their royal owners. No expense was spared when it came to providing for
their comfort: they slept in sumptuous beds, ate delicacies from exquisite
bowls, and had servants to attend to their needs. Pets were frequently
accorded greater privileges than many a favoured courtier and, in recognition of their peerless loyalty, enjoyed the unique honour of being granted
constant access to their royal masters.

DOG-COLLARS

Dog-collars, perhaps the most palpable expression of an owner's attachment to his pet, have a longer history than most breeds and can be reliably
traced back to the ancient Egyptians and Assyrians. Essential for training
and protecting hunting dogs, collars also identified ownership, reflected
social standing and established legal right, increasingly important when ownership of certain breeds became the exclusive prerogative of the nobility.
Hywel the Good, Prince of Wales from 942 to 950, undertook the first
classification of dogs in the British Isles; one of his famous laws deprived
greyhounds without collars of their privileges, while the 'Colwyn' breed, a
strain of spaniel so small it is unlikely to have had any function other than
as a pet, was deemed exclusive to the royal family and members of the
nobility. The fact that it was valued on a par with the royal buckhound
but at twice that of the greyhound is illustrative of how early lapdogs had

become as prized as hunting dogs in princely establishments where, throughout medieval Europe, rulers vied with each other to produce the best specimens. In the fourteenth century the spaniels and greyhounds belonging to Edward III, and kennelled at the Isle of Dogs, were attended by men themselves wearing collars. According to Chaucer in his Knight's Tale, the most noble dogs at the court were 'colered with gold and torretes filed round'.

The few medieval collars to have survived are made of iron with protective spikes and would have belonged to hunting dogs. From archaeological excavation, missals, bestiaries, Books of Hours and early literature, it is clear that collars were frequently made of precious metals. Archaeologists have recently unearthed the skeleton of a dog buried with the pre-dynastic King Cuo of China and wearing a collar of gold, silver and turquoise. Although the dog of Herculanium was no imperial pet, its beautifully wrought silver collar would have typified the sort worn by the pets of wealthy Romans of the first century AD.

The exquisite collars worn by the animals of early Renaissance princes can be seen in the art and tapestries of the period. The painter Pisanello (c. 1395–1455), who worked in his later years at the court of Ferrara, captured with the naturalist's accuracy of observation not just the different breeds of dog belonging to the ruling Este family but the jewels worn on their collars and adorning the horses' harnesses. In *The Vision of St Eustace* only the greyhounds wear collars. Leonello d'Este, Duke of Ferrara, considered life at his pleasure palace of Belfiore with his favourite greyhound as the acme of happiness. The dogs in the painting are almost certainly portraits of the ducal pets.

With the Renaissance the medieval emblematic notion of representing animals as symbols of fidelity or betrayal petered out. The dogs in the double portrait undertaken by Lucas Cranach the Elder in 1514 for the Duke and Duchess of Saxony are authentic animals; the Duke's hound wears an elaborate collar, redolent of his owner's noble status – as is his being on the point of unsheathing his sword – whereas the Duchess's lapdog wears none at all. These are ladies' dogs, devoid of chivalric associations. Nor were such collars confined to dogs: the 1557 portrait by Hans Mielich, court painter to Albert V, Duke of Bavaria, of Ladislas of

Fraunberg, Count of Haag 1505–66, who served in the armies of Charles V and Francis I, shows him beside a leopard with a magnificent collar. The noble rank of Ladislas is indicated by his hand resting on his sword and not by the leopard, an authentic pet and his constant companion.[1] The Renaissance rulers of Europe imported Indian cats, which they found could outpace their own hunting dogs. Few of Mielich's ladies' dogs at the Bavarian court wear collars, and the portrait of Albert's daughter, Maximiliana Maria (1552–1614), with a comforter on her lap wearing a collar bearing her initials and a fine pair of floral earrings, is exceptional. In a miniature dated 1552, where Mielich shows Albert V and his wife Anne playing chess, neither of their two toy dogs on the table beside them have collars, a sure indication that they never ventured from their masters' side.

Monarchs otherwise renowned for their thrift spent fortunes on their dogs. Renaissance princes set great store by extravagant displays of wealth, and everything that appertained to them had to reflect their magnificence. The colour of a collar was important in identifying ownership at a glance. Louis XI of France, a notorious miser, clad his favourite greyhound, Cherami, in a collar of scarlet velvet garnished with twenty pearls and eleven rubies.[2] Anne of Brittany, the wife of his son, Charles VIII, had twenty-four pet dogs each wearing a black velvet collar from which were suspended four ermine paws, the pure white of which was intended to recall the Brittany arms: *Potius mori quam foedari*.[3] At the court of Henry VIII, Regulations for the Royal Household stipulated:

Noe Doggs to be kept in Court.

The King's heighnes alsoe straightlie forbiddeth and inhibiteth that no person, whatsoever they be, presume to keepe anie greyhounds, mastiffs, hounds, or other doggs in the Court, then some small spanyells for ladies or others: nor bring any unto the same except it be by the King's or Queen's commandement. But the said greyhounds and doggs to be kept in kennell and other meete places out of court as is convenyent, soe as the premisses duelie observed, and the houses abroade, may be sweete, wholesome, cleane, and well furnished, as to a prince's house and state doth apperteyne.[4]

These royal spaniels were alone permitted to wear velvet collars; Henry VIII's inventories list many precious collars and caparisons made of hide and white silk:[5] 'two greyhoundes collars of crimsun velvett and cloth of gold, lacking torrettes' (spikes); 'two other collars with the kinges armes, and at the ende portcullis and rose'; 'item a collar embrawdered with pomegranates and roses with turrets of silver and gilt' (which must have belonged to Catherine of Aragon, whose emblem was the pomegranate); 'a collar garnished with stole-worke with one shallop shelle of silver and gilte, with torrettes and pendauntes of silver and guilte'; 'a collar of white velvette, embrawdered with perles, the swivels of silver'.[6] In the 1560s Mary Queen of Scots' small dogs wore blue velvet collars.[7] The thirty-six miniature greyhounds belonging to her brother-in-law, the French Valois King Charles IX, which he kept in his apartments, wore red and green velvet collars.

Collars inscribed with the owner's coat of arms were impractical on lapdogs whose diminutive size made them difficult to read. They were more commonly designed for large hounds and mastiffs. In his *Portrait of Cardinal Granvelle's Dwarf*, painted c. 1550, Antonis Mor portrays the Cardinal's hound wearing a collar of enormous dimensions with a prominent heraldic shield. Such pretensions on the part of the Cardinal may help explain his fall from grace in 1564. Collars not only mirrored the status of the dog's owner but also served propagandist and dynastic functions. With the Counter-Reformation, Hapsburg dog-collars frequently displayed the pilgrim's badge; a fine example can be seen in the picture by A. Sanchez Coello of the Archduke Albrecht (1559–1621), son of the Emperor Maximilian II, and his hound, painted in 1573, ten years after the Council of Trent. Pugs, introduced into Holland as a result of Dutch trading ventures in the Far East in the course of the sixteenth century, wore orange ribbons around their necks, symbolic of Dutch liberation from Spanish hegemony and the ascendancy of the House of Orange-Nassau. Similarly, when Peter the Great sent an embassy to the court of the Emperor of China, K'ang Hsi, in 1720–1, the Russian ambassador presented the Chinese envoy with a brace of greyhounds, each of which wore round its neck a yellow silk cord drawn through a hole in a little piece of wood which hung down the dog's neck, as a mark of its belonging to the Romanov court.

However enchanted K'ang Hsi may have been with his Russian grey-hounds, a thitherto unfamiliar breed in China, their collars must have seemed like trinkets when compared to that worn by the golden-coated chin, Mao Shih Tzu, which the Emperor presented to the court of Japan at the same period. The dog wore a collar adorned with bells and a ring through its ear which also had bells attached – such collars, inscribed in gold or silver, dated back to the Tang Dynasty (618–907). The bells were both functional and decorative: they ensured that the imperial servants were alerted to the whereabouts of the Emperor as he moved about the palace. As trade with the Far East opened up in the course of the sixteenth century, both oriental dogs and collars became the fashion at European courts. Titian's and Veronese's spaniels are constantly depicted wearing collars with bells. With the occasional addition of feathers and ribbons, such collars remained fashionable until the close of the nineteenth century.

In the late seventeenth century, collars bearing inscriptions became increasingly popular at European courts, largely as a result of the influence of La Fontaine's anthropomorphic fables. Raton, the diminutive pet of the celebrated French courtesan, Ninon de Lenclos, was named after the dog in one of the fabulist's tales. Black, with white stripes like those of a zebra, it was a gift from Louis XIV's morganatic wife, Madame de Maintenon, and was always seated on the table when she dined, acting as her *officier de santé* by forbidding her to drink alcohol but sharing her glass of water. Raton's collar was of silver filigree with a heart surrounded by marcasites and bore the legend:

> Faithful to my mistress, following her every step,
> Grateful for the style in which I'm kept,
> Ready to bite whomsoever does not like her,
> I've had no occasion to bite whatsoever.

Fashionable at Versailles, similar dog-collars inevitably soon found favour at the British court. The earliest inscriptions tended to be banal; in the Armoury at Windsor Castle there is a gilt copper collar, lined with red morocco leather and blue velvet, made by Bodely of London: 'This dog belongs to his Royal Highness George Augustus, Prince of Wales, 1715'. No trace remains of the collar belonging to the Great Dane presented by

Alexander Pope to Frederick, Prince of Wales, in 1738 and famously inscribed:

> I am His Highness' dog at Kew
> Pray, Tell me sir, whose dog are you?

It nonetheless set the pattern for British collars over the following two centuries and influenced Prince Albert when he commissioned a highly decorative pierced silver collar for his favourite greyhound, Eos.

The eighteenth-century preference for silver over velvet collars reflected the expansion of European trade which had led to the import of valuable precious metals. With the acquisition of the Asiento in 1713, Britain became the principal slave-trading nation, and the silver armbands of black slaves were frequently adapted for use as dog-collars after their release from bondage. In 1710 a comic letter appeared in *The Tatler* in which a black slave complained that his lady's 'parrot who came over with me from our country is as much esteemed by her as I am. Besides this, the dog has a collar that cost as much as mine.' Matthew Dyer, a London silversmith, specialised in 'silver padlocks for blacks or dogs; collars etc.'[8] The cost of the simplest collar was about ten shillings, although those lined with leather and cast with elaborate, pierced arabesque and foliate details were considerably more expensive. The silver dog-collar worn by the Italian greyhound of Bonnie Prince Charlie was ostentatiously engraved with the Jacobite royal arms. Towards the end of the century, collars became ever more extravagant, particularly on the Continent. Mimi, the spaniel of Madame de Pompadour, had a collar of solid silver, and Filou, the favourite dog of Louis XV, wore one of gold, studded with diamonds. It was with a diamond collar that the King of Sweden, Gustavus III, presented Madame de Pompadour's successor, Madame du Barry, in 1771 when he was attempting to enlist her support for a Franco-Swedish treaty of alliance. Marie Antoinette's dogs also had diamond collars. Such prodigality did not survive the Revolution and the Empress Josephine's pugs wore relatively simple collars, adorned with bells *à la chinoise*. Queen Victoria's lapdogs had velvet collars like those of their Tudor forebears while Edward VII heralded twentieth-century tastes by opting for leather.

PET ACCESSORIES

The coats worn by pets at Renaissance courts were not simply articles of prestige. They protected them outdoors and within the palaces themselves, which were cold and draughty in winter. Pets were also highly perfumed, as were all the creatures that came into contact with the prince, including mules. Isabel of Bavaria, wife of the French King, Charles VI, known as Charles the Mad, was devoted to both dogs and cats, her favourites among the latter being dressed in a coat of 'gay green'.[9] A miniature in the Froissart Chronicle shows her being greeted by her husband, who is mounted on a horse caparisoned from head to hoof in blue cloth emblazoned with fleurs-de-lis, as is the royal greyhound in the foreground. Charles VIII's bitch wore a velvet outfit of red and tan.[10] Henri II of France, as Dauphin, clad the dogs he had obtained from the court of Ferrara in white satin coats embroidered with silver thread.[11]

As the fashion for decorative collars and coats took hold, other items of body jewellery were added to canine attire. The painting by Tiberio Titi (1573–1627) of the Medici dogs in the Boboli Gardens shows the grand ducal pets clad in a resplendent array of accessories from ribbons to earrings. These refinements were brought to France by the Medici wives of Henri II and Henri IV. In the portrait undertaken by Pierre Mignard c. 1660 of Charles II's sister, Henriette d'Orléans, her dog is wearing a pair of elaborate drop earrings. The works of Antoine Pesne at the court of the Prussian King Frederick William I, and of Goya at the courts of Charles III and Charles IV of Spain, provide ample evidence of the continuation of this tradition late in the eighteenth century.

In the course of the nineteenth century, the taste for animal fashion developed into a profitable manufacturing industry. Princess Victoria upheld the tradition in Britain, proudly entering in her diary in 1833 how she had 'dressed dear sweet little Dash in a scarlet jacket and blue trousers'. Paris, however, was the Mecca for dog accessories, offering the choice of over a dozen shops catering in everything from gold and silver collars to rubber boots. Bouyer and Gotschif opened in 1835; Aux Etats-Unis advertised 'collars of the latest style, overcoats and kennels'; Lochet aîné and Dedertrand were established in 1864. They catered for both winter and summer costumes and

Pierre Mignard: Henriette-Anne d'Angleterre, Duchesse d'Orléans,
c. 1660. She was the sister of Charles II. Her spaniel is wearing earrings.

even made raincoats and beach-wear with sailors' collars embroidered with the names of the fashionable beaches of Cabourg and Trouville. In the Palais-Royal, underwear of Valenciennes lace was a popular item for *chiens de luxe*. Dogs also had their hairdressers and shops specialising in grooming equipment; the *caniche royal*, so named because of the poodle's popularity at the French court under the *ancien régime*, was particularly well suited to the latest styles.[12] The new dog and cat shows, in which princes eagerly participated, turned the taste for grooming into a mania.

In the twentieth century the tradition was maintained chiefly by the exuberant Indian princes: the Maharajah of Junagadh's favourite bitch not only wore necklaces but was scented, coiffed and carried on a silver palanquin. In Simla the Maharajah put his dogs into evening dress and sat them in rickshaws to annoy the Raj, in which he was singularly successful, being summoned to a stormy meeting with the viceroy.[13] The Duke and Duchess of Windsor's pugs not only wore wing collars and bow ties but their leads were woven from silver and gold thread. After a day at the beautician's in Paris they were frequently the guests of honour at the dog parties fashionable from the 1950s.

GROOMING

Many monarchs elected to groom their dogs themselves, finding in the ritual a release from tension. After her coronation, Queen Victoria hurried home, removed her state robes and gave Dash a bath. In 1898 her granddaughter Princess Victoria had the combings from her own brown poodle knitted into a large shawl. Edward VII personally clipped the coat of their borzoi, Alix, and the hair was spun at Sandringham at the King's direct instruction.[14] When the Dogs' Wool Association, founded to offset the shortage of wool during World War I, held its first exhibition at Claridge's both Queen Alexandra and Princess Victoria were keen to attend. Queen Victoria's granddaughter, HH Princess Marie-Louise, recorded how in 1914 the Kaiser, on hearing that war had been declared,

> was terribly upset. What he discussed with his generals I do not know,
> and if I did I should not be at liberty to say, but when his agitation
> had calmed down, he turned to my brother [Prince Albert of
> Schleswig-Holstein] and said 'Abbie, let us go and wash the dogs'. So
> they retired to the Emperor's cabin, took off their coats and scrubbed
> the dachshounds. Up to the last moment there were hopes – maybe
> very faint ones – of averting this terrible catastrophe of a World War,
> but they were of no avail. War was declared.

The requirements of favourite pets, always high on the royal agenda, could become paramount during political crises. Lt.-Col. C. E. Beddoes, who ran one of the smartest dogs' beauty parlours in London between the wars, never forgot the telephone call he received from Edward VIII in 1936:

It was a personal call from His Majesty to tell me that he was leaving the country for quite a time. As he was taking his two favourite cairns with him, would I please send by hand at once half a dozen of the special combs used for trimming, with full instructions as to their use, and also any other things that I thought he would require so that he could look after the dogs himself. At that moment the respect and affection I had for him welled up and almost brought me to tears. Here was a man of an exalted position in life who was beset by unprecedented worries, the outcome of which might fatally influence the future of our country . . . who could not only give thought to the welfare of two little creatures but who made it his personal business to ensure that they would be adequately looked after.[15]

In Paris, he must have soon found his newly acquired skills superfluous. The present Queen is also said not to be above washing her corgis herself after a muddy walk.

SERVANTS

As early as 1000 BC official dog-feeders and physiognomists, called Chancien, existed at the courts of China.[16] Not only did they have personal servants but Chinese dogs were granted titles and honours. Ling Ti, Emperor of the Han Dynasty from AD 168 to 190, kept his dog at his western garden in Lo Yang where it was presented with the official hat of the Chin Hsien grade, the highest literary rank of the time, which measured eight and three-quarter inches high in front, three and three-quarter inches high behind, and ten inches across. The Emperor's other favourite dogs were given the lesser ranks of K'ai Fu (viceroy) and Yi Tung (imperial guardian). Upon the consorts of these canine dignitaries were bestowed the ranks of wives of corresponding two-legged officials, and they had an escort of soldiers and personal bodyguards to accompany them on their walks. In AD 565 the Emperor Kao Wei of the Northern Chou Dynasty bestowed the name of Ch'ih Hu or 'red tiger' on a Persian dog, together with the rank and privileges pertaining to a Chun Chun (similar to a duke). The animal was fed on the choicest selection of meat and rice and granted the revenues of a prefecture. When Kao Wei went out on horseback, Ch'ih Hu sat on a mat placed on the saddle beside him.[17]

Considered as members of the imperial household, the chows favoured by the Tang Dynasty (618–907) were accorded all the privileges and honours to which their rank entitled them. One emperor owned no fewer than 2,500. Similarly, the Pekingese of dynastic China had hosts of personal servants and their toilet was executed with elaborate ceremonial. After their daily baths they were sprayed with perfume and laid to rest on silken cushions. They were taken out for regular exercise or carried around on sumptuous palanquins and much pampered by the emperor and his ladies. They accompanied him to the hall of audience, sat beside him on the throne and generally fulfilled their allotted part in palace ceremonial.

The Mongol emperors of the Yuan Dynasty (1206–1368) favoured mastiffs. Marco Polo, one of the very few travellers to penetrate into China at this period, described the dogs of Kublai Khan as being the size of donkeys, and numbering at least ten thousand. They were attended by two barons, Bayan and Mingan, known as *kuyukchi*, 'that is to say, keepers of the mastiffs. Each of them has 10,000 subordinates, who all wear livery of one colour; and the other 10,000 all wear another colour. The two colours are scarlet and blue.'[18] With the disintegration of the Mongol Empire and the accession of the ailurophile Mings, mastiffs disappeared from the Chinese court, and when Western merchants regained a foothold in the country at the beginning of the seventeenth century, these dogs became highly prized. In 1627, East India Company factors in Batavia were recommending that mastiffs be sent to China where they were so highly regarded that each dog 'has his attendants and is fanned from flies with as much observance as a principal personage'. This ferocious breed was much coveted in the East and therefore a lucrative article for export in the sixteenth and seventeenth centuries. When the British ambassador, Sir Thomas Roe, presented some mastiffs to the Great Mogul, Jahangir (1605–27), he was so enchanted by their savagery that he provided them with servants and fed them from his own hands off silver platters.

The Eastern notion of princely pets having servants lingered on well into the twentieth century, particularly in India: each of the Maharajah of

Junagadh's eight hundred dogs had its own room, servant and telephone at a total annual running cost of £5,000. The Maharajah of Jaipur's dogs had their own servants dressed in gold cummerbunds and high turbans whose duties included walking the royal dogs. The pets of the viceroys were accorded similar privileges. When her husband succeeded Lord Curzon in 1905, Lady Minto was amused to 'see old Dandy's departure from camp, lying at his ease on the soft mattress of a specially-made wooden bedstead, which was carried by four coolies with four relief men, and the one man in a red uniform, fully armed, and holding a sword at the salute, walking beside him to ensure that he should not fall out. The coolies speak respectfully of the Viceroy's dog as "Dandy Sahib", who accepts their homage and seems quite aware of his own importance.'[19]

At European courts responsibility for the supervision of pet dogs and cats was rarely an officially recognised post and was frequently foisted on whomsoever happened to be in attendance. The identification of lower servants, who did not always feature in court handbooks and whose duties can therefore be hard to establish, is necessarily somewhat speculative. Agnès Sorel, the mistress of the fifteenth-century French King Charles VII, entrusted her greyhound, Tapis, to her maid of honour, Mademoiselle de Bonneville, with an injunction to 'nourish him close beside you, not permitting him to go coursing with anyone; for he obeys neither whistle nor call, and would therefore be lost, the which would grieve me much'.[20] At the courts of Renaissance Italy, where pets were markedly fashionable, servants clearly existed to tend to their needs. When Francis I returned from Italy in 1516 he brought sixty greyhounds back with him and appointed six *valets de chien* to attend to them.[21] He also brought back with him Federico Gonzaga, and the dogs may well have been supplied by the Mantuan court; Federico, like his mother Isabella, was devoted to dogs. Henry VIII evidently had spaniel-keepers: on one occasion, forty-six shillings and nine pence were paid to a certain Robin for various disbursements including 'heir-cloth to rub the dogges with'.[22] According to Sully, the servants attending the dogs of the French King, Henri III, received extremely generous salaries, and the upkeep of the animals cost more than 100,000 crowns a year.[23] Marie de Medici, who married Henri IV in 1600, had her menagerie of monkeys, parrots and dogs superintended by

Pierre Grasseau, who bandaged them when necessary,[24] and Pierre Guilloret, 'la porte chaise',[25] who was paid an annual wage of seventy-five livres. Henri Dubois, the garçon de chambre, attended her greyhounds, each of which cost eight sous a day to feed.[26] In addition, Nicolas Guillois and 'little Gaspard' attended the birds of the femmes de chambre.[27] Her son, the Dauphin, ascended the throne as Louis XIII on the assassination of his father in 1610. It was his garçon de chambre, Haran, who looked after his beloved dogs in the early years of his reign,[28] and the satisfaction of the King is reflected in his purchase of a house for him at Gaigny for 3,500 écus in 1614.[29] The five dogs of his son, Louis XIV, named Pistolet, Silvie, Mignonne, Princesse and Dolinde, were initially looked after by his governess, whom he called Michelette, until they became too numerous and he appointed the brothers Pierre and René Bourlon as capitaines des levrettes de la chambre du Roi, an office that was only suppressed in 1786. They were assisted by three valets de chien.[30]

There were valets de chien at Versailles at the court of Louis XV in the eighteenth century but, through their intimacy with the monarch, the valets de chambre necessarily also had a great deal of contact with the royal pets. Comte Dufort de Cheverny recalled how, on one occasion, one of the King's premiers valets de chambre, Louis-Quentin de Champcenetz, played a practical joke on Louis XV's pet:

the King had a white angora tom-cat, prodigiously fat, very docile and very tame: it slept in the Council Chamber on a cushion of crimson damask, in the middle of the fireplace. The King always returned at half past midnight from the petits appartements. It was not yet midnight, and Champcenetz said to us: 'You did not know I can make a cat dance for a few minutes?' We laughed, we laid bets. Champcenetz then took a bottle from his pocket, stroked the cat and liberally poured eau de Cologne [eau de mille fleurs] over its four paws. The cat went back to sleep, and we thought we had won. Suddenly, feeling the effect of the spirit of wine, it jumped farting to the ground, ran across the King's table, cursing, leaping and pirouetting. We were all splitting our sides laughing when the King arrived out of the blue; everyone returned to their place, decency and serious demeanour were reestablished. The King demanded to know what accounted for our gaiety: 'Nothing

Sire, it was just a story we were relating' replied Champcenetz. At that moment the wretched cat started to dance again, and tore about like a thing possessed. The King stared: 'Gentlemen,' he said, 'What is happening here? Champcenetz, what has been done to my cat? I wish to know.' The question required an answer; Champcenetz hesitated, then succinctly related the facts, while the cat continued to cut capers. We smiled during the narration, to see from the eyes of the King how he would take the matter; but he frowned: 'Gentlemen,' he continued, 'I take my leave of you; but if you wish to amuse yourselves, please ensure that it is not at the expense of my cat.' These words were delivered with such curtness that thenceforth no-one ever made the cat dance.[31]

Valets de chambre were also at hand to shoo away unwanted dogs. When the Princesse de Talmond, a relation of the Queen of France, Marie Leszczyńska, was visiting the Marquise de Livry in the 1740s, they were joined by the Comte de Bavière, natural son of the Elector, whom Dufort de Cheverny described as

amiable, if scatty, he was an assiduous courtier. Madame de Livry had a large greyhound which took such liberties that, without fail, it would occupy an easy chair whenever one fell vacant, settling in comfortably until told to get down. Monsieur de Bavière paid her a visit; while chatting agreeably, he became engrossed with the dog, sometimes talking to it, sometimes going 'Chit! Chit!' to it. Madame de Talmond was announced; the *valet de chambre* chased away the dog; she sat in its place, and they started to talk. M de Bavière got heated; he became distracted. He forgot that the dog had a worthier successor; he stretched out his hand to Madame de Talmond, saying 'Chit! Chit!' She barely knew him and was completely nonplussed. Finally, losing patience, she asked him what had inspired such misplaced attentions. M de Bavière, taken aback, came back to reality and bowed humbly. 'Ah! Madame, forgive me,' he said, 'I thought you were the dog.'[32]

Madame de Boigne described summers at Bellevue before the Revolution when she would play with the dog of Madame Adelaide, Louis XV's daughter, who took long walks every day to supervise her workmen. She used to call me as she passed; my hat was put on, I got out of the window, and went off with her without any nurse. She was generally followed by a number of servants, and a little carriage drawn by one led horse, which she never entered, but which I often occupied. I preferred, however, to run by her side, and to carry on what I called a conversation. My rival and friend was a large white spaniel, a very intelligent dog, who shared these walks. If the road happened to be very muddy, he was put into a large white linen bag and carried by two of the servants on duty. I was extremely proud of being able to pick my steps without getting muddy as he did. When we came back to the castle, I fought with Visir for his red velvet cushion, which he abandoned more readily than he did the cakes which were broken up for us on the floor. The good Princess would often go down on all fours and join in our romps, to restore peace or to obtain the prize of the race. I can still see her tall, thin figure, her tucked violet dress (which was the uniform at Bellevue), her butterfly hat, and two large teeth, which were the only ones she had. She had been very pretty, but at this time was extremely ugly, and so I thought her.[33]

If there were no specific dog servants at the court of Louis XV's contemporary, Frederick the Great, his beloved greyhounds nonetheless travelled in a carriage drawn by six horses, and his coachman was ordered to address them with the utmost courtesy. They were principally looked after by Fredersdorf, officially Private Chamberlain, but whom Voltaire more aptly described as court factotum. The extensive letters between Fredersdorf and the Prussian King contain a wealth of detail concerning the health, love affairs and general wellbeing of his dogs.

The Empress Josephine's love of dogs was in no way moderated by Napoleon's dislike of them. When they travelled together, the favourite pug of the day would be relegated to the second carriage with a personal servant, selected from the Office of the Wardrobe. Until the latter years of their marriage, Napoleon and Josephine shared a room and the dogs were barred entry on the Emperor's orders. On these occasions they slept in an adjoining room. In 1806 the pugs' personal maid was Madame La Brisée, and their daily running costs were estimated at 568 francs.

DWARFS

Between the sixteenth and eighteenth centuries, human menageries were as popular at court as the animal variety, and the care of dogs was frequently entrusted to dwarfs who, considered as 'pets' of a sort themselves, were thought to enjoy an empathy with animals. To the emperors of ancient Rome dwarfs embodied ostentation and luxury. Suetonius mentions them at the court of Augustus and Tiberius consulted his dwarf on state affairs; Domitian had so many that he formed them into a troop of gladiators. The renaissance in the popularity of the dwarf coincided with a universal passion for curiosities of all kinds and a return to classical models. It originated in Italy, where up to thirty at a time, dripping with diamonds, might serve at table, justifying Lord Byron's description of them as 'monsters who cost a no less monstrous sum'. Isabella d'Este, wife of Francesco II, Marquis of Mantua (ruled 1484–1519), kept a large number of both dogs and dwarfs. To accommodate the latter she built a special apartment at the Reggia comprising some six or seven rooms with a miniature private chapel.

Detail of the dwarf from Tiberio Titi. Dwarfs were important figures at court until the eighteenth century.

Catherine de Medici introduced the fashion for dwarfs into France; she and her son, Charles IX, would send emissaries to scour Europe for the finest specimens, and they were exchanged between courts in much the same way as pets themselves. Dwarfs soon became a commonplace at all the courts of Europe. Marie de Medici's *second huissier affecté au Cabinet de la Reine* was the dwarf Jean Mauderon, known as Maudricart. She had a black woman called Madeleine, known as 'The Queen's Moor', as well as Greek, Turkish and Polish women in attendance. Exoticism was sought in all its manifestations. As *femmes de chambre* they were in constant intimacy with the Queen.[34] In 1610 her son Louis had a dwarf called Dumont whom he wished to marry to Marine, one of his mother's dwarfs, in much

Philip IV and His Dwarf Soplillo *by Rodrigo de
Villandrano. Soplillo was sent to the nine-year-old Prince from
Flanders in 1614 by his aunt the Archduchess Isabella Clara.
Being childless, she had a particular penchant for dwarfs.*

the same way as he match-made his pet dogs. Philip IV of Spain's dwarf
Soplillo was one of his most trusted companions. In 1621 Vincenzo
Gonzaga spent much of the proceeds from the sale of his pictures to
Charles I on buffoons and dwarfs; Maria Eleonora, consort of Gustavus

Adolphus of Sweden, spent a fortune in the same way. The close relationship between pets and dwarfs could lead to 'sibling' rivalry: Bébé (1741–64), the favourite dwarf of the deposed King of Poland, Stanislas Leszczyński, had entered the royal household in 1746 at the age of five and soon became so resentful of the attention his master lavished on his dogs that a footman was regularly required to remove him from the royal presence. The Duc de Richelieu described how Bébé 'would slip under an armchair like a spaniel in order to hide from the King. . . . He was given to tantrums and jealous of anything of a similar size to his own. He particularly despised the dogs of the court ladies and, believing that the caresses they lavished upon them would deflect the attention which he considered his exclusive due, threw many of the dogs out of the window.'[35]

The first dwarf to appear at the English court was John Jervis during the reign of Queen Mary I (reigned 1553–8). The favourite dwarf of Charles I and Henrietta Maria, Jeffrey Hudson, had formerly been in the service of the Duchess of Buckingham. At a dinner held in their honour the King and Queen were so impressed by the spectacle of the forty-two-inch dwarf leaping from a pie in the middle of the table that they instantly insisted on recruiting him. Such was the confidence that Charles I placed in Hudson that he was sent on missions abroad; in 1630 he was dispatched to France to find a midwife for Henrietta Maria. Hudson can be seen in a picture by Daniel Mytens of 1630–2 showing the King and Queen departing for the chase. He is in charge of the hounds. The painting also contains a portrait of Henrietta Maria's black page. The picture in HM the Queen's collection of Charles I and Henrietta Maria dining in public at Whitehall, although a work of imagination, shows a dwarf feeding a brace of Italian greyhounds.

Daniel Mytens: **Charles I and Henrietta Maria with Jeffrey Hudson,** *c. 1630. Shows Hudson, the favourite dwarf of the King and Queen, attending the dogs.*

Velásquez: **El Inglés with a Mastiff Bitch.** *The dwarf, Don Antonio, has sometimes been identified as Nicolas Bodson or Hodson. He was at the Spanish court from 1613.*

The animal–dwarf nexus is seen at its most explicit in the works of Antonis Mor, Veronese, Tiberio Titi and Velásquez. The hound in Mor's *Portrait of Cardinal Granvelle's Dwarf*, although on a lead, is familiar and relaxed with the dwarf who, in turn, betrays no signs of being ill at ease with a potentially fierce dog fully his equal in physical stature. The dwarf in Veronese's *Family of Darius before Alexander*, painted at the same date, 1560, is clearly in charge of the two Bologna spaniels. Similarly, the mastiff in Velásquez's portrait of El Inglés, one of the favourite dwarfs at the court of Philip IV of Spain, patently poses no danger to its diminutive keeper. The mastiff also features in a contemporary work by Juan Bautista del Mazo, Velásquez's son-in-law and successor as court painter. Here the mastiff requires no lead but stands obediently beside a black dwarf, in marked contrast to the hunting greyhound, elsewhere in the picture, which is being whipped for insubordination. Like pets, dwarfs were very popular with childless queens.

Mazo's painting of **The Hunt of the Tabladillo at Aranjuez,** *1666, includes portraits of the same dwarf and mastiff as appear in Velasquez's* **El Inglés**.

On succeeding to the Spanish throne in 1700, Philip V was so outraged by the insolence of the dwarfs that he promptly banned them from court. The last dwarf recorded at the English court was Coppernin, who was retained in the service of Queen Caroline, wife of George II. Catherine the Great recorded there being dwarfs at the Russian court in 1744[36] and they were still in evidence at the Polish and Portuguese courts at the end of the eighteenth century. During the First Empire, dwarfs were kept by Josephine in Paris and by the Murats in Naples, eager to bolster their fragile legitimacy with the aid of *ancien régime* courtly examples. At Perchino in Russia earlier this century, the borzois in the Grand Duke Nicholas's kennels had not only liveried servants to attend them but a dwarf to keep them amused.[37]

BLACK PAGES

Black pages similarly enjoyed great popularity at court from the Renaissance onwards. The first known portrait of a black page in attendance is in Titian's *Laura dei Dianti*, mistress of Alfonso I d'Este, Duke of Ferrara. As usual, the French were quick to follow suit and Charles VIII brought a black servant back from his campaign of 1494–5 as his official parrot-keeper.[38] Coming from distant lands they lent exoticism to a court and, if they did not enjoy the same privileges as aristocratically born white pages, they nonetheless occupied positions of considerable importance in close physical proximity to the prince. It is evident from contemporary paintings that one of their functions was to attend to the horses and domestic pets. They can be seen in many paintings from the early seventeenth century, such as the 1617 van Somer portrait of Anne of Denmark with her Italian greyhounds as well as the portrait by Titian's great admirer, Van Dyck, completed in 1634, of Henrietta of Lorraine. D'Aubigné described Corisande (née Diane d'Andouins, widow of Philibert de Gramont), mistress of Henri IV, attending Mass accompanied by a court jester, a moor, a lackey, a monkey and a spaniel. David Klocker von Ehrenstrahl's *African with Monkeys and Parrots*, painted in 1670, was one of the earliest to link black servants explicitly with exotic animals.

Black pages were *de rigueur* at the courts of the eighteenth century. In the 1713 portrait of Frederick the Great aged four with his sister, Wilhelmina, and their two dogs by Antoine Pesne at Charlottenburg, they are attended by a black page carrying a parasol in his right hand and a parrot on his left wrist. In the Labia Palace in Venice there is a fresco by Giambattista Tiepolo of a greyhound being prevented by a black custodian from interfering with the progress of Antony and Cleopatra as they embark. The most able black servants could hope to attain enviable positions. On the birth of the Prince of Wales, Lord Chesterfield presented George II with a black slave called Cato, who later became head gamekeeper at Richmond Park. Madame de Pompadour employed two, each of whom earned twice as much as a lackey and, theoretically at least, six times as much as Madame de Hausset, her *femme de chambre*[39] – one of them can be seen in the portrait by Carle van Loo in which she appears as a sultana being presented with a cup of tea.[40] The mentally unstable King of Denmark, Christian VII (1749–1808, King from 1766), who married George III's sister, Caroline Matilda, in 1766, used to go on the rampage in the Hirscholm Palace accompanied by his black page, Moranti, and his dog, Gourmand, removing the windows from their hinges.

In the early nineteenth century black eunuchs were much sought after at the imperial Chinese court.[41] The extent to which Queen Victoria came to depend on her Indian munshi, Hafiz Abdul Karim in the closing years of her reign caused consternation amongst her far less racially tolerant courtiers. In 1887 the *Daily Graphic* printed a large photograph of 'the Queen, sitting at her table with her dog at her feet, signing documents. There is a hint of a smile on her face. The Munshi, now no longer lithe and handsome but obese and opulent looking, holds one of these papers and stares out with an expression both smug and supercilious.'[42] The Duchess of Windsor employed Sidney Johnson, Edward's Bahaman valet, to look after her pugs.

HYGIENE

The keeping of pets became widespread with the development of single-family homes in the fifteenth century, and many of the most obvious and basic sanitary precautions were self-evident to people well aware of the precariousness of life. Late medieval English books of courtesy had reminded the page that before his lord went to sleep he should drive the dogs and cats out of the bedroom, and they cautioned guests at banquets against stroking dogs or cats while sitting at table. In the sixteenth century there were flea cravats or 'tippets', the grandest made in sable with a jew-elled animal head, intended to ward off the offending vermin. Into the notoriously fetid homes of the aristocracy during the seventeenth century crept a new fastidiousness, prompted largely by the experience of the plague. In 1668, the MP and lawyer William Lawrence confessed he had grown 'quite weary of the City ... where there is neither good air, nor good fire, nor good water, nor good earth ... the water polluted with dogs and vermin'. Allergies to cats were common at this period and the dangers of their breath were much discussed in medical books; but cats gained in popularity as standards of cleanliness improved: the ubiquity of the newly invented cat-flap reflected these sanitary developments.

These advances appear to have made little impression on royal animal lovers. The relatively lax standards that prevailed at court stemmed from the artificiality of palace life. Not only were servants at hand to attend to the depredations of royal pets but there was sufficient space to mitigate the noisome consequences. Notions of personal privacy were foreign at court, where virtually every bodily function was exercised in public. Pepys, who recorded several rows with his wife occasioned by her newly acquired puppy defecating in the house, was horrified by the low sanitary standards at the court of Charles II. When the plague broke out in London in 1665, the court fled to Oxford, 'leaving at their departure their excrements in every corner, in chimneys, studies, coal-houses, cellars'.[43] Pepys's views were shared by John Evelyn[44] who, upon the King's death in 1685, recorded with disapproval how he had taken 'delight in having a number of little spaniels follow him and lie in his bedchamber, where he often suffered the bitches to puppy and give suck, which rendered it very offensive, and indeed made the whole court nasty and stinking'. Charles's Gentleman of the Bedchamber, the Earl of Ailesbury, 'had a bed placed each night to be near him, and when the page of the backstairs lighted us from the room where we undressed, on his retiring we shut up the door on the inside with a brass knob, and so went to bed. Several circum-

stances made the lodging very uneasy – the great grate being filled with Scotch coal that burnt all night, a dozen dogs that came to our bed, and several pendulums that struck at the half quarter, and all not going alike, it was a continual chiming.'[45] Charles II cannot have been entirely impervious to the deleterious consequences of his passion for dogs; in 1683, he ordered from the Lord Chamberlain's Office 'a skreene of wire, with the frame of walnut tree sutable to chairs, for his Majesty's new Bedchamber to preserve the bed from being spoiled by the doggs'.

Detail of Danckerts' spaniels. The diarist John Evelyn complained that Charles II's dogs 'made the whole court nasty and stinking'.

Whether for practical reasons or not, pets enjoyed considerable licence at court and greater privileges than most courtiers – let alone royal consorts – including that of unrestricted access to the king's bedchamber. Finette, the miniature dun-coloured Italian greyhound of Peter the Great always joined the Tsar when he retired to bed for an afternoon nap. Peter's indifference to hygiene was such that he often kissed Finette on the mouth, an act of devotion witnessed in 1708 by a priest whose indiscretion in spreading the story resulted in his being put to torture in the Preobrajenski Prikaz. Frederick the Great not only emulated Peter in his choice of breed, showing a preference for miniature greyhounds, but displayed an equal disregard for hygiene, and the palace at Sans-Souci was notoriously filthy. His dogs had their own gallery where they gambolled on the furniture, tearing the fabric to shreds, much to the amusement of their royal master. The favourite slept on his bed and, when fire struck his palace in Berlin in 1753, he wrote to his sister Wilhelmina that he had been ill in bed but had managed to 'save his dog, his jewels [*pierreries*] and some books', incidentally revealing an interesting order of priorities.[46]

Versailles was filthy and Louis XIV's bed was infested with bugs. Nor did standards greatly improve in the reign of his successor when cows were led to the Princesses' apartments to provide them with their daily quota of fresh milk. The century was well advanced before dogs other than those belonging to the court or forming part of trick-performing troupes were barred entry to the palace. For Queen Marie Leszczyńska hygiene was of secondary importance to strict adherence to the elaborate code of etiquette that prevailed at Versailles. Madame Campan, her *femme de chambre*, described the Queen's indifference when her cat relieved itself on the cloak of an unidentified lady at court:

> Etiquette, or indeed I might say a sense of propriety, prohibited all persons from laying things belonging to them on the seats of the Queen's chamber. At Versailles one had to cross this chamber to reach the play-room. The Duchess de — laid her cloak on one of the folding-stools which stood before the balustrade of the bed. The usher of the chamber, whose duty it was to attend to whatever occurred in this room, whilst they were at play, saw this cloak, took it, and carried it into the footman's ante-chamber. The Queen had a large favourite cat, which was constantly running about the apartments. The satin cloak, lined with fur, appeared very convenient to the cat, who took possession of it accordingly. Unfortunately, he left very unpleasant marks of his preference, which remained but too evident on the white satin of the pelisse, in spite of all the pains which were taken to efface them before it was given to the Duchess. She perceived them, took the cloak in her hand, and returned in a violent passion to the Queen's chamber, where Her Majesty remained surrounded by almost all the Court.

The upshot was the Duchess being upbraided by the Queen: 'had you observed the forms suitable to your rank you would not have been exposed to the mortification of seeing your things thrown on the benches of the ante-chamber.'[47]

In 1747 Catherine the Great recorded how her husband, the Grand Duke Peter,

> to procure more amusement for himself during the winter . . . had eight or ten hunting dogs brought from the country and put behind the wooden partition which separated the alcove of my room from an immense vestibule at the back of our apartment. As the alcove consisted merely of a few boards put together, the stink of the kennels penetrated into our room and we both slept in this putrid air. When I complained, the Grand Duke replied that there was no other way, since the kennels had to be kept a great secret. So I had to put up with this discomfort in order not to betray His Imperial Highness and spoil his pleasure.[48]

Catherine the Great's aunt, Princess Hedwig-Sophie-Augusta, was prioress of the Lutheran convent at Quedlinburg, some thirty miles south-east of Magdeburg. She

> loved dogs and particularly those called 'mops'; one day, when I was a child, I was struck with astonishment upon finding in her room, which was no larger than six-feet square, sixteen mopses. A great many of them had litters, which also occupied this room where my aunt spent most of her time; they slept, ate, and performed all their functions in it; a maid was employed to keep them clean and she was busy the whole day with that task.
>
> There were, besides, a large number of parrots in the room, so it is easy to imagine the stink that permeated it. When the princess drove out, at least one parrot and half a dozen dogs accompanied her in the carriage; the dogs followed her even to church. I have never known anyone love animals as she did; they occupied all her time during the day and she took exercise only for their sake; such immobility had caused her to grow very stout, which disfigured her, particularly as she was small in stature.[49]

Another contemporary, Ferdinand IV of Naples, emulated his father, Charles III of Spain, in allowing three or four of his pointers freedom of the palace. The Hapsburg Emperor Joseph II recorded his impressions of the dogs with some disdain:

> These enjoy the privilege of entering everywhere, lying on all the furniture, which at Portici as at Naples is superb and in excellent taste, and filling all the rooms with their filth. After a few minutes' talk the King went to change his clothes. Several courtiers were in attendance; a chamberlain put on his shoes and stockings and a valet combed his hair, to the accompaniment of much tickling and childishness . . . all the palaces swarm with the most infantile amusements. The palace of Naples contains five or six frescoed and marbled rooms filled with chickens, pigeons, ducks, geese, partridges, quail, birds of all sorts, canaries, cats, dogs and even cages full of mice, which the King occasionally sets free and enjoys the pleasure of chasing.

Chiefly as a result of Louis Pasteur's bacteriological discoveries, attitudes to hygiene were revolutionised towards the end of the nineteenth century and royal pets were deprived of their privileged right to urinate and defecate whenever and wherever they so chose. Nonetheless, many princes continued, as Frederick the Great had done, to find the spectacle of their dogs' incontinence highly amusing, particularly if at the expense of their courtiers, and even fostered their delinquency. Feliz Yusupov, who later married the niece of Tsar Nicholas II, described how he acquired his French bulldog in Paris:

> Once, when I was walking in the rue de la Paix with my mother, I saw some dogs for sale. I took such a fancy to a small brown ball of fur with a black nose, who answered to the name of Napoleon, that I begged my mother to buy it for me. To my joy, she consented, but as I felt it disrespectful to call my dog after such a famous man I named it Gugusse.
>
> For eighteen years, Gugusse was my devoted and inseparable companion. He soon became quite famous, for everyone knew and loved him, from members of the Imperial family to the least of our peasants. He was a real Parisian guttersnipe who loved to be dressed up, put on an air of importance when he was photographed, adored candy and Champagne . . . He was most amusing when slightly tipsy. He used to

suffer from flatulence and would trot to the fireplace, stick his backside into the hearth and look up with an apologetic expression.

Gugusse loved some people and hated others, and nothing could stop him from showing his dislike by relieving himself on the trousers or the skirts of his enemies. He had such an aversion for one of my mother's friends that we were obliged to shut him up whenever she called at the house. She came one day in a lovely gown of pink velvet, a Worth creation. Unfortunately, we had forgotten to lock up Gugusse; no sooner had she entered the room than he made a dash for her. The gown was ruined and the poor lady had hysterics.

Gugusse could have performed in a circus. Dressed as a jockey, he would ride a tiny pony or, with a pipe stuck between his teeth, would pretend to smoke. He used to love going out with the guns, and would bring in game like a retriever.

The head of the Holy Synod called on my mother one day and, to my mind, stayed far too long. I resolved that Gugusse should create a diversion. I made him up as an old cocotte, sparing neither powder nor paint, rigged him out in a dress and wig and pushed him into the drawing room. Gugusse seemed to understand what was expected of him, for he made a sensational entry on his hind legs, to the dismay of our visitor who very quickly took his leave, which was exactly what I wanted.

I was never parted from my dog: he went everywhere with me and slept on a cushion by my bed. When Seroff, the well-known artist, painted my portrait, he insisted that Gugusse should be in the picture, saying that the dog was his best model.

Gugusse reached the ripe old age of eighteen and when he died I buried him in the garden of our house on the Moika.[50]

Kaiser William II, who was notoriously fastidious about personal cleanliness and would compel his valets and chasseur, who served him at table, to bathe two or three times a day, or as many times as they came into contact with him, had a lifelong passion for dachshunds, or Teckels, as they are known in German.[51] In 1902, shortly after she had taken up her duties as governess to the Kaiser's daughter Princess Victoria Louise, Anne Topham was bemused to see 'two dogs, little brown dachshunds which have travelled in the train from Homburg, waddle up and down on their queer, distorted-looking legs. William had a great fancy for those little animals and possessed a round dozen or so of them.'[52] An eyewitness at court described these pets as 'nearer to the Kaiser than all his faithful servants' despite their being

biting, snarling little brutes with jaws measuring half the length of their smooth bodies, and a corresponding penchant for people's calves, skirts, and petticoats. Except to the bedroom, from which they are excluded out of respect for the Empress's legs, these pets follow his Majesty everywhere, and when they make inroads on folks' flesh and blood, or clothes, William, who protects and coddles them, thinks it huge fun.

Whether the cunning Teckels know their imperial patron's overpowering position, I cannot say; but it looks almost like it, for, in the exuberance of their mischievous spirits, even the little propriety pounded into them in their earliest youth is now neglected, and Court-marshal von Eulenberg, whose pleasant duty it is to make both ends meet in the royal menage, has his hands full covering up the damage to furniture, decorations, and bric-à-brac in the Teckels' path, or to such articles as they are able to reach by high vaults and other caprioles that the Kaiser has taught them.

'Why don't you poison the beasts?' once said Eulenberg's colleague, pious Baron von Mirbach, who is on the Empress's staff, when his Excellency had wearied him with a jeremiad about the dachshunds' wickedness.

'I have thought of that myself, and would gladly go to this extremity, seeing that it meets with your most Christian approval, if I were sure that there would be no successors. But His Majesty might take it into his head to surround himself with Danish hounds, like Bismarck, and then none of us would be safe.'

A very funny incident in connection with the Teckels happened in the winter of 1893, at the Berlin Schloss, when a select company, in which the ladies in grand toilet predominated, had assembled at 1.15 P.M., in the Pillar Room, to await their Majesties coming, in order to form the usual procession to the dining-hall, where a ceremonious breakfast awaited us.

As is customary, her Majesty's Dames du jour, Countess Keller and Fraulein von Gersdorff, stood a little ahead of the rest, facing the door through which her Majesty was to enter, and, the august hosts being expected at any moment, everybody was on the alert.

Suddenly the portals opened – bowings and scrapings, and most submissive salutations – but, lo! only the dachshunds rushed in.

'Peste!' said Herr von Egloffstein, who stood at my side; while Prince Frederick Leopold, coming in just then, remarked: 'I would give anything to have on jack-boots and spurs! Wouldn't I whisk them off, or at least one of the litter, through the window!'

The Teckels, on their part, had no sooner caught sight of the silk stockings of the courtiers, than they began to bark menacingly, causing these worthies, who ten seconds before had paraded their calves with much gusto, to withdraw behind the ladies they were to escort. But these pre-cautionary measures were seemingly superfluous, as the Kaiser's pets showed no particular desire for a bite that afternoon. Instead, each separately squatted down before Mesdames von Keller and von Gersdorff, and conducted himself in the most reprehensible fashion. Perfidious Teckels! all the floggings and nose-rubbings the fancier had applied for that very thing were forgotten, and, worst of all, the Kaiser, her Majesty upon his arm, and, like her, *en grande tenue*, entered at that very moment; so withdrawal on the part of Keller and Gersdorff was out of the question. On the contrary, the unhappy ladies were obliged to bow low, bending from the waist at an angle of forty-five degrees, while the Teckels, much relieved, clambered up his Majesty's hussar boots, wagging their funny tails.

'Oh! you bad boys!' cried the Kaiser, having taken in the situation at a glance: 'if you do that again, I will have you birched – yes, indeed I will,' he added, seeing ironic smiles all around. Then he had a fit of laughter that made him hold his sides, and which resounded through the hall. He even sought to inveigle the Empress into joining in his merriment; but her Majesty ignored him, and blushing deeply, drew her consort out of the room.

The Teckels remained in the Pillar Hall while we breakfasted, and amused themselves by tearing into little pieces a beautiful fan which Countess Puckler, née Countess von der Schulenburg, who was one of the Empress's ladies before her marriage, had left behind.[53]

By the twentieth century the dangers arising from negligent pet ownership had been largely offset by achievements in the fields of science and medicine. Radclyffe Sidebottom, who flew with the Bengal Pilot Service between 1929 and 1946, nonetheless took a dim view of the Maharajah of Darbhanga's behaviour towards his dogs: he

> would see that a particular dog had won at Cruft's and he would immediately buy this dog and import it to India. He was very keen to show you his dogs and a man would follow regularly behind you with a bottle of methylated spirits and a rag to wipe over the place as soon as the dog had left his calling card. Some of these bits of furniture – the most beautiful modern furniture – smelt terribly. It was really very sad because five or six dogs in favour at the time lived in the palace and were made a great fuss of, whereas the dogs that had been favourites last year were relegated to the kennels and never came out again. You'd see thirty or forty beautiful pedigree dogs in these kennels which were never bothered about.[54]

PET BEDS

Pets, by definition, belong in the home and few princes before the nineteenth century kept anything other than hunting dogs kennelled outside the palaces. Even then, favourite hunting dogs frequently roamed the palaces when not required for the chase. The paucity of dog baskets and beds in court inventories suggests that most pets shared the beds of their masters. Such a privilege was seen as a befitting reward for the companionship they provided and physical proximity to their owners was believed to make them more human. Magnificent pet beds were a common feature at the ducal courts of Renaissance Italy; Pisanello designed a medal for Leonello d'Este, Duke of Ferrara 1441–50, which shows the Prince with his dog on the reverse and the dog sitting on an elaborate cushion. As with everything else, dog beds were soon conspicuous at the French court. One of Louis XI's (reigned 1461–83) favourite greyhounds, Mistodin, not only had its own bed but nightclothes to prevent its catching a chill. Charles VIII of France allowed his favourite dogs to sleep with him and an itemised expense records the provision of '18 aunes of linen to prevent the greyhounds of the King's Bedchamber soiling and ruining the sheets of toile de Hollande when they sleep on the bed'.[55]

According to his contemporaries, the extravagance of Charles IX's brother and successor, Henri III, was not confined to an annual outlay of one hundred thousand écus on his adored birds and dogs, of which he possessed no fewer than three hundred in 1586.[56] The King slept in a room strewn with roses and other flowers in a gilded bed covered in cloth of silver, supported by crimson satin pillows and wearing a face-mask of shining material dipped in odiferous oils which was occasionally adjusted by a servant to enable the King to consume sweetmeats and rolled spiced meats. Dressed in a nightshirt of white satin with silver spangles and tags around the neck and richly embroidered gloves, he was surrounded by little dogs which he alternatively fondled and incited to make a deafening noise. Determining which of them was to enjoy the privilege of accompanying him on his daily walk with his Queen, Louise, was a painful experience until he invented the novel expedient of a basket, suspended by a ribbon from the royal neck, and lined with crimson satin, in which he could allegedly carry between twenty and thirty of these diminutive creatures at any given time.

Under Louis XIV, the quantity and magnificence of the pet beds commissioned from the cabinet maker Gaudron is indicative of the number of pets at court, the affection in which they were held and his determination to let no opportunity slip for reflecting the splendour of the Sun-King. They were ordered for all the royal palaces, proof that these animals were their owners' constant travelling companions. The two ordered for Marly in 1688 were four and a half feet long and eighteen inches wide and high. Each was made of veneered walnut with ebony marquetry and inlaid flowers. There were two curved entrances and the whole of the interior was lined with crimson velvet, specially sent from Holland. Louis XIV's miniature greyhound Zette slept in one of gilded bronze lined with red crimson.[57] The *cabinet de chiens* at Versailles where the King fed his dogs himself was imitated across Europe, as were so many other aspects of the seventeenth-century French court. Charles II's wife, Catherine of Braganza, had 'ye room where the Queen's dogs are kept' at Whitehall – in marked contrast to her husband, whose dogs slept with him.

Jean Ranc: Portrait of Liseta, the favourite dog of the Spanish Queen Elizabeth Farnese, lying on a crimson cushion.

The crimson dog beds favoured at Versailles were introduced to the court of Spain from 1700 when the Bourbon dynasty was established under Philip V, a King anxious to emulate Louis XIV in virtually every detail. One can be seen in the portrait of Liseta, the favourite dog of Queen Elizabeth Farnese, by Jean Ranc. Both Madame de Pompadour and Marie Antoinette had ornamental beds for their dogs; the picture by Desportes of a dog kennel covered in blue damask from which a long-haired dog appears to be emerging was in the collection of Madame de Pompadour.[58] It is clear from the memoirs of Marie Antoinette's *lecteur*, the Abbé de Vermond, that the dogs she had in her early years at Versailles were kept in her room.

One of the most squalid rulers of the eighteenth century was Gian Gastone, last of the Medici, who succeeded in 1723. The Rev. M. Noble reckoned it impossible to give much of the personal history of a Prince who, from mere indolence and sloth, was never dressed for the last thirteen years of his life, and who never left his bed for the last eight. His appearance was singularly whimsical; he received those whom he suffered to approach him, in his shirt, without ruffles, a cravat of considerable length, made of muslin, none of the finest, and a nightcap; all of which was besmeared with snuff. The late Earl of Sandwich acquainted this writer that this filthy habit so far grew upon Gian Gastone towards the latter part of his life, that to stifle the disagreeable smells of the bed, the room was covered entirely, when his lordship was introduced to His Royal Highness, with new-gathered roses.

This damning indictment was corroborated by the Baron de Pollnitz, who in 1731 found the Grand Duke 'sitting upright in bed, accompanied by several lap-dogs ... and truly there was nothing neat nor grand about him'. Scattering rose petals was standard practice at court for neutralising unpleasant odours.

The Empress Josephine's pugs slept near her on cashmere shawls or valuable carpets. On the eve of the coronation in 1804 her *première femme de chambre*, Madame Marco de St Hilaire, made an inventory of her belongings which included a monkey basket but mentioned none for dogs, thus confirming that her pugs enjoyed greater privileges. Eugenie, the wife of Josephine's grandson, Napoleon III, showed the same indulgence towards her favourite Maltese. In August 1855, during her visit to the Emperor and Empress, Victoria 'went for a moment, when dressed to go to St-Germain, to see the dear Empress, who was in bed with nothing on her head, and her hair merely twisted and combed back, but looking very pretty, with her very funny, very little dog, a little Cuba one, and a dear little thing called Linda, which the Empress generally carries on her arm, on her bed'.[59]

Keeping a favourite pet close by at night helped ward off the loneliness of separation. Victoria's granddaughter, Alexandra, Tsarina of Russia, always kept their dogs nearby at night when Nicholas II was away. She wrote to him on 24 June 1900 from Peterhof, 'Good-morning lovy! Well, both dogs slept in my room and did not move all night not even when I woke up several times and drank water. I got up at 7:30 and walked with them for an hour.'[60] Edward VIII also suffered from loneliness when Wallis left England during the abdication crisis. She left behind the cairn terrier the King had given her, Slipper, and 'in the bitter days that followed I was to be grateful for his companionship. He followed me around The Fort; he slept by my bed; he was the mute witness of my meetings with the Prime Minister . . . Except for Slipper, the living bonds between us had momentarily parted.'[61]

MEALTIMES

Mealtimes afforded manifold opportunities for pampering pets, and paintings from the Renaissance until the nineteenth century consistently depict dogs attending royal feasts. At the Burgundian court small dogs wandered freely across the tables and on occasion participated in lavishly orchestrated entertainments. Mathieu de Coucy described how, during one such banquet at the court of Duke Philip the Good in 1453, an enormous meat pie was brought in from which there suddenly sprang 'miniature greyhounds and *valets de chien* and poachers who sounded the trumpets as though they had been in the forest'.[62] Favourite dogs not only ate the same food as their masters but were frequently fed by them personally. Courte, the greyhound of Charles IX, ate biscuits and marzipan from the royal hand while sitting on the royal table.[63] Such was the King's devotion to Courte that, when it died, he had the animal's hide made into a pair of gloves which he always wore when hunting. In 1606, Héroard witnessed the Dauphin, Louis, 'giving his bread to his little dog; Mme de Montglat told him, "Monsieur, you shouldn't give bread to dogs, you should give it to the poor" – "Are dogs rich?"' quipped the Prince. In 1607, when the Dauphin joined his royal parents for supper, 'the King threw on the table for his dog, Cadet, [a spaniel] a sugared-almond; the dog licked it, the dauphin picked it up and ate it'.[64]

Detail of greyhound being fed from the **Très Riches Heures***. Dogs continued to be fed from horns until porcelain bowls became the fashion in the eighteenth century.*

Portrait by Diego Velásquez of the young Infante Felipe Prosper, 1659. Velásquez's meteoric rise at court culminated in 1658 when he was made a Knight of Santiago, an honour never previously accorded to a commoner.

Portrait of the Three Eldest Children of Charles I *by Anthony Van Dyck showing Charles II breeched. Like that other great British royal maecenas, the Prince Regent, Charles I was dilatory when it came to payment and Van Dyck longed for an appointment at the French court.*

A 1637 portrait of the five eldest children of Charles I by Van Dyck.

Portrait by Joshua Reynolds of Princess Sophia Matilda of Gloucester as a child with a shih tzu. Reynolds was appointed as Principal Painter to George III in 1784, even though the King allegedly 'could not endure the presence of him'.

Portrait by Pierre Mignard of the Grand Dauphin and his family. The most fashionable and prolific painter of his day, Mignard was appointed premier peintre in 1690, on the death of Le Brun.

Picture by Hendrik Danckerts depicting Charles II being presented with a pineapple while attended by tv

niels. Like Largillière, Danckerts was compelled to flee England in 1679 because of his Catholicism.

George Knapton: The Family of Frederick, Prince of Wales, *1751, showing a pug and a spaniel. A founder member of the Society of Dilettanti in 1736, Knapton was appointed Surveyor to the King's Pictures in 1765.*

The portrait by Nicolas de Largillière of Louis XIV and his Heirs *includes a Bolognese and a pug. All three princes represented in the picture had died by 1712.*

Gainsborough: Queen Charlotte with her spaniel. Gainsborough's double portrait of his Pomeranians, Tristram and Fox, held pride of place above the chimney-piece in his house in Pall Mall.

Portraits of Madame de Pompadour's bitches Iñes and Mimi, after the 1759 painting by Jean-Jacques Bachelier, on a gold box made by Louis Roucel.

Again, in 1610 he gave some water to his dog,[65] Gayan, asking 'Why do dogs need to drink?' and when he received the answer that it was to prevent rabies, the Dauphin reflected 'drunks run no risk of rabies then; they drink all the time'.[66] With thinly veiled disapproval Héroard noted every occasion when the Prince fed his dogs at table. Louis was only imitating the ways of his parents; Marie de Medici's dog, Brigantin, had the extraordinary privilege of being allowed to sit next to her on a stool during meals.[67]

Louis XIV also personally fed each of the privileged dogs housed in his *cabinet des petits chiens de la chambre du Roi*. His pastrycook baked special biscuits daily for this purpose, it being the King's belief that, by training them to eat from his own hand, they would learn greater obedience during the hunt.[68] Louis XV's favourite spaniel, Filou, was fed by the King from two horns handed to him by his *premier maître d'hôtel*.[69] The daily delivery of a chicken to the bedside of Marie Antoinette was a custom at Versailles dating back generations and owing its origin to a queen having once required one for her pet dog, though nobody could recall the identity of the particular queen in question. Many dogs enjoyed greater privileges than courtiers. In the painting by Luis Paret y Alcázar of the Spanish King Charles III lunching before his court c. 1770–2, the royal hounds appear to enjoy greater access to the monarch than the grandees who were not so much as allowed to sit in his presence.

Frederick the Great also fed his greyhounds himself. Jean-Baptiste de Boyer, Marquis d'Argens, at the court of Prussia from 1742, once entered the King's apartment to find him sitting on the ground with a big platter of fried meat, from which he was feeding his dogs. He had a little rod, with which he kept order among them, and shoved the best bits to his favourites. Frederick's behaviour was not dissimilar to that of Maria Amelia, Electress of Bavaria (1701–56), 'who loved dogs as well as she did men, rather better perhaps on the whole; and was never more pleased than when she dined in no better company than with a dozen of these canine favourites, whose unceremonious cleaning of the dishes before their hostess could help herself, only excited her hearty laughter'.[70] Another example of Bavarian table manners was furnished by the Duchess Ludovica of Bavaria, mother of the Empress Elisabeth of Austria, who

In Luis Paret y Alcázar's portrait of Charles III of Spain at table the King is seen with his 'perr
were fed from the royal hand on biscuits dipped in sweet wine.

le caza' whom the memorialist Count Fernán-Núñez described as enjoying pride of place. They always dined with two spitz on her lap which she fed continuously, simultaneously amusing herself by killing their fleas and depositing them on her plate.[71]

In contrast, some pets had perfect table manners: in the early nineteenth century, Monsignor Capecelatro, Archbishop of Taranto, of whom Prince Henry of Prussia famously said 'When one comes to Naples, one must see Pompeii, Vesuvius and the Archbishop of Taranto', had more than ten cats. Lady Morgan recalled dining with the eccentric Archbishop:

> Between the first and the second course, the door opened, and several enormously large and beautiful cats were introduced, by the names of Pantalone, Desdemona, Otello, and other dramatic *cognomina*. They took their places in chairs near the table, and were as silent, as quiet, as motionless and as well-behaved, as the most *bon-ton* table in London could require. On the bishop requesting one of the chaplains to help the Signora Desdemona to something, the butler stept up to his lordship and observed, 'Desdemona will prefer waiting for the roasts'. After dinner they were sent to walk on the terrace, and I had the honour of assisting at their *coucher*, for which a number of comfortable cushions were prepared in the bishop's dressing-room.[72]

Some of Queen Victoria's dogs were allowed into the dining room at mealtimes;[73] Albert's favourite greyhound, Eos, was fed from a fork at the luncheon table.[74] The Queen noted in her journal in 1869: 'Good Sharp was always in the dining-room, but remained quietly lying down.' The same privilege was not granted to all her dogs: in 1873 she noted in her journal,[75] 'my favourite collie Noble is always downstairs when we take our meals, and was so good, Brown making him lie on a chair or couch, and he never attempted to come down without permission, and even held a piece of cake in his mouth without eating it, till told he might. He is the most "biddable" dog I ever saw, and so affectionate and kind; if he thinks you are not pleased with him, he puts out his paws, and begs in such an affectionate way.' Exceptionally, Noble was allowed to attend their meals during the expedition to Loch Maree in the Highlands in 1877. Wearing a large white apron, Victoria often fed her animals herself in pairs after lunch in the 'Apron Room', next to the kennels at Windsor.

The far greater liberties extended to her dogs by Queen Alexandra were sometimes frowned upon by members of her intimate circle. Baroness de Stoeckl's daughter, Zoia, was appalled by the antics of one particular Pekingese to which the Queen was especially devoted and 'used to protest as this animal was allowed to walk on the dinner table and eat off the plates. It was so small that it jumped once and nearly disappeared in the Queen's décolleté.' Dogs were always present during the meals of Edward and Alexandra, and the King's fondness for his pets was one of the few subjects on which he and his mother agreed. It is not altogether surprising that, as a child, the future George V had such poor table manners that Victoria insisted he eat under the table, as would the dog he was apparently trying to emulate. He removed all his clothes, saying that as dogs wore none, neither would he.[76]

Although royal eccentricity assumes less flamboyant forms than it did in the past, it has not been altogether stifled. At Windsor Castle in 1944, when Princess Alexandra, daughter of the King of Greece, met George VI and Queen Elizabeth for the first time, she was bemused by the spectacle of the feeding of the royal pets:

> tea was brought in, and the little corgi dogs woke up. Lilibet gave an enquiring look at her mother, who nodded. With a 'Come on, Margaret' to her sister, she trotted out of the room. In a moment the sisters were back, followed by a footman who carried four little bowls. With great precision these were set out at some distance apart, a little way away from the low tea table. Then with much concentration the little girls prepared a meal in each of the bowls. 'Ready,' Margaret sang out, and Elizabeth, giving a final inspection, nodded. Two more small dogs answered their call. Then there were four of them, each eating from his own bowl. Not until the dogs were feeding happily did the girls come to have their tea.[77]

As Queen, Elizabeth II has maintained this protocol and a footman brings her the ingredients on a silver tray which she then personally mixes for her corgis and dorgis – corgi/dachshund hybrids – each receiving its food in order of precedence.

Diets

The ancients fed their dogs on a vegetarian diet of wholemeal bread, broth made from barley meal, milk and cooked beans, and by William the Conqueror's time the diet had little changed. The hounds belonging to the Prioresse in Chaucer's *Canterbury Tales* were clearly hunting dogs for:

> She was so charitable and so pitous,
> She wolde wepe if that she saw a mous
> Caughte in a trappe, if it were ded or bledde.
> Of smale houndes hadde she, that she fedde
> With rosted flesh, and milk, and wastel brede.
> But sore wept she if on of hem were dede,
> Or if men smote it with a yerde smert:
> And all was conscience and tendre herte.

As part of the process of blooding, hunting dogs received their share of the game which, according to Edward, second Duke of York, in his *Mayster of Game* (1406–13), consisted of the 'paunches and guts'. Small palace dogs which were discouraged from developing any interest in the chase continued to be restricted to a farinaceous diet. The sixteenth-century Counts d'Artois collected a special manorial due in oats for dog feed, and both Henri II and Henri III kept a baker who catered exclusively for their little dogs.[78] Mary Queen of Scots fed hers on a daily ration of two loaves of bread in the 1560s,[79] and the dogs of Marie de Medici consumed two pounds of bread a day.[80] A hundred years later the wisdom of a meat diet was still being questioned; in 1627 a factor of the East India Company complained that dogs being exported to China 'grow faint and die for want of fresh water and too much salt meat aboard, fresh oaten meal or ground barley is the only food for dogs, and a chain and a comely collar to grace them ought ever to be remembered'.

The argument against feeding dogs meat was still raging in the 1830s and beyond. Veterinary pathologists came to consider vegetables mixed with biscuits more appropriate for the health of small dogs. Spratts Patent Meat 'Fibrine' Dog Cakes were the first widely successful commercial dog food manufacturers with, by 1907, factories in Berlin, New York and

Sydney, largely as a result of advertising themselves as 'Suppliers to the Royal kennels'. When the Siberian sheepdog Luska (painted by Maud Earl c. 1908), presented to Edward VII in 1908, fell ill and refused all meat, Alexandra personally fed him on a diet of fish and rice until he recovered. By the 1920s British dog specialists were advising owners to shape the diet to the breed: for the hugely fashionable Japanese chin, batter puddings, with the occasional supplement of oatmeal porridge, was considered particularly suitable. King Charles spaniels were obviously keener on pure British fare: 'brown bread, cut up dice size, and moistened with good stock gravy, together with minced, lean, underdone roast beef, with the addition, two or three times a week, of a little well-cooked green vegetable, varied with rice or suet pudding and plain biscuits. Fish may be given occasionally.' For the Pekingese to flourish, fish, rice and 'bread well soaked in a very strong stock, sheep's head, and liver are always better as regular diet than meat, but in cases of debility a little raw meat given once a day is most beneficial, and Virol is always a good tonic'.[81] How nostalgically the dogs must have recalled the splendour of life under the Dowager Empress of China, who had stipulated that should a Pekingese fall ill: 'anoint it with the clarified fat of the leg of a snow-leopard and give it to drink from throstle egg-shells full of juice of custard-apples, in which are three pinches of shredded rhinoceros horns, and apply piebald leeches; and, if it dies, remember that man is not immortal and thou too must die'.[82]

R. Mathieu: Catherine the Great with Peter and Paul, *1756. Shows the imperial family with a pure black spaniel. When her favourite dog died, Catherine had it stuffed and buried in a tomb modelled on the Cestia pyramid.*

CHAPTER FOUR

Cruelty and Kindness

P RINCES WERE DEVASTATED when their pets got lost, fell ill or
died and frequently displayed a tenderness unparalleled in their attitude
to their subjects or even other members of their families. Although they
were willing spectators and sponsors of the cruel sports universally popular in
the early modern period, monarchs desisted from attending long before their
subjects were compelled to by legislation in the nineteenth century and were
often in the vanguard of movements to prevent cruelty to animals.

LOST PETS

Royal memoirs and correspondence testify to the heartache caused by the
loss of a favourite pet, be it through death, kidnapping or mere accident.
In dynastic China, heavy penalties were imposed on those who stole
imperial Pekingese, including death by torture. Western monarchs were
prepared to pay generously to recover a pet, a practice which increased the
temptation to steal them. Such sentimentality was often in marked contrast
to their attitudes to human life: Henry VIII rewarded a man with ten
shillings, 'for bringing Cut the kinge's spanyell ayen' and five shillings for
'bringing home Ball the kinge's dog that was loste in the forrest of
Waltham'. Cut was evidently an errant creature for another payment of
four shillings and eight pence was made 'to a poure woman in Rewarde, for
bringing ayenne of Cutte, the kinge's dog'.[1] Given that ten shillings in the
1530s was approximately equivalent to £150 in today's currency, the £30
offered by Prince Charles when his Jack Russell, Pooh, went missing in

April 1994 might appear somewhat derisory were it not borne in mind that Henry VIII was the richest prince in Christendom at the time. Anxiety was heightened when the pet was a bitch. When Marie de Medici lost Turquette she sent footmen and other palace officials to scour the palace grounds lest, 'during her escapade, the poor creature meet some galant both unworthy and overattentive'.[2] The recovery of Negrite, another of the Queen's dogs to go astray, prompted Henri IV to write her a letter of effusive congratulation.

The Stuarts were frequently subject to dog theft. Elizabeth I's godson, Sir John Harington, wrote to James I's son, Prince Henry, in 1608 explaining the difficulties he had persuading the Spanish ambassador that the dog to which he had become immeasurably attached was in fact his own spaniel, Bungey:

> Nor did the householde listen to any claim or challenge, till I rested my suite on the Dogge's own proofes, and made him performe such feats before the Nobles assembled as put it past doubt that I was his master. I did send him to the hall in the time of dinner, and made him bring thence a pheasant out of the dish, which created much mirthe; but much more, when he returned at my commandment to the table and put it again in the same cover. Herewith the companie was well content to allow me my claim, and we bothe were well content to accepte it, and came homewardes.[3]

The kidnap of Jowler, the favourite hound of James I, was politically motivated, as Edmund Lascelles explained in a letter to the Earl of Shrewsbury:

> There was one of the King's speciall hounds called Jowler, missing one day. The King was much displeased that he was wanted; notwithstanding went a-hunting. The next day, when they weare on the feild, Jowler came in amongst the rest of the hounds; the King was told of him, and was very glad, and, loking on him, spied a paper about his neck, and in the paper was written: 'Good Mr. Jowler, we pray you speake to the King (for he hears you every day, and so doth he not us) that it will please his Majestie to go back to London, for els the country wilbe undoon.'

James ignored the message and continued hunting for the next fortnight.[4] In 1654, the King's daughter, Elizabeth Queen of Bohemia, wrote to Sir Edward Nicholas, secretary of state, thanking him for congratulating her on the recovery of Apollo: 'you know how great a favorit [sic] he is'.[5] When her son, Prince Rupert, lost his dog in Dean's Yard, Westminster in 1677, he placed an advertisement in the *London Gazette* describing his pet as a 'young white spaniel about six months' old, with a black head, red eyebrows and a black spot on his back, belonging to His Highness Prince Rupert. If anyone can bring him to Prince Rupert's Lodgings in the Stone Gallerie at Whitehall, he will be well rewarded for his pains.'[6] Publicity proved successful and Charles II had recourse to the same stratagem when his 'black dog, between a greyhound and a spaniel' went missing. The cause of the animal's disappearance was explicitly stated and the royal *cri de coeur* exacerbated by the memory of the theft of a buckhound in 1663: 'It was his Majestie's own dog, and doubtless was stolen, for the dog was not born nor bred in England, and would never forsake his master. Will they never leave robbing His Majestie? Must he not keep a dog? This dog's place (though better than some imagine) is the only place which nobody offers to beg.' Charles II's cavalier attitude to disciplining or training his dogs frequently caused him embarrassing situations: their tendency to bite made him liable to demands for financial compensation. The mother of a boy bitten in Oxford by the King's dog, Cupid, petitioned for hefty compensation.[7]

The favourite Italian greyhound of Frederick the Great, Biche, was kidnapped during the Battle of Soor in 1745 by the Austrian General Radaski, who presented his trophy to his wife. The Prussian King was distraught at the loss of Biche, the dog he accredited with having saved his life when she refrained from barking at the approach of an enemy dragoon patrol close to where they were hiding. After protracted negotiations his friend, General Rothenburg, managed to persuade his Austrian adversary to restitute Biche. Stealing into the King's room at Sans-Souci, where he was writing letters, Biche jumped on to his desk and placed her paws around the royal neck, reducing him to tears of unbridled joy at being thus reunited with the creature he described as his 'best friend'.[8]

RABIES AND QUARANTINE

Towards the end of the nineteenth century the two greatest scourges of dog owners were rabies-paranoia and thieves. As a result of the former any unidentified dog was liable to be picked up by the authorities without further investigation and taken to the laboratory for experimentation, where many of these 'Unknown Soldiers in the battle of the human mind against disease and death', as Axel Munthe described them, 'looked as though they had seen better days'.[9] By identifying ownership, collars might help obtain a stay of execution but, by the same token, they played into the hands of the increasingly professional dog thieves who preyed on the new, luxurious hotels to which the aristocracy and royalty were attracted and which, with the revolution in mobility engendered by the railway and steamship, they were able to frequent relatively easily. As Munthe noted: 'With the opening of the Grand Hotel, Ritz had dealt a final blow to the vanishing simplicity of Roman life. The last invasion of the barbarians had begun, the Eternal City had become fashionable.'[10] Thieves hoped to reap rich rewards for finding the very animals they had stolen. When Axel Munthe lost his dog, Gorm, in Rome, the Queen of Sweden, who had given it to him, instantly alerted the police and launched a three-day search, happily crowned with success.

Axel Munthe had first-hand experience of rabies, having worked with Louis Pasteur at his institute in Paris. In *The Story of San Michele*, written in 1929, he expressed scepticism as to the virulency of the disease and remained convinced that 'the majority of dogs killed suspected of hydrophobia, are suffering from other relatively harmless diseases' and that 'fear of hydrophobia is as dangerous as the disease itself'.[11] Pasteur first successfully inoculated a child against rabies in 1885, and among the patients who immediately rushed to Paris for preventative treatment were seven London policemen. It was Pasteur who recommended the system of quarantine in Britain, on the basis that full-scale vaccination was superfluous on an island with the natural protective barrier of the sea. Quarantine was introduced in 1901 and Britain declared rabies-free a year later.[12]

It was ironic that a French scientist should be the motivating force behind the introduction of quarantine regulations, given that their first proponents were xenophobically inspired. The idea had been mooted initially in 1794 by the Manchester physician Samuel Argent Bardsley, who recommended a confinement of eight months for all dogs entering the country. The French Revolution was then at its height and England had given sanctuary to numerous *émigrés* escaping from the Terror. Whenever possible, they fled with their dogs, equally at risk as their masters but excoriated in some British circles as four-footed fifth columnists. Ignorance of the causes of rabies and resistance from an aristocratic and cosmopolitan ruling class, who had themselves acquired a taste for extensive travel – generally accompanied by dogs – in Europe before the outbreak of the Revolution, put paid to any such schemes, and a compromise was reached with the introduction of dog licensing in 1796. As a direct consequence, thousands of dogs were slaughtered across the country including four hundred in Cambridge and one thousand in Birmingham.[13]

Attempts to find an antidote to rabies were far from new. Pliny the Elder (AD 23–79) was probably responsible for the theory of 'the hair of the dog', recommending that a mixture of some hairs from the mad dog's tail mixed with livers from drowned puppies belonging to the same sex as the offending dog be applied to the wound.[14] One of the first works in France on the chase, the *Livre du Roy Modus et de la Royne Racio*, written in the early fourteenth century, isolated two strains of the disease and prescribed a highly original treatment:

> In order to be cured, some go to the sea, which is a good remedy. But better still, immediately make a mixture of coarse salt and fine vinegar, heat it up and wash the wound with a combination of this sauce and some nice small nettles. Another proven remedy for man, woman or beast bitten by a rabid dog is to find a cock as quickly as possible, pluck its backside . . . and to the bite wound or wounds apply the anus of the bird which will suck out the poison; each wound should be given this treatment over a protracted period. If the wound is too small it should be enlarged with a lancet. If the cock swells and dies the victim will recover; if the cock does not succumb, it is proof that the dog was not rabid.[15]

The Duke of York, in his *Mayster of Game*, written between 1406 and 1413, considered the standard remedy of going to the sea and causing nine waves to pass over the victim as being of 'litel helpe' compared to the application of a potion consisting of leeks, garlic, rue, nettles, salt, vinegar and olive oil.[16] George Turbervile, writing in the late sixteenth century, enumerated seven types of the disease.

In the sixteenth and seventeenth centuries suspected rabies victims in France, whether canine or human, were most commonly sent to the sea at Dieppe. Henri IV's dog, Famor, was taken there when he was bitten,[17] as were three prominent ladies at the court of Louis XIV in 1671, including Marie-Elizabeth de Ludres, the King's mistress, 'to be thrown three times into the sea'.[18] On 20 December 1610, while playing in the Tuileries gardens, Louis XIII encountered

> a rabid dog, which molested several of his own dogs and, in particular, his favourite, Gayan, together with the man who attended them. He struck the dog with his riding-crop, which pounced at him before it could be stopped by Monsieur de Meurs, standard-bearer of the Scotch Guard, but who then managed to hold it at bay with his cudgel and would have killed it had the King, naturally humane, not prevented him from doing so. Brought home at 10:30 in a carriage, he told the Queen what had happened to his dogs and begged her to send them to the sea. Her Majesty immediately gave the order to the huntsman [who had been bitten]; at 11:00 the King came to dine, did me the honour of telling me the whole story, with tears in his eyes, of his huntsman and Gayan, saying he wished he had not taken Gayan to the Tuileries today.[19]

On another occasion, chasing hares in Ville l'Evêque, the Prince insisted on bringing back a fierce dog he had encountered while chasing hares, saying it was but a 'poor creature searching its master'.[20]

The sanguine approach to rabies at seventeenth-century courts contrasted strongly with attitudes in eighteenth-century Britain; the physician of the Princess Dowager of Wales wondered whether they were 'occasioned by any real cause, which infected dogs'? Public alarm was largely fuelled by the press, the disease being no better understood then than it would be a hundred years later.[21] Indeed, rabies was probably in decline as a result of the virtual extinction of the wolf caused by royal hunting in western Europe. Of the 150,000 dogs received by the Battersea Dogs' Home between 1860 and 1877, only one was found to be rabid. In 1887, the veterinarian William South challenged the members of the Select

Committee of the House of Lords and his fellow witnesses to cite one single example of a mad dog they had seen in the streets; no one volunteered a reply.[22] In 1897 *Country Life* inveighed against 'the folly of creating needless panic by the insistence of the assertion that hydrophobia is prevalent at the present time', pointing out that 'the statistics upon which the assertion of the prevalence of the disease is founded, have been mainly made out by the police, who can scarcely be regarded as infallible authorities'. Rabies had become associated with dirt, disorder and sin, notions alien to most sovereigns where their dogs were concerned. When six Russian peasants succumbed to the disease in the 1880s, the Tsar personally paid for their transportation to the Pasteur Institute in Paris.[23] When quarantine was introduced in 1901, monarchs decided to ignore it.

Edward VII travelled annually with his favourite terrier Jack until its death in 1903, and subsequently Caesar, to Paris, Biarritz, the Mediterranean, Berlin, Vienna, St Petersburg, Athens, Copenhagen and Marienbad. 'During the visit paid by Monsieur Clemenceau, then French Premier, to King Edward at Marienbad in August 1908, Monsieur Clemenceau slyly asked whether the King would take Caesar back with him to England, breaking the quarantine regulations. With mock gravity he remarked, "Surely Your Majesty will not set an example in law-breaking?" The King laughingly replied, "I make the laws, can't I break 'em?" '[24] Prince Yusupov acquired a bulldog, Punch, while an undergraduate at Oxford:

Detail of Caesar. Edward VII refused to abide by the new quarantine regulations introduced in 1901.

Like all of his kind, he was most eccentric. I soon noticed that checks on linoleum or on any kind of material drove him wild. One day when I was at Davies', my tailor's, a very smartly dressed old gentleman, wearing a check suit, came in. Before I could stop him, Punch rushed at him and tore a huge piece out of his trousers. On another occasion, I went with a friend to her furrier's; Punch noticed a sable muff encircled by a black and white check scarf. He immediately seized it and rushed out of the shop with it. I, and everyone else at the furrier's, ran after him half-way down Bond Street, and it was only with the greatest difficulty that we managed to catch him and retrieve the muff, happily almost intact. When the holidays came, I took Punch to Russia, not thinking of the stringent law governing the entry of dogs into England. As six months in quarantine was out of the question, I decided to evade the law. On my way to Oxford in the autumn, I passed through Paris and went to see an old Russian ex-cocotte whom I knew. I asked her to come to London with me; she would have to dress as a nurse and carry Punch, disguised as a baby. The old lady agreed at once, as the idea amused her immensely, although at the same time it frightened her to death. The next day, we left for London after giving 'Baby' a sleeping draught so as to keep him quiet during the journey. Everything went smoothly and not a soul suspected the fraud.[25]

The Prince of Wales and Wallis Simpson travelled with their cairn, Slipper, in the summer of 1935 and quarantine was flouted even after the abdication.[26] Despite being the Queen's physician, Axel Munthe himself felt little compunction about smuggling his dachshund, Waldmann, into Sweden.

Attempts to flaunt the quarantine laws were not always successful as the former Queen of Greece found in 1941 when she arrived in England after a year's wandering across the globe. Her daughter, Queen Alexandra of Yugoslavia, remembered how, despite having disembarked

safely in solid imperturbable Britain, seated comfortably in the boat train for London . . . mummie was weeping as though her heart would break. And the simple cause of all this grief? Her little dog, Tulip, had been taken from her and sent to quarantine.

There is a proverb – 'it is the last straw which breaks the camel's back,' and this, for poor mummie, was the last straw.

In war-time, when thousands were losing their lives, millions separated from their families, it may sound absurd to record our distress at a normal, temporary separation from one small dog. But as in all families, it is often the smallest, most trivial sorrow which brings the tears, not only for itself, but for all the other great stresses and griefs which have been endured.

Tulip was very special to mummie. I think her natural love for animals had been strengthened by my father's affection for them. She had never been without a long-haired dachshund, and Tulip was the one who had shared the greatest part of all our shifting fortunes.

Now Tulip had been taken away, and for quite an hour there was no consoling mummie.

One person who didn't attempt to console her was Uncle Georgie. To be honest I think he was feeling that this abrupt quarantine order served mummie right! There was good reason for his somewhat harsh sentiments. Uncle Georgie had a dog, too, which he had 'openly' declared when we landed, knowing it would be taken from him to go to quarantine. He was quite furious when he discovered that mummie had successfully smuggled tiny Tulip ashore, under her coat. So when poor Tulip gave a revealing squirm and whine, and officials spotted and abducted her, Uncle Georgie felt that justice had been done.[27]

DOCTORS

The distinction between veterinary surgeons and medical practitioners remained blurred until the late eighteenth century because man, and not the beast, was the object of physiological research. All the early botanists were apothecaries primarily in pursuit of medical remedies for humans. Animal welfare grew out of the needs of war and hunting and was concentrated on horses and hounds. The attachment felt for their sick pets by most monarchs nevertheless generally outweighed considerations of function and they would go to great lengths to ensure their comfort and relief from pain. When one of his dogs fell ill, Louis XI ordered that it be transported in a litter by water to his chateau at Plessis-les-Tours, in order to ease its suffering. His apothecary, Guion Moreau, supplied various ointments, powders and plasters for the treatment of his sick dogs.[28] The French King Henri IV was exceptional in abandoning a dog in old age. Age and physical incapacity were of little consequence at court where servants attended to the irksome duties imposed by animal decrepitude. The poet Agrippa d'Aubigny (1552–1630), who was at one time equerry to the King, rescued the royal spaniel and expressed his disapprobation of his monarch's behaviour in verse:

La Folie du Jour. *In this nineteenth-century French coloured engraving a lapdog is being subjected to an enema. The mixing of eroticism and medicine was a common theme in art of the period.*

Faithful Citron who once did sleep
Upon your sacred bed, now sleeps rough.
This is the faithful dog which learned from nature
To distinguish friend from traitor.
Courtiers, who turned with scorn
From this forsaken dog, left to starve on the streets,
Expect to reap the same reward for your fidelity.[29]

Apothecaries and doctors submitted their patients – whether humans or animals – to the same ineffectual tortures. Both were bled, purged, induced to vomit and subjected to enemas in the hope of forcibly evacuating the 'evil' humours believed to be the cause of sickness. The only diseases to have been accurately diagnosed before the end of the eighteenth century were bubonic plague and smallpox.

Frederick the Great displayed a tenderness to his sick pets quite unparalleled in his dealings with his fellow men. When the Prussian King's favourite, Biche, fell ill, no fewer than ten doctors were summoned. The dog nonetheless died in 1752 and thereafter Frederick nursed his greyhounds himself on a diet of whey. Such a diet is indicative of how little progress had been made in veterinary science since the ancients. Virgil had prescribed the same treatment in *Georgics* III:

> Nor, last, forget thy faithful dogs; but feed
> With fattening whey the mastiff's generous breed.[30]

Describing Frederick the Great in a dispatch from Berlin in 1776, the British ambassador, Sir James Harris, was struck by

> that motley composition of barbarity and humanity which so strongly
> marks his character. I have seen him weep at tragedy, known him pay
> as much care to a sick greyhound as a fond mother could to a
> favourite child, and yet, the next day, he has given orders for the
> devastating a province, or, by a wanton increase of taxes, made a whole
> district miserable; and, what will perhaps appear still more
> contradictory, contribute to his own brother's death, by continuing to
> him marks of his displeasure, the whole time of his last illness.[31]

Later that same year, when Frederick was confined to bed with an attack of gout, he had no option but to send for a doctor. The man he chose, Cuttenius, had one redeeming feature: he had refused to prescribe for Biche when she lay dying and was thus uniquely absolved from responsibility in the greyhound's death.

The majority of doctors before the nineteenth century enjoyed an influence at court wholly disproportionate to their ability. In order for them to tend their patients, etiquette and protocol were necessarily relaxed in their favour and they had easier access to the monarch than many a privileged courtier. To obtain an audience with Louis XIV, Saint-Simon had to apply through the King's doctor, Fagon, despite being far better born. The great diarist had an unfortunate aversion to the chase; doctors accompanied princes

Detail of the sick spaniel by Velásquez. Before the nineteenth century, ailing pets received the same treatment as their owners.

179

during the hunt, lest an accident should befall them, and thus had enviable opportunities to solicit favours and further their careers. Ailing monarchs were susceptible to any quack or charlatan who promised relief from the physical torment that was the everyday lot of all mortals before the nineteenth century. Equally, a doctor who could cure a cherished pet could expect to be royally rewarded.

By the summer of 1796, Napoleon desperately wanted Josephine to join him in Italy where he was in command of the army. He wrote sardonically and imploringly: 'As if a pretty woman could give up her routine, her friends, her Madame Tallien or a dinner-party at Barras' house and the performance of a new play or Fortuné, yes! Fortuné! You love them all more than your husband...'[32] Fortuné was Josephine's pug to which she was particularly devoted, not least because, during the Revolution when she was imprisoned at the Carmes, her children, Eugène and Hortense de Beauharnais, had succeeded in getting messages to her by hiding them in the dog's collar. Far from giving him up, she brought the dog with her to Mombello where he was suffocated by a huge mongrel belonging to the cook. The cook, mortified, would not allow his dog to enter the park until Napoleon pleaded with him to 'bring him back. Perhaps he will rid me of the new dog too.'[33] The 'new dog' was a gift in 1797 from Hippolyte Charles, Josephine's lover, but it soon fell ill and, for all his canophobia – not to mention ignorance of the donor's precise place in his wife's affections – Napoleon called in the most famous Milanese doctor of the day, Pietro Moscati, to tend it. The dog recovered and Moscati owed his meteoric rise in no small measure to Josephine's gratitude, becoming a member of the Cisalpine Directory and, after the creation of the Kingdom of Italy, count, senator, and Grand-Officer of both the *Légion d'honneur* and the *Couronne de fer*.

Although never a doctor, Rasputin was already beginning to attract attention as a faith-healer when he was invited in 1905 to the home of the Grand Duchess Militsia, daughter of the King of Montenegro and wife of the Grand Duke Peter Nicolaevich. On arrival, Rasputin found the Grand Duke patting a small sick dog and instantly fell on his knees in prayer. Half an hour later, when Rasputin rose to his feet, the dog was cured. He was introduced to the Tsarina, Alexandra, and nothing was more indicative of his hold over the imperial family than his demand (one of the few to be rejected) that their borzoi, Minka, be put down after biting him. His astonishing career ended only with his murder in 1916 at the hands of Prince Yusupov, the assassin suffering no remorse beyond that occasioned by having 'to shoot one of my best dogs and lay it out in the courtyard where the snow was stained by the blood of the murdered *staretz*. I did it in case our Sherlock Holmeses find a first lead to Rasputin's disappearance and decide to analyse the blood or resort to police dogs.'[34]

In 1791 the first British Veterinary College was founded in St Pancras under the professorship of the Frenchman Charles Vial de Sainbel, himself educated at the Veterinary College of Lyons, established some thirty years earlier in 1760. George IV was the first British monarch to employ a veterinary surgeon, Joseph Goodwin (1786–1845), to oversee the royal stud and kennels. When it came to the care of favourite pets, however, monarchs continued to treat veterinary surgeons with a great deal of circumspection throughout the nineteenth century. Queen Victoria always sought a second opinion from her personal physician when one of her dogs fell ill and allowed no pet of hers to be destroyed, regardless of the nature of the disease. In 1881, when her favourite collie, Noble, whose principal function at court was to guard her gloves, fell ill, both her vet, Charles Rotherham, and her own doctor, Sir James Reid, were called in to prescribe. 'On one occasion she was anxious that Noble should be fed at night, for "I have such a dread that he may sleep away!" Rotherham declared "I think you will have him for a long time yet, if he does not get any bones and is regularly, but not overfed". Noble lived for another 3 years, dying at the advanced age of 16.'[35]

By the end of the nineteenth century medical science had advanced considerably. The introduction of anaesthesia, of which Queen Victoria was one of the earliest beneficiaries, had transformed doctors into demigods at the courts of Europe. So enhanced was their social prestige that Victoria boycotted the appointment of C. F. Watts to the Privy Council because, unlike Huxley, he was not a scientist;[36] her own doctor, Sir James Reid, was the first member of his profession to stand beside the coffin at his sovereign's funeral. Doctors continued to enjoy privileged access to the royal person, accompanying their peripatetic monarchs across the world, ever at hand to attend to illness and injury at a time when the spread of revolutionary movements was taking its toll of crowned heads.

Nobody was more aware of Edward VII's devotion to dogs than his veterinary surgeon, A. J. Sewell. When the King's French toy bulldog, Peter, had to be destroyed on the eve of the coronation after being run over by a butcher's cart, it was Sewell who found his replacement, Jack, a rough-coated fox-terrier. Jack also came to an untimely end, choking to death on some food, and Edward had some of the dog's hair made into a bracelet, which occupied pride of place on his desk. The next Irish terrier was put down on Sewell's advice as soon as cancer was diagnosed. By the time Caesar appeared on the scene, the King was taking no risks and, when the dog fell ill in Marienbad in 1907, his assistant private secretary, Sir Frederick Ponsonby, recalled how: 'His Majesty wanted to send for Sewell from London. Sewell's charge was £200 for coming out. I expostulated with the King on the extravagance of having out a man who charged so much, but His Majesty said that if his dog was ill he would get the very best man, and he did not care what it cost. Luckily a first-class vet was found in Vienna who came and cured the dog.'[37] Not only were Viennese doctors considered the best in the world at the time but Ponsonby was doubtless also anxious to avoid a repetition of the ugly scene which had occurred at Friedrichshof in 1901, when the Kaiser's physicians, Renvers and Spielhagen, had refused to address a word to Edward's doctor, Laking. The Kaiser, and the whole German medical establishment, were still smarting over the death from cancer of Frederick III in 1888, for which they blamed Dr Morell Mackenzie, who had been preferred by the Kaiserin Victoria, sister of Edward VII, above all practitioners of German nationality. The Kaiser's suspicion that his father's death resulted from wilful misdiagnosis never ceased to rankle and was one of the many grudges he harboured against the British.[38]

Axel Munthe, who described himself without exaggeration as 'a consulting dog-doctor famous among all dog-lovers of my clientele',[39] was nonetheless a physician by training and his clientele reflected the new social prestige attained by medical practitioners. He was amused when his assistant, Miss Hall, started another diary, entirely devoted to our associations with Royalty. The previous Monday she had had the honour to carry a letter from the doctor to HRH the Grand Duchess of Weimar at the Hotel Quirinale. . . . On Wednesday she had been entrusted with a letter for HRH the Infanta Eulalia of Spain in the Grand Hotel. . . . One afternoon, as she was with the dogs in the Villa Borghese, Miss Hall had noticed a tall lady in black walking rapidly up and down a side alley. She recognised her at once as the same lady she had seen in the garden of San Michele, standing motionless by the Sphinx and looking out over the sea with her beautiful, sad eyes. As the lady passed before her now, she said something to her companion and stretched out her hand to pat Gialla, the borzoi. Judge of Miss Hall's consternation when a detective came up to her and told her to move on at once with the dogs – it was HIM the Empress of Austria and her sister Countess Trani! . . . Had she not last summer for weeks been watching at a respectful distance a granddaughter of her own beloved Queen Victoria, painting in the pergola! Had not a cousin of the Tsar himself been living there for a whole month! Had she not had the honour to stand behind the kitchen door to see the Empress Eugenie pass before her at arm's length the first time she came to San Michele. Had she not heard with her own ears HIH say to the doctor that she had never seen a more striking likeness to the great Napoleon than the head of Augustus the doctor had dug up in his garden! Had she not several years later heard the commanding voice of the Kaiser himself . . .[40]

Munthe's principal patient was Queen Victoria of Sweden, who frequently visited Capri with her favourite poodle. Such was the respect he commanded that, when the First World War broke out and the Queen – the daughter of the Grand Duke of Baden – sided with the Germans, Munthe, an ardent anglophile, resigned and sought naturalisation as a British subject. The Queen never formally accepted his resignation and, after the war, he not only resumed his duties at court but dedicated the first edition of *The Story of San Michele*: 'To Her Majesty Queen Victoria of Sweden, Protectress of Oppressed Animals, and Friend of All Dogs'. The day before her death a year later, in 1930, she made Munthe promise that the dedication would stand in all future Swedish editions of his book.[41]

Recent British monarchs have proved themselves as attentive to their pets' wellbeing as any of their forebears. Edward VIII not only had steps built for his favourite cairn, Cora, when she could no longer jump on his bed, but ordered spectacles for her in order to counter the effects of altitude when flying.[42] When Crackers, one of the Queen Mother's favourite corgis, became too decrepit to walk, she had a miniature Bath chair constructed, in which the dog would rest on a plush cushion while pushed around the grounds. Having been bitten on more than one occasion by her corgis, Queen Elizabeth II wisely employs an animal psychologist, Dr Roger Mugford, to attend to their mental health.

PARTURITION

In the days when death in childbirth remained common, the confinement of a cherished pet inevitably gave many a monarch cause for anguish, and the news of a successful delivery warranted special mention. George Turbervile, in his *Book of Faulconrie* of 1575, described puppies born under the signs of Gemini or Aquarius as being exempt from madness, and couplings may well have been arranged in the hope of guaranteeing that dogs were astrologically advantaged. When her favourite greyhound had a litter, Marie de Medici wrote to a friend, 'I hasten to inform you my little Bichette has given birth and she has produced three handsome little dogs, of which the prettiest has two noses and which I intend for you.' Nor did she hesitate to impart the glad tidings when Roquette was delivered of '*petits roquetons*' – little mongrels.[43] Interest in canine parturition could help remedy the tedium of life at court. Madame, the Duchesse d'Orléans, wrote to the Raugravine Louisa from Versailles in 1702: 'the Court will soon be deserted. But that doesn't worry me much, because I shall not miss the society. I am alone all day in my cabinet and time does not hang heavily; in fact, I find the days too short. I have plenty of flowers outside my window, many little dogs which I love dearly, my medals, and lots of books. One of my prettiest little bitches is at present having her puppies here in my cabinet.'[44] In 1709 she wrote again, this time from Marly:

One of my little bitches has just jumped up on the table, seized my paper and torn a word, as you see. The lady who did this fine trick is called Candace or Robe, which latter name was given to her because her mother Charmille, who was behind me, began to whimper and fidget as she always did when she wanted to be caressed. The Princess said to me, 'Your little dog is restless, what is the matter with her?' I said, 'She wants me to stroke her.' I put my hand behind me to pet her, and felt it all wet, she had just had her puppies on my gown, which was spread out all around me. The Princess had a good laugh at the affair, but this is ancient history and three years have gone since then.[45]

On occasion, the birth of a litter might engross the whole court. When the dog of Henrietta Howard, Countess of Suffolk and mistress of George II, was in labour in 1720, Horace Walpole reported how: 'it was the humour of the Court for them to go down to my lady Suffolk's apartment to drink caudle on Marquise lying in. Lord Chesterfield heard of it & writ her a letter, with directions for the education of the Puppies, into which he introduced the chief personages about the Court, allotting them employments according to the several ridicules for which they were most remarkable.'[46] Caudle, a spiced hot wine, probably mixed with egg, was given to bitches – and their mistresses – during labour.

Frederick the Great's greyhounds were all bitches and he was so over-joyed when they had puppies that he would hasten to spread the good news among friends and relations. On 30 November 1769, when Diane had a litter, he wrote a verse to his sister, in which he purports to be the proud mother and exhorts her to ape the dog's example:

> A bitch today sets a great example.
> I have had two little ones;
> All the curious who come to see them
> Find them beautiful like me, well-made and kind,
> Be god-mother at their christening,
> And my wishes will be fulfilled,
> If, Madam, you shortly follow suit.[47]

DEATH

The death of a pet, in labour or otherwise, could reduce even the most martial ruler to paroxysms of grief, and animal cemeteries and monuments have an ancient history. An inscription at Giza records how the burial of a dog that guarded the King of Egypt was carried out with all the ritual ceremony due to a great man. The King presented the dog with a coffin, linen and incense together with a jar of ointment for the burial chamber. The bodies of dogs interred at Cynopolis were embalmed, placed in wooden dog-shaped coffins, and buried in graveyards at public expense. In the necropolis of Thebes, there is a statue of King Hana of the XI Dynasty (c. 2000 BC) with his cat Bouhaki recumbent at his feet.

Cats were first tamed by the Egyptians in 3000 BC to protect grain from rodents and had been kept as pets for more than a thousand years before they became sacred.[48] Herodotus described how, when a cat died, 'there is great mourning in Egypt. Dwellers in a house where a cat has died a natural death shave their eyebrows and no more; when a dog has so died, the head and the whole body are shaven. Dead cats are taken away into sacred buildings, where they are embalmed and buried, in the town of Bubastis; bitches are buried in sacred coffins by the townsmen, in their several towns.'[49] There were cat cemeteries along the Nile.

No ruler before or since ever honoured the memory of a dead animal as magnificently as did Alexander the Great. According to Plutarch,

after this battle with Porus, Alexander's horse Boukephalus died, not immediately, but some time afterwards. Most historians say that he died of wounds received in the battle, but Onesikritus tells us that he died of old age and overwork, for he had reached his thirtieth year. Alexander was greatly grieved at his loss, and sorrowed for him as much as if had lost one of his most intimate friends. He founded a city as a memorial of him upon the banks of the Hydaspes, which he named Boukephalia. It is also recorded that when he lost a favourite dog called Peritas, which he had brought up from a whelp, and of which he was very fond, he founded a city and called it by the dog's name. The historian Sotion tells us that he heard this from Potamon of Lesbos.[50]

The ancient Romans wrote elegies and epitaphs for their dead pets and the Emperor Hadrian built sepulchres in honour of his dogs at the end of the first century AD.

It was to the example of the Romans that Renaissance princes turned in the fifteenth century. William Beckford, travelling in the environs of Padua in 1780, felt he was 'too near the last and one of the most celebrated abodes of Petrarch, to make the omission of a visit excusable', and went to Arqua where, in the poet's parlour, 'a niche in the wall contains the skeleton of his favourite cat, with a Latin epigram beneath, of Petrarch's composition. It is good enough to deserve being copied; but the lateness of the hour did not allow me time.'[51] Isabella d'Este's

> pet animals were buried with great solemnity in the terraced gardens of the Castello opposite the Corte Vecchia, and cypresses and tombstones inscribed with their names marked their graves. All the ladies and gentlemen of Isabella's household were present on these occasions, and her favourite dogs and cats joined in the funeral procession. And it was characteristic of the age that every incident, from the birth of a prince or the fall of an empire, to the death of a fool or pet dog, became an occasion for producing Latin epitaphs and sonnets and elegies in the vulgar tongue.[52]

In 1511, Isabella was distraught at the death of Aura, caused by its falling over a cliff while being pursued by a larger dog.

> The poor little dog was laid in a leaden casket, and a fine tomb was prepared for her in a new Loggia which the Marchesa had built that autumn. Meanwhile, not only at Mantua, but in Rome and Ferrara, elegies, epitaphs, sonnets, and epigrams were poured out by the best poets of the day, and the tragic fate of the 'chaste and noble Aura' was lamented in Latin and Italian verses, by Tebaldeo and Scalona, Equicola and Celio Calcagnini, and a score of well-known humanists. Federico shared his mother's grief for this lost favourite, and sent her Latin verses in praise of Aura, composed by Monsieur Filippo Beroaldo and others.[53]

Giulio Romano: Design for Memorial to a Dog. *Giulio Romano settled in Mantua c. 1524. The dog belonged to Federico Gonzaga.*

In c. 1525, Isabella's son, Federico Gonzaga, first Duke of Mantua, commissioned Giulio Romano to erect a monument with an epitaph for the south wall of the Secret Garden when his beloved little bitch (*cagnolina*) died in labour. Amore, the favourite dog of Alessandro, Duke of Florence, had earned the opprobrium of contemporaries by its unpleasant habit of biting, scratching and urinating over anyone with whom it came into contact. When it died, c. 1534, Francesco Berni (1498–1535), one of the most important Florentine poets of the sixteenth century, was asked by the grieving Duke to write its epitaph, and he obliged by producing a uniquely unflattering verse:

> He lies buried in this dark hole,
> A vile and treacherous cur;
> Nastiness itself, he was called Love.
> He had but one virtue: he was the Duke's dog.

Love was probably a large shaggy retriever of the sort given by the Duke to Benvenuto Cellini, who named his dog Barucco and greatly appreciated its ability as a watchdog. On one occasion Cellini accredited it with recognising a thief who had stolen from his shop and bringing the terrified malefactor to justice.[54]

French kings and courtiers were deeply impressed by the culture they observed during the invasions of the Italian peninsula. Louis de Ronsard, father of the poet, had accompanied the armies of Francis I in his capacity as *maître d'hôtel des enfants de France* and returned imbued with a taste for the arts which profoundly influenced his son, himself a courtier from the age of twelve when he was appointed page to the dying King. On the accession of Charles IX, twenty-four years later in 1560, Ronsard was lavishly rewarded for the years he had spent at court composing all the occasional verse and literary amusements for royal festivities. Upon the death of the King's favourite dog, aptly named Courte because of its diminutive size, Ronsard was asked to write the epitaph:

> Courte is dead, who when alive
> Did for her King uniquely strive.[55]

When Chateaubriand was sent as minister plenipotentiary from the French court to Berlin in 1821, he was horrified by the sight of the tombs erected by Frederick the Great in honour of his beloved greyhounds: 'The blasphemous King took pleasure in profaning the religion of the tombs, by erecting mausolea to his dogs; he intended his own sepulchre to lie beside them, less out of hatred for mankind than out of a desire to parade his belief in nothingness.'[56] Although undoubtedly a religious sceptic, the Prussian King's devotion to his dogs was absolute. The first tomb was erected on the terrace at Sans-Souci in 1744 and was followed in the course of his long reign by a further ten, all fashioned in white marble. The King himself wrote the couplet inscribed on the grave of his favourite, Biche.[57] Every event in the short lives of the royal greyhounds was considered of sufficient significance to be imparted to members of the family and close friends; Frederick's letters to Fredersdorf trace every detail of their existence.

When Biche died in 1752 Frederick was inconsolable. He wrote to his sister Wilhelmina on 29 December:[58]

> I have had a domestic loss which has completely upset my philosophy.
> I confide all my frailties in you; I have lost Biche, and her death has
> reawoken in me the loss of all my friends, particularly of him who gave
> her to me. I was ashamed that a dog could so deeply affect my soul;
> but the sedentary life that I lead and the faithfulness of this poor
> creature had so strongly attached me to her, her suffering so moved me,
> that, I confess, I am sad and afflicted. Does one have to be hard? Must
> one be insensitive? I believe that anyone capable of indifference towards
> a faithful animal is unable to be grateful towards an equal, and that, if
> one must choose, it is best to be too sensitive than too hard.

A decade later, in 1763, he wrote to his brother Prince Henry: 'I have a
domestic sorrow; my poor dog is about to die and, to console myself, I
tell myself that if death does not spare crowned heads poor Alcmene cannot expect a different fate.'[59]

Wilhelmina, who was as devoted to dogs as her brother, described in
her memoirs how she felt when her dog died in 1736.[60]

> I had a domestic upset. A little Bolognese dog which I had for 19 years
> died. I loved this creature, my companion throughout all my misfortunes.
> Animals strike me as being rational types of beings; I have seen some so
> spiritual, that all they lacked was speech to articulate their thoughts. I
> find Descartes altogether ridiculous on this subject. I respect the fidelity
> of a dog; it seems to me they have this advantage over humanity, which is
> so inconstant and changeable. If I wanted to examine this matter in
> depth, I would undertake to prove that animals are more rational than
> humans. But I am writing my memoirs and not a panegyric on animals,
> although this article could serve as an epitaph to my little dog.

Wilhelmina later constructed a magnificent mausoleum to this dog's successor, Folichon, in Bayreuth, adjacent to which Pius of Bavaria later face-
tiously added a rococo chapel festooned with cows.

While the *philosophes* of the eighteenth century endlessly debated the
existence of the animal soul, the Philosopher-King quietly interred his
greyhounds at Sans-Souci and princes at the French court mourned and
elegised their dead pets with scant regard for the lofty theological arguments bandied in the salons. Madame, the Duchesse d'Orléans, like her

Folichon's tomb at Bayreuth. The monument was erected by Frederick the Great's sister Wilhelmina.

Prussian cousins, felt the death of a dog acutely. In 1702 she wrote to the Duchess of Hanover: 'I don't know whether you are fond of dogs, and whether you will understand the true sorrow I feel today as I write. My little dog Mione, who was my favourite, has died.'[61] The philosopher who chiefly earned her opprobrium – as he did that of Wilhelmina forty years later – was Descartes with his insistence that animals were unfeeling automata, inferior to man because of their incapacity to acquire knowledge. In 1696 Madame had written to the Duchess of Hanover:

> Please give Monsieur Leibnitz [1646–1716, German philosopher and mathematician] my thanks. I consider that his treatise is very well written, and I admire the lucidity with which he writes on such a complicated subject. It is a great consolation to me to know that animals do not entirely die, because of my dear little dogs. Descartes' remarks on the subject of the wheels of watches struck me as very ridiculous. The other day I confronted a Bishop who completely agreed with this way of thinking. He is by nature of a very jealous disposition and I said to him:

'When you are jealous are you being an object or a man, because, except for my dogs, you are the most jealous thing I know, so I am wondering whether it is a movement of an object or a passion of the soul.' He flew into a rage and went off without replying to me.[62]

Louis XIV's daughter-in-law, the Duchesse de Maine (1676–1753), lived at the chateau of Sceaux surrounded by cats and courted by the literary world. The duchesse dedicated a *rondeau Marotique* to her cat, Minon, and the death of Marlamain was described by Paradis de Moncrif in a letter to a friend:

half an hour before he died, we could see that he wanted to be carried to the apartment of his illustrious Mistress. Scarcely had he arrived than he gathered all that remained of his strength to bid her the most tender farewell; a few moments later, it being noticed that he clearly wished to leave, doubtless in order to spare her the spectacle of his death, he was taken back to his bedroom, where he expired. His last breath was a tender and gentle mewing of the sort he was accustomed to make, when he was honoured with those caresses which have made him so famous. I have just tried to write his Epitaph. I include it, but do not read it if you are familiar with that of which Monsieur de la Mothe [La Mothe le Vayer, 1588–1672, tutor of Louis XIV and Monsieur] is author. It taught me the little that mine is worth:

> Puss passer-by, within this simple tomb
> Lies one whose life fell Atropos hath shred;
> The happiest cat on earth hath heard her doom,
> And sleeps for ever in a marble bed.
> Alas! what long delicious days I've seen!
> Oh cats of Egypt, my illustrious sires,
> You who on altars, bound with garlands green,
> Have melted hearts, and kindled fond desires,
> Hymns in your praise were paid and offerings too,
> But I'm not jealous of those rites divine,
> Since Ludovisca loved me, close and true,
> Your ancient glory was less proud than mine.
> To live a simple pussy by her side
> Was nobler far than to be deified.[63]

Portrait by Sir Francis Grant of Queen Victoria with the Princess Royal and the Prince of Wales. Grant, who owed his popularity as a painter to his ability to draw animals, was bound to appeal to Victoria, whose devotion to 'those four-footed friends whom no bribe can buy' was legendary.

ABOVE *Edwin Landseer:*
Portrait of Eos, *1841.*
Notwithstanding the injuries the
bitch sustained in a shooting
accident, Eos lived until 1844,
when this painting was used as a
model for the funerary monument
erected on the slopes of Windsor by
the sculptor John Francis.

RIGHT *Edwin Landseer:*
Princess Alice Asleep. *Alice,*
born in 1843, married the Grand
Duke of Hesse.

Franz Xaver Winterhalter: Albert, Edward Prince of Wales and Prince Alfred. By 1838 Winterhalter was the most sought-after portrait painter in Europe. He received his first commission from the British court in 1842.

Tray after Landseer showing Hector, Nero and Dash with the parrot, Lory. Lord Melbourne considered Victoria's 'dear sweet little Dash' 'a plebeian ill-conditioned dog'.

ABOVE *J. B. Oudry:*
Bitchhound Nursing her
Pups, *1752. The picture was
purchased by the philosophe
Baron d'Holbach and much
admired by Denis Diderot.*

BELOW *George Stubbs:* Fino
and Tiny, *1791? The fiord in
the background denotes the
northern European origins of the
Pomeranian.*

Edwin Landseer: Queen Victoria at Osborne, *1867. Landseer fell prey in his last years to melancholia and alcoholism. He commented ruefully: 'If only people knew as much about painting as I do, they would never buy my pictures.'*

ABOVE *R. Marshall:* A Jemmy Shaw Canine Meeting, 1855. *Jemmy Shaw was the landlord of the Queen's Head Tavern in the Haymarket, London. Nine different breeds can be recognised in the picture. 'Canine meetings' were the precursors of the dog shows.*

BELOW *Charles Burton Barber:* Cat and Dogs Belonging to the Queen. *Victoria's dachshund Paul, fox-terrier Vic and pug Princess are depicted in an orchard gazing at a kitten.*

RIGHT *Charles Burton Barber: Marco, 1893. Interviewed in 1891, Barber revealed: 'One great aim of my pictures is to help people to love and understand dogs better.'*

BELOW *Thomas Blinks and Frederick Morgan: Queen Alexandra with her Grandchildren and Her Favourite Pets, 1902. The obligatory weekly visit to the kennels was not always relished by the Queen's guests.*

Michael Leonard: Her Majesty Queen Elizabeth II, *1985–6. With her corgi Spark, whom the artist considered 'a great asset at the sittings. She did all that was asked of her, and provided the occasion for Her Majesty to adopt a pose that was unforced and natural, lending the composition a degree of liveliness and movement.'*

Fashionable at the French court, pet epitaphs soon appeared in England. One of the earliest, written in 1693 by Matthew Prior (1664–1721), was dedicated to True, the dog of Queen Mary II:

> If wit or honesty could save,
> Our mouldering ashes from the grave,
> This stone had still remain'd unmark'd,
> I still writ prose, True still have bark'd.
> But envious Fate has claim'd its due,
> Here lies the mortal part of True,
> His deathless virtues must survive,
> To better us that are alive.
>
> His prudence and his wit were seen
> In that, from Mary's grace and mien,
> He own'd the power, and lov'd the Queen.
> By long absence he confest
> That serving her was to be blest. –
> Ye murmurers, let True evince
> That men are beasts, and dogs have sense!
>
> His faith and truth all Whitehall knows,
> He ne'er could fawn or flatter those
> Whom he believ'd were Mary's foes:
> Ne'er skulked from whence his sovereign led him,
> Or snarl'd against the hand that fed him –
> Read this, ye statesmen now in favour,
> And mend your own, By True's behaviour!

True may have been a spaniel; a portrait by an anonymous artist of c. 1690 shows her with one at her feet.

The reign of Victoria, most of it spent by the Queen in lugubrious widowhood, marked the zenith of the royal cult of animal death in Britain. Her journals repeatedly testify to the bereavement she felt whenever one of her pets perished. Her childhood favourite, Dash, died on 24 December 1840 and was buried at Adelaide Cottage with a tombstone bearing an inscription advising the visitor to follow the example set by the spaniel during its short life. When Eos died in 1844, Landseer's portrait was used as the model for the monument erected on the slopes at Windsor by the sculptor John Francis (1780–1861) and worked on in part by Prince Albert himself. The death of Däckel, her favourite dachshund, in 1860 prompted the Queen to lament 'that these charming creatures live so short a time'.[64] He was in fact fifteen, not such a mean age for a dog; Dandie Dinmont was nineteen when he died in 1858.[65] Many of these pets, such as Boz, the Skye terrier that had once belonged to her mother, the Duchess of Kent, were buried by the lake at Frogmore and, from 1868, when he received his first royal commission, almost all had statues modelled of them by the Hungarian sculptor Joseph Boehm, in Boz's case in 1881. James Reid, who was present at the death, in 1884, of the Queen's favourite collie, Noble, recorded how

> Her Majesty was much upset, and cried a great deal, said she was so fond of those that were gone, and that everything in the world comes to an end: that she believes dogs have souls and a future life: and she could not bear to go to see his body, though she would have liked to kiss his head. Kingsley and many people, she says, believe dogs have souls. I had to increase the strength of her sleeping draught, and only left her at 12.45 a.m. when she gave me the accompanying note of instructions for his burial:

> *I just write down what was done in the case of the Prince's beloved old dog, EOS who died 43 years ago and is buried in the slopes in a small bricked grave under her statue at the top of the slopes at Windsor. The grave was bricked, and coins were placed in the bag in which the dear dog (who was only 10 years old) was placed. I wish the grave to be bricked. The dear dog to be wrapped up in the box lined with lead and charcoal, placed in it, as well as some coins. I feel as if I could not bring myself to go and choose the spot. Dr Profeit would perhaps suggest it. I will then tell Mr Profeit to write to Mr Boehm to get a repetition of the statue of the dear Dog in bronze to be placed over the grave.*[66]

The Duke of Windsor recalled how at Balmoral and Osborne, Victoria

> in her craving to immortalize her own private memories and ward off the encroachments of time, had surrounded herself with countless monuments commemorating her past associations. The hills and crags over the river Dee lent themselves to a profuse display of these

tangible signs proclaiming her dedication to the dead. On the summit of nearly every hilltop within sight of the Castle was a granite memorial cairn, and as one walked around the grounds, every turn of the paths brought one face to face with a statue erect or recumbent, an inscribed granite drinking-fountain, or a granite seat dedicated to the memory of a relation or a faithful retainer or even a pet dog.[67]

He himself also erected tombs at the Moulin de la Tuilerie and, when the house was sold, a clause was inserted protecting the graves of his canine favourites.[68]

One of the few areas of common ground between Victoria and the Prince of Wales was their love of animals. Edward wrote to his mother in 1869 expressing his opinion that 'except a wife and children, no man could have a greater companion than a dog'.[69] Alexandra was no less devoted to animals than Edward and they both erected tombs for them when they died. Edward's first dog was a retriever, Duck, a gift on his eleventh birthday and so gentle that the Queen recorded with pleasure its tolerance of all the children's boisterousness. When the dog died in 1854 the Prince entered in his diary: 'Unfortunately today Poor Duck Died having been with me 1 year and a 1/4, he was six years old, and I am sure I never saw or knew a nicer dog.'

When Alexandra's favourite Pekingese died in 1914 the Baroness de Stoeckl heard from her daughter how

the Queen was really in despair and had it laid on cushion in her bedroom. She used to look at it and sob. This went on for two days. At last Zoia went in to the bedroon and was nearly knocked down by the smell. She scolded the Queen and said she could catch typhoid fever, etc. But Her Majesty would not hear of the 'dear little thing' being taken away. General Probyn [Sir Dighton Probyn, Comptroller of the Queen's household] came to Zoia and said, 'You must insist.' 'But no use insisting,' answered Zoia, 'she refuses.' That day at tea there were some egg sandwiches. The Queen smelt them and then said with tears in her eyes, 'Just like my sweet little Togo.'

Zoia started laughing and she became almost hysterical. The Queen saw the joke and started herself and they laughed and laughed. Zoia,

Tomb of Togo at Marlborough House. Queen Alexandra was devastated by this dog's death.

seeing the good mood, said, 'For goodness sake, Ma'am, have him taken away or I shall never be able to look at an egg.' 'All right,' said the Queen. So Zoia flew out of the room, met a page and gave the order. Togo was buried. The next day a new Togo arrived, a gift from Lady (Arthur) Paget, and all was in order once more.[70]

Alexandra paid tribute to the late Togo with the words she had engraved on the dog's tomb at Marlborough House: 'My darling little Togo. Given to me by the Empress of Japan. My constant companion for 12 years. The Joy and Pleasure of my Life. Died May 25th 1914.'

From the Renaissance to the present day bereaved royal pet owners lauded the same timeless qualities which they valued most highly precisely because they were so rarely exhibited by their courtiers and relatives: loyalty and devotion. It was as a 'loving little dog and loyal to its mistress' that Francis I's mother, Louise of Savoy, most regretted her dog Hapegai when it died in October 1502.[71] Four hundred years later, almost to the day, Tsar Nicholas II wrote to his mother, the Dowager Empress Marie: 'My other sorrow, a completely personal one, was the loss of good old Iman, which happened at the beginning of October, almost on the same day as poor Raven [his horse]. He had been ill since the summer. He was such a good, clever, devoted dog!'[72] Since the reign of Queen Victoria all British monarchs have continued to erect headstones for their pets. HM Queen Elizabeth II's record not simply the breed and dates but also bear a brief legend summarising their most endearing qualities: Sandringham Brae A GENTLEMAN AMONGST DOGS; Sandringham Fern TIRELESS WORKER AND MISCHIEVOUS CHARACTER; Sandringham Salt DEVOTED AND ALWAYS WILLING TO SERVE.

Each of HM the Queen's dog graves bears a brief legend celebrating the animal's most endearing characteristics. Sandringham Sidney was Field Trial Champion in 1979.

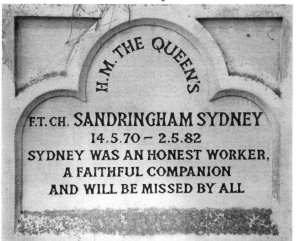

Living in the lap of luxury was no safeguard against mortality and royal pets were as vulnerable to death as their owners from causes both natural and unnatural. Although mawkish accounts of animal suicide should be regarded with some scepticism, pets might be immolated to save them from a fate considered worse than death. The vast majority of the imperial Pekingese found during the storming of the Summer Palace in 1860 had been slaughtered to prevent their falling into the profane hands of the invading Anglo-French forces. In India at the turn of the century, one of the discarded mistresses of the lubricious Jagatjit Singh, Maharajah of Kapurthala, was so fearful of assassination that, one day in Delhi, she ordered the purdah car, took all her little dogs, and together they all jumped off the top of the Kutab Minar, the monument celebrating the coming of Islam to India.[73] Whether he most regretted his mistress or her dogs is open to speculation.

Illness and accident were nevertheless the principal causes of animal death. Favourite hounds were particularly vulnerable to their masters' love of the chase, and anyone who inadvertently killed one justifiably trembled for the consequences. The fury with which James I initially reacted on hearing of the accidental death of his favourite hound Jewell in 1613 was soon dispelled on learning the culprit was his wife, Queen Anne:

> The K. is in progresse and the quene gon or going after: at theyre being at Toball's [Theobald's] wh was about a fortnight since, the Q. shooting at a deere, mistooke her marke and killed iewell, the Ks. most principall and speciall hound, at wch he stormed excedingly a while, but after he knew who he did yt, he was sone pacified, and wth much kindnes wisht her not to be troubled wth yt, for he shold love her never the worse, and the next day sent her a diamond worth 2000L as a legacie from his dead dogge: love and kindnes increases dayly between them, and yt is thought they were never in better termes.[74]

Dogs could make or break careers at the court of Louis XV. In 1763 Marie, Comtesse de Rochefort, wrote to her lover, the Chevalier d'Eon, in London: 'People are talking sadly about a sad thing that has happened to the Duc de Duras who is in the deepest distress. He had the misfortune, last time he went out hunting with the King, to kill his master's favourite dog, the one who never left his side, the one who slept in his bedroom; in fact the most permanent rival of the Marquise de Pompadour. This loss has caused general desolation and we do not know how this is all going to end; it is a terrible misfortune for a courtier.'[75] She need not have worried; the unfortunate incident was pardoned and the Duc de Duras died peaceably at court on the eve of the Revolution.

Comte Dufort de Cheverny watched with bemused detachment as Etienne-Michel Bouret (1710–77) rose from *trésorier-général de la maison du Roi* in 1738 to *secrétaire du cabinet du Roi* in 1769, largely through the good offices of the *garde des sceaux*, Monsieur de Machault, whose

> spaniel, to which he was very attached, sickened and died. Bouret scoured Paris for a similar dog, found one, had a wig and a magistrate's cassock like those worn by M de Machault made, had the dog sleep in his room and dressed in the wig and cassock to feed it. The dog once trained, he took it to his patron and said: 'Your dog is not dead, I saved its life!' The dog, by now accustomed to the court dress, could not have given a warmer welcome to its new master. M de Machault was delighted and most impressed by Bouret.
>
> How to refuse him anything?
>
> Not only was he made *administrateur des postes* but he was invited to share Machault's office . . . and, before long, every member of his family occupied the highest position in Finance.[76]

Even in the twentieth century the anguish caused by the death of an adored pet at a critical moment in its owners' lives could be heightened when superstitious interpretations were attached. The wedding of Wallis Simpson and the Duke of Windsor in 1937 was seriously marred by the accidental death of their favourite cairn at the chateau of Candé in France in December 1936. She explained in her memoirs how, on leaving England to escape the furore caused by their affair, she had

> decided, because of the uncertainties ahead, that I could not take with me the little cairn, Slipper, whom David had given me at the beginning of our friendship [in 1934] and whom I had come to love dearly . . . David must have guessed something of my inner state. One evening, he telephoned to say that he was sending back to me my dog

Slipper, to be a companion on my walks. A rarity among animals, Slipper seemed to find equal joy with either of us. Two days later, Chief Inspector Storrier, of Scotland Yard, who had been assigned to David in Austria, arrived with certain important papers and the Cairn. The dog's joyous recognition was like a signal to me that, along with Slipper, David had sent part of himself.

Next afternoon a terrible thing happened. Bernard Rickatson-Hatt, an old friend from London, was stopping at Candé. He and the Rogers decided to play golf, while I chose merely to walk around the course with them. Slipper tagged along behind. Katherine and Herman had a pair of Scotties, and shortly after we started down the second fairway, Slipper and the Scotties suddenly tore off into the woods in pursuit of a rabbit. The Scotties reappeared, but Slipper was missing. That struck me as a little odd; Slipper was always at my heels. We went on to the next tee. Still no Slipper. I became worried. 'It's not like Slipper to run off,' I remember remarking to Herman, who whistled and whistled in the notion that Slipper was probably rooting in the underbrush close by. Then, with Bernard, I started back through the woods to look for him. As we emerged near the first green, I saw what seemed to be a grey rag on the grass. It was Slipper. I called; he did not move. But on coming closer I saw that his eyes were open and staring. When I tried to come near he raised himself as in a spasm. I had a dreadful time picking him up. He twisted and tried to bite me. There was no mistaking what had happened to Slipper. In his foray into the undergrowth he had run afoul of a viper. And I realised as I half-ran to the car that it was already too late to save him.

Slipper died early that evening at the veterinary's in Tours. He was a tiny creature; the poison must have gone rapidly to his heart. I cried. His loss on the eve of my reunion with David seemed to me a frightful omen. He had been our companion in joy and trouble; now he was gone. Was everything that I loved to be destroyed?[77]

Wallis wrote to Edward,[78] 'Even God seems to have forgotten WE for surely this is an unnecessary sorrow for us. He was our dog – not yours or mine but ours – and he loved us both so. Now the principal guest at the wedding is no more. I can't stop crying but we must be brave and suf-

Wallis Simpson and Slipper. Slipper's death from a snake bite on the eve of Wallis's marriage to Edward VIII cast a cloud over the proceedings.

fer the next three weeks. We are both feeling the strain – I can hear it in your beloved voice – that defeated sound. . . .' Edward replied, 'Oh! how utterly cruel that our darling Mr Loo should be taken from WE like this. My heart is quite breaking this morning my beloved sweetheart from sadness and above all from not being able to be with you and hold you so tight which is the only help when WE are unhappy . . . I feel quite stunned and dread the remaining three weeks until I am to be with you never to be parted ever again my sweetheart.' After the dog's funeral at Candé on 6 April 1937 its memory was immortalised by a diamond-encrusted slipper embedded in a medallion and inscribed 'Our Mr Loo', to which the Windsors gave pride of place in their mansion in the Bois de Boulogne.[79]

CRUELTY TO ANIMALS

Although the sincerity of the Duke of Windsor's affection for his dogs cannot be gainsaid, he had, as a boy, been known to enjoy tormenting animals. His erstwhile neighbour at Windsor, the Hon. Sylvia Lady Brooke, Ranee of Sarawak, had lived nearby at Orchard Lea and recalled an occasion when the eight-year-old prince came over with his sister Mary to play. The two of them disappeared only to return 'red in the face and looking guilty, but they refused to tell us where they had been. All the time we were playing Prince Edward seemed inattentive and listless. Suddenly my father appeared in a furious temper. A message had been sent from the house opposite to the effect that all the baby ducks had been killed and were laid out in a row beside the lake.'[80] Possibly he shared the feelings of his distant ancestor, Edward VI, who, as a child, seized a falcon and pulled out its feathers one by one in front of his tutors before tearing the bird into four pieces, saying 'that he likened himself to the falcon, whom everybody plucked, but that he would pluck them too hereafter, and tear them in four parts'.[81]

Such an isolated act of savagery on the part of the future Edward VIII would be of little significance were it not for the subsequent rumours that he wished to slaughter the Clumber spaniels kennelled at Sandringham and which had been the pride and joy of both his father, George V, and his grandfather, Edward VII. He explained how, on succeeding to the throne, his 'enquiring gaze fell upon the Sandringham accounts' where he discovered that 'no expense had been spared to maintain Sandringham as a model property; but that praise-worthy reputation had been preserved only by dipping into the Privy Purse with a prodigality that was the wonder of my father's neighbours. And game birds for the King and his guests to shoot were still being raised on a scale that could hardly have been surpassed in the country.'[82] In the event the kennel-master at Sandringham, Alfred Higgs, had the dogs dispersed rather than put down, easily as effective a cost-cutting exercise as their destruction. Potential purchasers for royal dogs of any breed, least of all Clumbers, a dog not only rare but, as Edward VII asserted, capable of doing the work of three beaters, were unlikely to be in short supply. While their royal association alone was sufficient to guarantee

Fabergé model of a Clumber, belonging to Edward VII, and one of their cats. The King greatly admired these spaniels, which he held could do the job of three beaters.

a profitable sale, the better specimens would have commanded even higher prices for their stud potential. George V had won a first prize at Cruft's in 1932 and 1934 with his Clumber Sandringham Spark.

Most allegations of cruelty to animals made against members of royal families lack both foundation and probability. The legend that Henry VII had all the mastiffs in the land executed for baiting a lion is patently false given the ubiquity of these dogs in sixteenth-century England; it was allegorical, hinting at the consequences attendant upon tampering with the natural hierarchy of the animal kingdom, and reflects the insecurity of the newly established Tudor dynasty.[83] Louis XI, described by the chronicler of his reign, Philippe de Commynes, as a man who 'loved hunting and hawking but nothing pleased him more than dogs', was later said to have broken a dog's back with a stick out of sheer sadism.[84] Lestrange[85] described the young Louis XIII crushing the head of a sparrow between two stones and being severely reprimanded by his parents, Marie de Medici and Henri IV. He also suggested that Louis XV, as Dauphin, gratuitously shot at and maimed a hind he had been given, inflicting the *coup de grâce* as it limped towards him seeking protection.[86] Louis XVI was said to have shot at stray cats at Versailles. Such stories were apocryphal, metaphors for the royal abrogation of responsibility to their subjects. No eyewitnesses ever made such a claim; on the contrary, Héroard, the physician of Louis XIII, frequently referred to the almost reckless kindness to animals exhibited by the King. In 1610, at the Tuileries, when the gates were open to the public (as they always were when there was no hunting), Louis saw 'a dog thrown at a lion which was attached to a tree; the lion killed it. This displeased him so much that, in his fury, he insisted that the man who had hurled the dog be punished'.[87] Louis XVI, although he kept no pets as such, took enormous pains to ensure the safety of his packs of hounds at the outbreak of the Revolution, and Hébert, leader of the sansculottes and the man who did more than any other to blacken the reputation of the monarchy in the press during their captivity, was reduced to tears after the King's execution when he remembered how 'the tyrant was very fond of my dog; he often used to stroke it; I couldn't help recollecting'.[88] When Paul, the son of Catherine the Great, was on his grand tour in 1781–2, travelling under the assumed title of Comte du Nord, he told Louis XVI, 'without hesitation, and before a considerable number of persons, that he should be very sorry to have with him even a poodle dog that was much attached to him, because his mother would take care to have it thrown into the Seine, with a stone round its neck, before he should leave Paris'.[89] Not only is there a touching portrait by R. Mathieu painted in 1756 of Catherine with Paul clutching a black spaniel, but her own love of animals was beyond question and far exceeded her love of humanity. Indeed, Catherine's last lover, Prince Zubov, became so insufferable as a result of his elevation that 'even Paul was forced to humble himself before a petty officer of the guards, who, but a short time before, had begged his pardon for having offended one of his dogs'.[90] Paul's unfounded accusation was no more than an expression of his emotional bitterness, an oblique reference to crimes that could not be named and humiliations he did not wish to reveal, cloaked in a metaphor that could not fail to curry sympathy at the dog-obsessed French court.

With an eye to posterity, and deeply conscious of her part in his murder in 1762, Catherine the Great's descriptions of the acts of cruelty perpetrated against his dogs by Peter III were almost certainly exaggerated. Catherine maintained that:

Morning, noon and night the Grand Duke, with rare perseverance, trained a pack of hounds, chasing them with much cracking of whips and beaters' cries from one end of his two rooms to the other. Any dog which could not stand up to this treatment and stole away was punished severely, and so whined and howled more than ever. When he finally tired of this exercise he took the violin which he scraped with such unskilful violence and walked up and down the rooms with it, until it was time to resume the education of the pack and its punishment, which often seemed to me very cruel indeed. One day I heard a dog whine piteously for a long time. I opened the door of my bedroom where I was sitting and I saw that the Grand Duke was holding one of the dogs in the air by its collar, while a young boy of Kalmuk origin who was in his service held its tail; it was a poor little English King Charles, and the Grand Duke was flogging the dog as hard as he could with the handle of a whip. I tried to intercede for the poor animal but this only increased the blows. Unable to stand a spectacle that seemed quite horrible to me, I retired to my room in tears. Generally tears and cries, instead of inspiring the Grand Duke with pity, only made him angry; to him, pity was a painful and even unbearable emotion.[91]

By 1753 Peter's condition had deteriorated yet further and he had taken to flogging his Kalmuk servants and putting animals on trial:

One day I walked into His Imperial Highness's apartment [and] . . . was struck by the sight of an immense rat which he had hanged, with all the paraphernalia of torture, in the middle of a small room which he had had partitioned off. I asked what was the meaning of this; he then told me that the rat had been convicted of a crime and deserved the severest punishment according to military law. For it had climbed over the walls of a cardboard fortress standing on a table in this recess and eaten two sentinels on duty, made of starch, one on each of the bastions, and he had had the criminal court-martialled. His setter had caught the rat which had at once been hanged, as I had seen, and would be exposed to the public for three days as an example.[92]

The court-martialling of a rat was a novel idea, characteristic of the militaristic Grand Duke, even if rat trials themselves were not. There had been four in Europe between 1710 and 1733, and in the sixteenth century

Bartholomew Chassenée had made his reputation at the Bar as counsel for some rats that had been put on trial before the ecclesiastical court of Autun in France on the charge of having feloniously eaten and wantonly destroyed the barley crop of that province. When the accused failed to appear in court on the appointed day, Chassenée pleaded the 'length and difficulty of the journey and the serious perils which attended it, owing to the unwearied vigilance of their mortal enemies, the cats, who watched all their movements, and, with fell intent, lay in wait for them at every corner and passage'.[93] Although animal trials were unknown in England, where *lex talionis* did not apply, James I ordered a bear that had killed a child to be baited to death, as reported by Stow:

> the King, Queene, and Prince, the Lady Elizabeth, and the Duke of Yorke, with divers great Lords, and manie others, came to the Tower to see a triall of the Lyons single valour, against a great fierce Beare, which had kild a child, that was negligently left in the Beare-House. This fierce Beare was brought into the open yard, behind the Lyons Den, which was the place for fight: then was the great Lyon put forth, who gazed a while, but never offred to assault or approch the Beare: then were two mastife Dogs put in, who past by the Beare, and boldly seazed upon the Lyon.

Clemency was not granted, however, and two weeks later, 'according to the kings commandement, this Beare was bayted to death upon a stage: and unto the mother of the murthered child was given xx.p., out of part of that money which the people gave to see the Beare Kild'.[94] In 1679, a woman who had committed bestiality was hanged alongside her offending dog. As part of the community animals received the same punishments meted out to humans.[95]

Popular superstition was fostered by the Church because it constituted one of the mainstays of their power. Formally linked with sorcery in the thirteenth century by Pope Gregory IX, who founded the Inquisition to suppress heretical sects like the Cathars, dogs and cats were hounded from monasteries and nunneries by the ecclesiastical authorities. Cats — and rats — were inadvertently brought back to Europe aboard the ships of the returning Crusaders. Ignorance of the causes of plague led to the extermination of the very creatures that might have contained the spread of the disease: in London in 1665, two hundred thousand cats were destroyed by order of the Lord Mayor.[96] Pope Innocent VIII (1484–92) confirmed the powers and duties of the Inquisition and, in 1484, issued the Bull *Summis desiderantes affectibus*, which led to cats being slaughtered by the thousand. Mere possession of a cat by an unpopular woman was sufficient to invite denunciation, and witches were sometimes drowned in cat-filled sacks. At the coronation of Elizabeth I, a wickerwork dummy of the Pope was filled with live cats and finally thrown on an enormous bonfire, the shrieks being interpreted as 'the language of the devils within the body of the Holy Father'.[97] There are echoes of this widespread fear of cats in Shakespeare's *A Midsummer Night's Dream* (III. ii) when Lysander tells Demetrius: 'Hang off, thou cat, thou burr! Vile thing, let loose, Or I will shake thee from me like a serpent!' In 1638 a live cat was roasted in Ely Cathedral and hounds were used by parliamentary troops to hunt cats in Lichfield Cathedral.[98] In contrast, Archbishop Laud was one of the first people in England to import a tabby in the 1630s.

Throwing stones at tethered cats was a universal practice on Shrove Tuesday, when excessive behaviour was tolerated as a prelude to Lenten self-denial, and, in certain areas of France such as Metz, on St John's Eve (24 June), the slaughter of cats in celebratory bonfires lingered on well into the nineteenth century. Although the spectacle had earlier been witnessed by the court, there is little evidence that it was relished. In 1604 the Dauphin, Louis, 'obtained mercy for the cats which were about to be put to the torch of St John',[99] and when his father, Henri IV, was offered a cat in 1595, he ridiculed the idea that the creature would poison him.[100] Louis XIV is known to have attended the St John's Eve festivities in 1648, but there is no evidence to suggest he repeated the experience. By 1713, when Alexander Pope pointed out 'the conceit that a cat has nine lives has cost at least nine lives in ten of the whole race of them', scientific advance had reduced superstition and weakened religious belief to such an extent that the cat had become a popular pet. In the eighteenth century the clergy themselves attacked the idea that God showed His purpose through animals and asserted it was wrong to see cats as dangerous.[101] At the French court they were particularly cherished and both

Louis XV and the Queen kept them as pets. Wilhelmina, the sister of Frederick the Great, killed a cat in 1735, explaining to her brother[102] that 'I was told it was possessed . . . It looked at me so sadly, having received the mortal blow, and miaowed so forgivingly and melodiously that I have repented my cruelty.'

Superstition also attached to dogs, legend having it that they were the only animals to copulate in the Ark and that the Devil sometimes assumed a canine form. Heathens were systematically likened to dogs. To hear one howling was long deemed unlucky, and Duke Filippo Maria Visconti (ruled 1412–47) locked up his wife after a dog howled on their wedding night.[103] At the Escorial in Spain in 1577, a succession of disasters led people to believe the monastery was possessed: it was struck by a thunderstorm and, in August, at the height of the summer, there was a hail-storm so serious the hail did not melt for eight days. Monks, hearing the agonised groans and desperate barking of a dog, became convinced 'it was the phantom-Dog, the howling-Dog of the Escorial, which had long been talked about . . . throughout Spain'.[104] Rumour had it that an enormous black dog wandered nightly through the building while it was still under construction, dragging its chains and barking horribly. This was interpreted as a manifestation of satanic rage unleashed against the monastery for the huge cost of the Escorial. The sound of chains symbolised the slavery of Spain and the barking was said to be particularly loud under the royal bedchamber. Eventually one of the monks, Fray Antonio de Villacastin, found a dog in the monastery which had broken its chain, and they hanged it from the balustrade of the cloister. The next morning the monks heard Mass with the creature suspended above their heads.

The most famous dog-familiar was probably Prince Rupert's white poodle, Boy, a gift in 1634 from Lord Arundel, the English ambassador in Vienna, while the Prince was imprisoned in Linz. Boy accompanied Rupert to England and remained at the Prince's side throughout the Civil War until killed at Marston Moor in 1644. The reluctance of Rupert to be parted from his dog, and its apparent indestructibility, made it the butt of Roundhead propagandists and pamphleteers, who became increasingly obsessed with the idea that Boy was the Prince's familiar and attributed to it the most fantastic powers. Boy was reported as being fluent in several languages, invulnerable in battle and able to put a hex on the enemy. In an anonymous pamphlet of 1643, 'Observations upon Prince Ruppert's White Dogge Called Boy', which carried the dog's portrait as frontispiece, Rupert was criticised for allowing it to sit beside him during council meetings and for turning to kiss it in debate. Charles I was said to have succumbed to the poodle's charms, letting it sit in his chair and play with his children and feeding it the choicest delicacies from his own hand, 'even with sides of capons, and such christian-like morsels. . . . It is thought the King will make him Serjeant-Major-General Boy. But truly the King's affection to him is so extraordinary that some at court envy him. I heard a Gentleman-Usher swear that it was a shame the dog should sit in the King's chair, as he always does; and a great Lord was seriously of opinion that it was not well he should converse so much with the King's children, lest he taught them to swear.' At church services, Boy was said to have conducted himself 'most popishly and cathedrally. He is very seldom at any conscionable sermons, but as for public prayers, he seldom or never misses them.' After the Royalist victory at Birmingham, Prince Rupert and his officers were said to have sat up all night 'drinking healths upon their knees – yea, healths to Prince Rupert's dog!' Given the deeply superstitious nature of the Prince, the story probably had foundation. The Roundheads vainly tried both prayer and poison to destroy this 'Popish, profane Dog, more than halfe a divell, a kind of spirit.'

Prince Rupert must have nursed reservations about Boy's immunity for, when the poodle finally died, it was as a result of his having omitted to tie it to the baggage wagons. Although now over ten years old, Boy faithfully followed his master into battle and fell to a Roundhead bullet, the Puritans subsequently claiming in a verse entitled 'A Dog's Elegy, or Rupert's Tears', published in London on 27 July 1644, that the dog had been 'killed by a valiant souldier who had skill in Necromancy':

> Lament poor Cavaliers, cry, howl and yelp
> For the great losse of your Malignant Whelp

Rupert was described as 'Prince of Robbers, Duke of Plunderland', determined 'to kill,

A
DOGS ELEGY,
OR
RVPERT'S TEARS,

For the late Defeat given him at *Marston-*
moore, neer *York,* by the Three Renowned
Generalls, *Alexander Earl of* Leven, *Generall of the Scottish*
Forces, Fardinando *Lord* Fairefax, *and the Earle of* Manchester *Generalls of the* English *Forces in the North.*

Where his beloved Dog, named *B O Y,* was killed by a Val-
liant Souldier, who had skill in *Necromancy.*

Likewise the strange breed of this Shagg'd Cavalier, whelp'd of a Malignant
Water-witch; *With all his Tricks, and Feats.*

Sad Cavaliers, *Rupert* invites you all } Close-mourners are the Witch, Pope, & devill,
That doe survive, to his Dogs Funerall. } That much lament yo'r late befallen evill.

Printed at *London,* for *G. B.* July 27. 1644.

Prince Rupert and Boy, 1644. The Roundheads
believed that the dog put a hex on them.

burne, steele, ravish, nay anything,
And in the end to make himself a King.
Sad cavaliers Rupert invites you all
That doe survive, to his Dog's Funerall,
Close mourners are the witch, Pope, and Devill,
That much lament your late befallen evill.'[105]

His death was also recorded in the parliamentary journals: 'Here also was slain that accursed cur, which is here mentioned, by the way, because the Prince's dog has been so much spoken of, and was valued by his master more than creatures of more worth.'[106] More than fifty years later Boy's reputation remained undimmed: Madame, Duchesse d'Orléans, wrote from Versailles in January 1717,[107] 'I have heard it said that in England people looked upon my uncle – the late Prince Rupert – as a great sorcerer, and thought the great black dog, which was his companion, was the devil. When he was with the army and marched against the enemy, whole regiments used to flee before him for that reason.' The imputations of sorcery had, with time, transmogrified the dog from white to black, the traditional colour of the Devil.

ROYAL SPORTS

If hunting had been practised since time immemorial, animal combats were a Renaissance revival and princes continued to take an unconscionable pleasure in the sanguinary spectacle of such sports until the eighteenth century. Although wild animals had been imported throughout Europe during the Middle Ages to be housed in the royal menageries that lent prestige to a court, the expansion of trade with Africa and Asia from the late fifteenth century accelerated the pace and widened the variety of creatures entering Europe. They were increasingly considered as symbols of the state, and great superstition was attached to animal behaviour. In 1459, at a reception held to honour the visit to Florence of Pope Pius II and Galeazzo Maria Sforza, bulls, horses, boars, dogs, lions and a giraffe were turned out into an enclosed space of the Piazza della Signoria, where the lions lay down and refused combat. Such a peaceful demonstration by the kings of the animal creation was deemed an excellent augury.[108] Similarly, during the siege of Florence in 1529, when an eagle that had been shot at fled into the city, the Signoria gave the bearer four ducats, because the omen was good.[109] In Paris in 1583 Henri III ordered the killing of all the 'lions, bears, bulls and other like beasts which he reared for combat with his dogs' because he had dreamed the previous night that he would be devoured by wild animals.[110]

The dogs pitted against these wild animals at the Valois court were almost certainly mastiffs. The French ambassador at the court of Elizabeth I had watched bull-baiting with the enthusiastic Queen in 1559, and been sufficiently impressed by the breed to take some back when he returned to his native land. He and his colleagues 'were brought to Court with musick to dinner, and after a splendid dinner they were entertained with the baiting of bears and bulls with English dogs. The Queen's Grace herself and the Ambassadors stood in the gallery looking on the pastime till six at night.' On another occasion they took the barge at St Paul's Wharf to Paris Garden (at Bankside in Southwark) for another baiting of bulls and bears, 'and the Captain, with an hundred of the Guard, kept room for them against they came, that they might have space to see the sport'.[111] In 1586 the Danish ambassador was similarly entertained at Greenwich: 'for upon a green, verie spatious and large, where thousands might stand and behold with good contentment, there beare-bating and bull-bating (tempered with other merie disports) were exhibited; whereat it cannot be spoken of what pleasure the people took ... their eies full bent upon the present spectacle, diverse times expressing their inward conceived joy and delight, with shrill shouts, and varietie of gesture.'[112] In 1591, by order of the Privy Council, plays were banned on Thursdays, the traditional day for baiting, because their popularity was threatening a sport 'maintained for her Majesty's pleasure'.[113]

Bull dogs were not used for baiting before 1631[114] and mastiffs were still the preferred protagonists at the close of the seventeenth century. James I shared the predilection of his precedessor, and John Evelyn saw the young Louis XIV enjoying the spectacle in 1649,[115] although he himself considered it 'a barbarous custom'.[116] One of the last occasions on which a bull was baited at the French court was in 1682 to celebrate the birth of the Duc de Bourgogne. Pepys, like Evelyn, was unusual in thinking it 'a very rude and nasty pleasure'[117] for, as late as 1694, John Houghton still described it as 'a sport the English much delight in; and not only the baser sort, but the greatest lords and ladies', not least because of the enormous potential gains that might accrue from a successful bet.[118] In 1801, at Bury St Edmunds, 'a bull's hoofs were cut off and the wretched animal was forced to defend himself as best he could against the dogs set upon him, on his mangled and bleeding stumps. Fires were occasionally lighted under them to prevent their lying down from exhaustion, spikes thrust into their most tender parts, and their tails frequently twisted to dislocation, by the yelling and hellish miscreants who encompassed them. At the end of a bait young dogs were brought, with a view to initiate and encourage them, to lick the bloody nostrils of the bull.' Every town in England had a bull-ring.[119] The sport was not finally abolished until 1835, along with most other forms of animal baiting.[120] Not only was it popularly believed that the quality of the meat was improved by the animal being baited to death, but many in Parliament shared the view of William Windham, as expressed in 1802, that the sport was preferable to Jacobinism,[121] of which those supporting the humanitarian treatment of animals were accused. Cruelty to animals was positively fostered in certain parliamentary circles after the French Revolution as providing the best antidote to popular unrest.

Another popular royal sport was bear-baiting. When Henry VIII and Anne Boleyn travelled to France in 1532 to meet Francis I, it formed part of the entertainment. In 1575, when Elizabeth I stayed at Kenilworth with the Earl of Leicester (whose emblem was a chained bear), she was treated to the spectacle of thirteen bears being set upon by a pack of mastiffs: 'with fending and prooving, with plucking and tugging, skratting and byting, by plain tooth and nayll to a side and to other such exspens of blood and leather waz thear between them, az a moonths licking I ween wyl not recoover', noted an eyewitness.[122] In London both Bear Gardens were situated on the South Bank and baitings originally took place twice a week, on Sundays and Thursdays, until prohibited on the Sabbath by James I. The King employed a Master of the King's Games, Edward Alleyn, to supervise the bears, bulls and mastiffs; so well was he remunerated that he was able to found Dulwich College on the proceeds. The Stuart King's Master of the Cocks was paid more than the combined salaries of two secretaries of state, evidence of the importance attached to these sports at court.[123] In 1623 the Spanish ambassador was 'much delighted in bear-baiting. He was the last week at Paris-Garden, where they showed him all the pleasure they could both with bull, bear, and horse, besides jackanapes, and then turned a white bear into the Thames, where the dogs baited him swimming; which was the best sport of all.'[124]

Both bull- and bear-baiting continued to be considered appropriate entertainments for visiting princes and diplomats until the eighteenth century. In the early seventeenth century Frederick, Duke of Württemberg, was treated to both spectacles:[125]

In order to gratify His Highness, and at his desire, two bears and a bull were baited; at such times you can perceive the breed and mettle of the dogs for although they receive serious injuries from the bears, are caught by the horns of the bull, and tossed into the air so frequently to fall down again upon the horns, they do not give in but fasten on the bull so firmly that one is obliged to pull them back by the tails, and force open their jaws. Four dogs at once were set on the bull; they, however, could not gain any advantage over him, for he so artfully contrived to ward off their attacks that they could not well get at him; on the contrary, the bull served them very scurvily by striking and butting at them.

When the London Bear Garden, closed during the Interregnum, was reopened in 1663, a theatre was erected to improve visibility. Thomas Woodman, appointed Serjeant of the Bears, was paid a wage of 7½d. daily and 22s. 6d. annually for his livery; many of the bears were presented by the Russian ambassador.

Nor were lions, bulls and bears the only creatures to be baited. In 1667 John Evelyn refused to attend when 'there was now a very gallant horse to be baited to death with dogs; but he fought them all, so as the fiercest of them could not fasten on him, till the men run through with their swords. This wicked and barbarous sport deserved to have been punished in the cruel contrivers to get money, under the pretence that the horse had killed a man, which was false. I would not be persuaded to be a spectator.'[126] The ambassador of the Emperor of Fez and Morocco watched a horse of Lord Rochester being torn to shreds by mastiffs in 1682. In 1721 a polar bear was baited for the first time in Europe: 'it is not doubted, from his uncommon size, excessive weight, and more than savage fierceness, but he will afford extraordinary entertainment, and behave himself in such a manner as to fill those who are lovers of diversion of this kind with delight and astonishment', announced *Read's Weekly Journal*. In 1747 tigers were added to the catalogue of victims. A foreigner visiting England at the period noted: 'The

English have games which are peculiar to them, or at least which they affect and practice more than people do elsewhere. . . . Everything that is called fighting is a delicious thing to an Englishman.'[127] The last lion-baiting in England took place in Warwick in 1825.

Paul Hentzner, a German travelling in England in 1598, was one of the many foreigners struck by the cruelty towards animals displayed by the English at this period, a reputation enjoyed until the late eighteenth century when it was usurped by Catholic Europeans. Hentzner described

> whipping a blind bear, which is performed by five or six men, standing in a circle with whips, which they exercise upon him without mercy; although he cannot escape from them because of his chain, he nevertheless defends himself rigorously, throwing down all who come within his reach and are not active enough to get out of it, tearing the whips out of their hands and breaking them. At these spectacles, and everywhere else, the English are constantly smoking the Nicotian weed, which in America is called Tobaca.[128]

Cruel sports were not, however, an exclusively English phenomenon. In 1606, when the six-year-old Dauphin Louis was staying at Fontainebleau, he was 'taken to the King in the ball-room to see dogs baiting bears and a bull; a bear having overwhelmed one of the dogs, he started to yell "Kill the bear! Kill the bear!" Taken back to his room at 9:45 he did not want to sleep, put on his tunic, and had himself held by his leading strings in imitation of the dogs he had witnessed pulling against their leads in their eagerness to throw themselves on the bears.'[129] Five years later, while being served breakfast by

the Duc de Guise, the young King was informed 'that an Englishman had arrived at court with some very savage dogs and bears and that, if His Majesty cared to provide a pension of 1,000 écus, he would maintain five or six of these dogs throughout the year for the pleasure of the King who, when he so wished, could see them fight to the

English mastiffs were highly prized for their ferocity.

215

bitter end. The King listened in silence before saying, "No, no, not to the bitter end; I don't want that." He was too good-natured.'[130] Nonetheless, later that same day he went to the Oval Room to see the Englishman's dogs pitted against a bear and clearly enjoyed the sport for, in about 1617, Alleyn petitioned James I for money owing for bears and dogs conveyed to France by a man called Starkey to amuse the French King.

Bear-baiting, long popular in Russia, was abolished by order of Tsar Alexis (1629–76, Tsar from 1645) in 1648 as part of his campaign for moral regeneration. The people were instructed to 'shun sorcerers; they must not play immoral or devilish games, nor bait bears or dance with dogs'.[131] This did not prevent Alexis from staging a fight between an old bear and a wolf in the winter of 1668/9 and organising a battle between wolves and hounds which left most of the latter either dead or maimed.[132] Bears are baited in Russia and eastern Europe to this day.

Not only was there increasing concern that popular participation in such sports might incite people to perpetrate similar acts of violence against their fellow men, but many began to question whether such activities were not an abrogation of man's duty of stewardship over the animal kingdom. The first country to legislate against cruelty to animals was America, where the *Liberties of the Massachusetts Colony* of 1641 stipulated that 'No man shall exercise any tyranny or cruelty towards any brute creatures which are usually to be kept for man's use'.[133] In England, during the Commonwealth, the readiness of dogs to fight with bears was seen as an unseemly reminder of original sin[134] and, in 1654, a Protectorate ordinance prohibited cockfighting and cock-throwing. Public – not private – bear-baiting was abolished and, although these sports resurfaced with the Restoration, Quakers and dissenters continued the battle for the suppression of activities that John Wesley considered the 'foul remains of Gothic barbarity'.[135] Attitudes were changing; in June 1670, John Evelyn

> went with some friends to the Bear Garden, where was cock-fighting,
> dog-fighting, bear- and bull-baiting, it being a famous day for all these
> butcherly sports, or rather barbarous cruelties. The bulls did exceedingly
> well, but the Irish wolf-dog exceeded, which was a tall greyhound, a
> stately creature indeed, who beat a cruel mastiff. One of the bulls tossed

a dog full into a lady's lap, as she sate in one of the boxes at a considerable height from the arena. Two poor dogs were killed, and so all ended with the ape on horseback, and I most heartily weary of the rude and dirty pastime, which I had not seen, I think in twenty years before.[136]

The notorious ferocity of mastiffs accounted for their popularity in baiting sports and, in 1625, the East India Company lodged a complaint that the seizure of the best specimens by the Master of the Bear Garden for the King was causing their business to suffer.[137] They were not alone; the royal officers sent into every county in the land to seize arbitrarily bulls, bears and mastiffs to replace those killed in the Bear Gardens were often molested. When mastiffs were in short supply, wolfhounds and greyhounds were substituted. Elizabeth I had earlier enjoyed the spectacle of sixteen head of deer being torn to pieces by a pack of greyhounds, and a dog of this breed successfully challenged a wolf at the French court in 1682. Dogfights were also a popular diversion at this period, being staged in London at the famous dog-pit in Westminster well into the nineteenth century. By this time the combatants were bulldogs and, in the decade following Napoleon's defeat at Waterloo, one of the most ferocious of these creatures enjoyed such a reputation for invincibility that it was rather illogically named Boney. The sport was particularly favoured in the East. Pekingese were considered excellent little fighters by the Chinese and combats were frequently held at the imperial palaces. In Japan, Takatoki of the Hojo Regency (reigned 1316–26) had kept two thousand fighting dogs and staged twelve combats a month, each of which resulted in the death of between one and two hundred. The champion was carried in splendour on a sedan chair through the streets of Kamakura to popular acclaim. So fascinating did he find the sport that Takatoki ordered his subjects to bring him fighting dogs in lieu of taxes and, not surprisingly, he found himself the proud owner of no fewer than five thousand. Imperial fighting dogs were fed on a diet of fish and fowl, dressed in brocade and kept in elaborate and costly kennels.[138]

As sensibilities changed and attitudes softened so, by the eighteenth century, the vogue in animal entertainment had shifted to trick-performing, once popular in ancient Rome where Plutarch had witnessed the spaniel, Zoppico, enacting pantomimes before the Emperor Vespasian. Henry VIII is recorded as having paid 'twenty shillings to the fellaw with the daunsing dogge' in 1529.[139] The Tsar Alexis staged a reindeer race with Samoyeds as jockeys[140] and the Tsar's Dutch contemporary, J. Steen, was one of the earliest artists to depict a performing white clipped poodle in *The Dancing Lesson*. In France, at the close of the seventeenth century, troupes of poodles were trained to accomplish unprecedented feats such as playing cards and dominoes.[141] One such troupe, from Louvain, and known as 'The Ball of Little Dogs', crossed the Channel in 1700 to entertain Queen Anne at her special request. Bearing aristocratic names such as the Marquis de Gaillerdain and Madame de Poncette, they danced before their royal hostess.[142] The painting by John Wootton (1682–1764) of four *Dancing Dogs*, Lusette, Madore, Rosette and Mouche, which was completed in 1759, testifies to the undiminished popularity of performing poodles in eighteenth-century England. Although the attribution of the performing poodle in Jean-Jacques Bachelier's *Dog of the Havannah Breed* to Marie Antoinette seems improbable, given that it is dated 1768 – two years before she arrived in France – there is no doubt that the breed was extremely popular at the French court at this period. The first circus was established in Lambeth in 1769 by Philip Astley, who subsequently moved to France where he went into partnership with the celebrated Franconi. Poodles, long familiar to those attending fairgrounds, had come of age. The most famous circus poodle was probably Munito, which shared an act with the tightrope-walking goat, Amalthée, in Paris in the 1820s,[143] and as late as 1897 dogs performed before Queen Victoria at Windsor Castle.[144]

Nor were poodles mere circus animals. In the early nineteenth century the fashion for dog drama swept across Europe and America, the most popular being *The Dog of Montargis* starring Vendredi, the poodle of an actor called Karsten. This traditional tale illustrating the sagacity and fidelity of dogs was based on an allegedly true event said to have occurred in 1371: Aubrey de Montdidier, the owner of the dog of Montargis, was murdered by his companion, Macaire, to whom the animal then showed a marked hostility. The dog led the agents of justice to the spot in the forest of Bondy where Montdidier had been buried and Charles VI granted the ordeal of battle to test Macaire's guilt. The dog won and thus avenged his master's death. The play opened in London in 1814 and ran to over 1,100 performances before being transferred to Germany in 1817, where the news soon reached Goethe, officially Court Librarian but also in charge of the theatre in Weimar, and a man who detested dogs. The Duke of Weimar's mistress, Caroline Jagemann, herself an actress who deeply resented Goethe's authority, now used the dog to engineer his downfall:

> The duke, whose fondness for dogs was as marked as Goethe's aversion to them, was craftily assailed, from various sides, to invite Karsten and his poodle to Weimar. When Goethe heard of this, he haughtily answered, 'In our Theatre regulations stands: no dogs admitted on the stage' – and paid no more attention to it. As the duke had already written to invite Karsten and his dog, Goethe's opposition was set down to systematic arbitrariness, and people artfully 'wondered' how a prince's wishes could be opposed for such trifles. The dog came. After the first rehearsal, Goethe declared that he would have nothing more to do with a theatre in which a dog was allowed to perform; and at once started for Jena. Princes ill brook opposition; and the duke, after all, was a duke.

He was dismissed. Although the Duke later repented, 'no entreaty could make Goethe resume the direction of the theatre, and he withdrew his son also from his post in the direction. He could pardon the hasty act and unconsidered word of his friend; but he was prouder than the duke, and held firmly to his resolution of having nothing to do with a theatre which had once prostituted itself to the exhibition of a clever poodle.'[145] Goethe got his revenge in *Faust* by casting Mephistopheles in the shape of a black poodle.

> In length and breadth how doth my poodle grow;
> With bristling hair now doth the creature swell
> Huge as a hippopotamus,
> With fiery eye, terrific tooth,
> Ah! now I know thee sure enough.

Faust first addresses Mephistopheles with the words:

> Cease thus to gnash
> Thy ravenous fangs at me! I loathe thee

RELIGIOUS OBJECTIONS

The vogue for trick-performing animals at the turn of the nineteenth century reflected the wholesale revolution in the attitude towards animals that had taken place since the Renaissance. The Bible, long scoured for justification of man's dominion over nature, had difficulty competing with scientific evidence which struck at the very foundation of the theological edifice on which anthropocentrism was based. Animals had previously been seen as existing exclusively for man's benefit, and created by God for his recreation and needs, and there could therefore be no injustice in either killing or tormenting them. The tamer the beast, the closer to God, for savagery was deemed the consequence of the Fall. By the late eighteenth century, even the Comte de Buffon (1707–88) who subscribed to the view that the taming of the dog was the crucial act in man's development, nevertheless felt compelled to jettison biblical chronology in the light of archaeological discoveries that refuted the Old Testament assertion that the world was only six thousand years old.

It is unlikely that many princes followed the complicated philosophical debate on the animal soul which gathered momentum from the Renaissance and was largely exhausted after the French Revolution, when laws were finally passed throughout Europe making cruelty to animals a criminal offence. That princes had long overruled the Bible as far as pets were concerned was clear from the quasi-religious ceremonial with which they buried them. However, they did not listen gladly to arguments that threatened to undermine their authority, and exhibited an inconsistent orthodoxy when faced by the spectre of real or imagined sedition. The Church had a vested interest in buttressing this orthodoxy and exalted faith over reason in response to physiological discoveries that exposed many of their shibboleths as intellectually untenable. The animal kingdom was monarchical, a mirror of human society. Ironically, René Descartes (1596–1650), the philosopher who gave the greatest sanction to cruelty to animals, with his insistence that they were insensate machines, was also the most universally execrated by princes: 'this ruthless statement had proved acceptable to Jansenists, vivisectionists, fervent Cartesians who did not question the master's obiter dicta, Christian apologists who liked to have difficult problems simplified, and citizens who disliked their neighbours' dogs.'[146] Descartes considered Montaigne a heretic for suggesting that man and beast were equal and for denouncing cruelty.

Both Descartes and Montaigne held positions at court, the former in Sweden at the court of Queen Christina, the latter in France under Henri III as *gentilhomme de la Chambre du Roi* from 1571. It was to that passionate royal dog lover that he dedicated his celebrated *Essays*. Court patronage was the cynosure of all aspiring men and a glowing dedication could earn a writer rich rewards. The enormously ambitious Jean Racine (1639–99), premier poet at the court of Louis XIV, rose from relatively humble beginnings to become an intimate of the King and *secrétaire du Roi* in 1696. Racine, who believed that animals were a vehicle for God's wisdom, echoed royal contempt for Cartesianism in the *Epistle to the Duchesse de Noailles*:

> This gentle dog which accompanies and flatters me,
> In response to my orders meekly offering up a paw,
> Bringing terror to the thief who seeks to break my door,
> Baring his teeth ready in pieces to tear;
> Despite all this assistance, my inflexible Reason
> Pitilessly declares him an unfeeling automaton.
> Inanimate machine, walking with blind eyes
> Feigning passions it does not recognise,
> Destroying without rage, crying for me without pity,
> Flattering me without affection, evading me without fear,
> Drawn to an object it unseeingly pursues,
> Obeying my will though ignorant of its virtues.

It was under Louis XIV's successor, Louis XV, that the battle royal over animal immortality was engaged. The *libertins*, or freethinkers, as those sympathetic to the idea were called, suffered relentless persecution during the reign of this most libertine of French kings. Claude-Adrien Helvétius (1715–71) had to retract the 'heresies' of *De L'Esprit*, a work in which he suggested that, if a horse had hands instead of hooves, it would be indistinguishable from man in intelligence. Maupertius (1698–1759), who believed that the difference between man and beast was merely one of degree, had to flee to Prussia where Frederick the Great appointed him

President of the Berlin Academy of Sciences in 1746. Julien Offray de La Mettrie (1709–51), author of two controversial books *L'Histoire Naturelle de l'Ame* and *L'Homme Machine* in the 1740s, was also forced into exile, finding sanctuary with Frederick. Denis Diderot (1713–84) was imprisoned at Vincennes for his unorthodox views and his hugely influential *L'Interpretation de la Nature* had to be published anonymously in 1753. His advocacy of uninhibited natural, and specifically sexual, physical drive was found particularly repellent by clerics at the court of the lubricious Louis XV.

If La Mettrie was accused of degrading man with his emphasis on education alone making him superior to the beast, he compounded the sin by insisting that it was only by imitating animals that man could raise himself to their level. His exile was spent in Switzerland and England. Like Rousseau, Voltaire granted both speech and souls to animals, albeit of an inferior kind. Rousseau's *Discours sur l'origine et les fondements de l'inégalité parmi les hommes* was published in Amsterdam in 1755. Voltaire wrote to congratulate the author: 'One is tempted to walk on all fours after reading your book. However, as it is more than sixty years since I lost the habit I feel that it is unfortunately impossible for me to resume it, and I leave this natural posture to those who are worthier than you or I.'[147] Voltaire had spent the years 1750 to 1753 in Berlin where he was, initially at least, warmly received by the Philosopher-King. Despite his many talents and attempts to curry favour, Voltaire never succeeded in rehabilitating himself at the French court and retired to Switzerland. Paradis de Moncrif was execrated by Academicians not because of his famous *Histoire des Chats*, written between 1727 and 1748, but because he was the Queen's *lecteur* and owed his appointment to her patronage. Dupont de Nemours, who argued strongly in favour of animal language, listing, in 1813, with meanings, twenty-five words he maintained he had heard used by crows, lived undisturbed in the France of Napoleon, only going into exile in 1815 with the restoration of the Bourbons.[148]

The court of Prussia, where the French language was *de rigueur*, philosophy appreciated and dogs worshipped, appealed to many of these exiles. Others went to England where some of the greatest thinkers on the subject – Bacon, Newton and Locke – had managed to convey their opinions without risk of persecution. Hobbes expressed serious doubts about man's inherent right to superiority: 'I pray, when a lion eats a man and a man eats an ox, why is the ox more made for man than the man for the lion?'[149] In his poem '*Homo Sapiens*', the Earl of Rochester, one of the favourite courtiers of Charles II, wrote:

> Were I (who to my cost already am
> One of those strange, prodigious creatures, man.)
> A spirit free to choose, for my own share,
> What case of flesh and blood I pleased to wear,
> I'd be a dog, a monkey, or a bear,
> Or anything but that vain animal
> Who is so proud of being rational.

The fact that neither Hobbes nor Rochester suffered persecution owed less to the greater tolerance of the Protestant Church than to their living in a more secular society. Superstition and mummery could work in dogs' favour. In folk culture killing dogs was considered very unlucky and, in France, the Lyonnais elevated a shrine to Saint Guinefort, the legendary greyhound credited with having saved a child from a snake, which continued to attract pilgrims until well into the nineteenth century despite repeated efforts to suppress the cult.[150] The Prussia of Frederick the Great was exceptional; such tolerance would never have been manifested by his father, Frederick William I, and, when Napoleon entered Lutheran Frankfurt in 1806, he ordered the removal of notices from public buildings barring entry to dogs and Jews.[151] Dutch artists continued to represent dogs as symbols of man's basest instincts long after they had shed such stigmas in Catholic art. In England, where there was no Inquisition and no Roman law, where papal authority was far weaker than on the Continent, long before the Reformation, and where the Church had long enjoyed substantial independence, unorthodox views could be voiced relatively freely.[152] It was not the Protestants but the Quakers and Methodists, and later the evangelicals, who led the movement against cruelty to animals.

The British public of the late eighteenth century benefited from a far higher level of literacy than existed on the Continent and was therefore more influenced by the new sensibility disseminated through prints and novels. There was also no censorship. Currents of humanitarianism and sentimental feeling which had affected attitudes towards relationships within the family were extended to animals. As Jeremy Bentham observed in 1789, the question was no longer '"Can they *reason?*" nor, "Can they *talk?*" but, "Can they *suffer?*"' Latin countries were considered cruel to animals not simply because their religion proscribed animal immortality but also because they continued to countenance the eating of creatures that had long ceased to form part of the diet in prosperous countries like Britain. When Edward Topsell, author in 1607 of *A Historie of Four-Footed Beasts*, criticised the Spanish for eating cats, it was not from a moral standpoint but because he considered the flesh poisonous. In 1634 Lord Spencer entertained Charles I at Althorp to a banquet consisting of ruffs, reeves, redshanks, dotterels, godwits, curlews, swans, bitterns, mallards, peewits, herons, storks and dozens of other birds.[153] The consumption of dogs and cats was universal during food shortages. The English ate them during the Civil War, the French during the Religious Wars of the sixteenth century and during the Commune in 1870. Zoo animals were consumed by the French in 1870 and the Russians in 1917. The Chinese considered certain breeds of dog and cat – though not the Pekingese – gastronomic fare. In Berlin in 1917 the Kaiser's dentist, Arthur Davis, recalled how 'dogs too nearly vanished from city life. A man I knew who had kept a fine Newfoundland dog told me that it had disappeared one night, and the next day its skin was found hanging on the fence, with a sign running, "Died for the Fatherland".'[154]

Many nineteenth-century socialists, like Fourier, Engels and Saint-Simon, advocated the complete lordship of man over beast in a manner redolent of early modern orthodox Christianity.[155] Pets, unnecessary animals, symbolised the contamination and decay of defunct regimes. They were a waste of national resources, undeserving recipients of food much needed by the people. In the sixteenth century, when there had been far more animals than men on the planet, the life of the ordinary smallholder was a daily struggle for dominion over predatory animals likely to destroy his meagre livelihood. The hounds of the aristocracy were usually far better nourished, and often better housed, than their servants, and the gentry frequently compelled their tenants to rear puppies at their own expense.[156] By the nineteenth century foreign dogs were increasingly execrated in nationalist circles and the epizootic disease that wiped out so many French dogs in the nineteenth century, including half the King's hounds in 1769–70, was later held to have originated in England.[157] In republican France nearly ten thousand dogs were destroyed in a single year, 1879, although the annual average of death by rabies had never exceeded twenty-five.

HECATOMBS

Although animals were destroyed as a sanitary precaution during plagues and eaten when starvation threatened, the worst atrocities perpetrated against them were nonetheless generally committed by republican regimes after the overthrow of monarchical government. One of the earliest modern animal hecatombs occurred during the French Revolution when the small luxury dogs abandoned by their owners in the first wave of emigration were rounded up and burned in the Place des Grèves.[158] In the popular mind, not only did such dogs symbolise unacceptable levels of waste and privilege, but they also invoked images of uncontrolled sexual licence. Artists like Fragonard and Watteau, and writers like Diderot, repeatedly used small dogs as metaphors for female carnality. By 1789, these dogs embodied the moral laxity of eighteenth-century society so abhorrent to Robespierre and his ilk. Furthermore, as putative carriers of smallpox, they were associated with disease. Jenner, inventor of the vaccine, had even taken the precaution of inoculating his pet dog. In rural areas, hounds were also persecuted, many breeds disappearing altogether during the Revolution. Most of those that survived had been given cosmetic surgery to disguise their pedigree.

The collapse of so many dynasties in the twentieth century spelt disaster for innumerable breeds of dog, particularly where closely associated with the monarchy and ruling class. In China in 1912 nearly all the Pekingese in the royal breeding establishments were destroyed. By the 1920s the Chinese had already come to realise the economic folly of the slaughter and a fair was held each month, lasting six days, at the Lung Fu Ssu Temple in Peking, where the dogs were sold for up to thirty dollars each. In 1918 the same fate befell the imperial Russian borzois. In 1861, when serfdom was abolished, many aristocratic kennels had been dispersed and the dogs sold off at exorbitant prices to covetous purchasers. One Russian exchanged eighty acres of land for a particularly fine pair. Prize dogs occasionally formed part of dowries. Not all the dogs could be reaccommodated, however, and the risk of extinction led to the formation in 1873 of the 'Imperial Association for the Propagation of Hounds', and the Grand Duke Nicholas Nicolaevich, uncle of the Tsar, resigned as commander of the Imperial Hussars in 1887 to devote himself to the borzoi kennel he purchased at Perchino. This became the fore-

Alix, Queen Alexandra's borzoi. The Bolsheviks were responsible for the wholesale extermination of the breed in Russia.

most hunting establishment in Russia in the thirty years preceding the Revolution. Kept in considerable luxury and fed on horsemeat, the borzois were superintended by a large staff. Although many were sold at lucrative prices, others were offered as gifts to the imperial hunt. They walked beside the Tsar on state occasions. In 1918 the Bolsheviks razed the eighteenth-century palace at Perchino to the ground, although the kennels were preserved as human accommodation, which they remain to this day.

With the expansion of communism, the dogs of eastern Europe were similarly targeted. In Romania in 1947, the government ordered the extermination of the Transylvanian hounds and Hungarian greyhounds on the basis that these breeds were 'reminders' of the Hungarian aristocracy, regardless of the fact that only the former were indigenous. In Estonia, Latvia and Lithuania native dogs met the same fate. In Poland, the *ogar Polski*, a large bloodhound-type scenting dog, and the *gonczy Polski*, a shorter-limbed strain, all but disappeared, as did the *Czesky fonsek*, or pointer, in Czechoslovakia. Here the tiny *Prazsky krysavik*, a prized lapdog before the communist takeover, continued to be bred in secret, its diminutive size militating in favour of its survival. In most of these countries, the resurgence of nationalism following in the wake of the collapse of communism has led to the introduction of intensive breeding programmes aimed at re-establishing the very breeds previously vilified.[159]

Mussolini was exceptional and turned Capri into a bird sanctuary in response to the long campaign waged by Axel Munthe. Munthe was overjoyed and claimed the birds sang the Fascist anthem, 'Giovinezza', to him out of gratitude.[160] Munthe had done all in his power to protect the birds that came to Capri:

> wood pigeons, thrushes, turtle-doves, waders, quails, golden orioles,
> skylarks, nightingales, wagtails, chaffinches, swallows, warblers,
> redbreasts and many other tiny artists on their way to give spring
> concerts to the silent forests and fields in the North. A couple of
> hours later they fluttered helplessly in the nets the cunning of man
> had stretched all over the island from the cliffs by the sea high up to
> the slopes of Monte Salaro and Monte Barbarossa. In the evening
> they were packed by hundreds in small wooden boxes without food
> and water and despatched by steamers to Marseilles to be eaten with
> delight in the smart restaurants of Paris.[161]

Munthe paid dearly for his championship of birds when both his pet dogs were murdered by locals resentful of being deprived of sport and revenue.

ROYAL PROTECTION OF ANIMALS

The collapse of monarchies in the East has had an equally devastating effect on the animal kingdom. The princes of India, however keen on hunting, were careful to preserve game and wildlife and treated their pets with oriental magnificence. It was not simply eccentricity which prompted the Maharajah of Junagadh to order his whole court into mourning and the Chopin funeral march to be played whenever one of his dogs died. Like the subject of Alexander Pope's 'Indian and his Dog', the Maharajah:

> Asks no angel's wings, no seraph's fire:
> But thinks, admitted to that equal sky,
> His faithful dog shall keep him company.

Most of the animals now at risk of extinction were venerated at Eastern courts. White elephants, believed to be animated by human spirits, were

227

sacred in Burma, India and Siam, as was the tiger in Korea. Dogs, in all but the Moslem faith, were protected by their divinity, no essential difference, in spiritual terms, being deemed to exist between dog and man, whose soul was believed to transmigrate into the dog on death. The Zoroastrians thought dogs were gods in disguise and crimes against them were severely punished. In 1834 Parsees in Bombay rioted when an order was issued to destroy all the dogs. They collected together as many dogs as they could and shipped them off to a desert island where, overcome by thirst and hunger, the animals devoured each other.[162] The Pekingese of China were bred to resemble the Buddhist lion as closely as possible. The pedigree of the dog reflected the life of the man whose soul it possessed; in Tibet, pariah dogs were credited with being reincarnations of faithless priests. The fact that a lack of male progeny was attributed to having killed living things in a former life made dynastic rulers particularly attentive to animal welfare. All life being sacred to the Hindus, animals were cherished without distinction. The Hindu for cat means clean.

Hospitals for sick creatures were in existence in the East centuries before they appeared in the West, where Christian dogma insisted on the beast's subservience to man. In Japan, the eighteenth-century shogun Tsunayoshi had special surgeons to tend sick dogs and nurses who sat up with them. They allegedly received better treatment than children.[163] In India in the 1930s, the Maharajah of Junagadh's eight hundred pet dogs had a white-tiled hospital and an English vet. The Maharajah's dogs benefited from an infinitely higher standard of medical treatment than did his subjects. Their protection of animals often endangered the human species: in 1912 the Maharajah of Jaipur had to construct a large plague camp outside his capital because of his refusal to allow any rats to be killed.[164] Moslems have protected cats since Mohammed, whose own cat, Muezza, used to curl up in the sleeve of his robe. Once, when he was addressing the faithful in Damascus, he cut off his sleeve rather than disturb its sleep. Tabby cats were so named after the Governor of Mecca in the seventh century, who was also a companion of Mohammed.

In Buddhist Japan the protection of dogs was taken to extremes by the shogun Tokugawa Tsunayoshi (ruled 1680–1709), as the German traveller Kaempfer recorded:

Since the now reigning Emperor came to the throne, there are more Dogs bred in Japan than perhaps in any one Country whatever, and than there were before even in this Empire. They have their Masters indeed, but lie about the Streets, and are very troublesome to passengers and travellers. Every street must, by special command of the Emperor, keep a certain number of these Animals, and provide them with victuals. There are Huts built in every street, where they are taken care of when they fall sick. Those that die, must be carried up to the tops of mountains and hills, as the usual burying-places and very decently interr'd. Nobody may, under severe penalties, insult or abuse them, and to kill them is a capital Crime, whatever mischief they do. In this case, notice of their demeanour must be given to their Keepers, who alone are empower'd to chastise and punish them. This extraordinary care for the preservation of the Dog-Kind is the effect of a superstitious fancy of the now reigning Emperor, who was born in the Sign of the Dog . . . and has for this reason so great an esteem for this Animal, as the great Roman Emperor Augustus Caesar is reputed in Histories to have had for Rams. The natives tell a pleasant tale on this head. A Japanese, as he was carrying up the dead carcass of a Dog to the top of a mountain in order to its burial, grew impatient, grumbled and curs'd the Emperor's birth-day and whimsical commands. His companion, tho' sensible of the justice of his complaints, bid him hold his tongue and be quiet, and instead of swearing and cursing, return thanks to the Gods, that the Emperor was not born in the Sign of the Horse, because in that case the load wou'd have been much heavier.[165]

The edicts protecting dogs were passed in 1687 and, in the next two years, fifty thousand were kept and fed on a diet of rice and dried fish at the expense of the taxpayer.[166]

Long before Kaempfer reached Japan, other travellers had returned from the East impressed by the Eastern belief in metempsychosis – the transmigration of the soul – and the Manichean idea that man had no right to kill or harm animals. Renaissance humanists found similar ideas in the writings of ancient philosophers such as Pythagoras; the clown in *Twelfth Night* (IV.ii) bids farewell to Malvolio with the words: 'Remain thou still in darkness: thou shalt hold the opinion of Pythagoras ere I will allow of thy wits; and fear to kill a woodcock, lest thou disposses the soul of thy grandam.' Both Plutarch and Aelian described animal reason and morals as far superior to man's and Lucretius declared their state in the natural world to be both higher and happier. Pliny the Elder went so far as to suggest that animals were dearer to the gods than man because of their ability to protect themselves from birth. Many of these classical authors had not been translated into French before the eighteenth century, and several works of the period, such as Paradis de Moncrif's *Ames Rivales* of 1738, reflect interest in the transmigration of the human soul after death. Those classical authors who combined a discourse on the animal soul with sound physiological investigation were read with keen interest by natural historians moving ever closer to the discovery of the process of evolution. Of these, the father of zoology, Aristotle, was easily the most eminent, having distinguished between vertebrates and invertebrates three hundred years before the birth of Christ. The revelation of the close similarity between the bodies of Man and Beast made a mockery of Cartesianism and all but removed any justification for cruelty to animals.

It was the French Revolution which administered the *coup de grâce* to man's belief in his own superiority. The natural historian the Comte de Buffon, employee of the Crown as *Intendant du Jardin du Roi*, and the man who had argued most cogently against animal equality, died in 1788, just in time to be spared the spectacle of his son, an officer in the army, mounting the guillotine. The idea that cruelty to animals led ineluctably to cruelty towards humans was not new: William Hogarth had explored the theme in his series of blatantly propagandist prints *The Four Stages of Cruelty*, published in 1751; Immanuel Kant (1724–1804) also believed brutality to be contagious, reckoning in 1790 'we can judge the heart of man by his treatment of animals'. In France itself, where the Terror was experienced at first hand, many came to believe man more bestial than the beast and shared the view that cruelty to animals was but an apprenticeship. A new word entered the French language, *animaliser*, coined by L. S. Mercier in 1801 when he launched an attack on 'those guilty philosophers who seek to explain everything by bodily functions, to reduce everything to purely physical operations; dangerous philosophy, which aimed to animalise man'.[167] In France, the Rights of Animals were conceived as an extension of the principles enshrined in the Rights of Man, and the Code Napoléon incorporated articles outlawing cruelty against domestic pets which were subsequently imposed on all the countries of the Empire. Under Napoleon III, in 1850, further preventative measures were incorporated into the Loi Grammont. The Société Protectrice des Animaux had been founded in 1845.[168] Bear- and bull-baiting nonetheless still took place at the end of the nineteenth century under the Third Republic. One of the first *dogues de Bordeaux* to be seen in Britain, Matador du Midi, received grudging admiration from *Country Life* on 6 February 1897 for having, 'before he was sixteen months old, made a name for himself in the arena, having won four matches besides having twice fought the bear. He comes from a strain which has for generations been noted for prowess in the arena, counting amongst his ancestors the celebrated "Corporal" who recently died of old age in Paris, after having borne the name of "The Invincible" for the reason that he was never beaten by either bull or bear. These brutal combats are still to be occasionally seen in the extreme South of France.'

As early as 1790, European governments began to legislate against activities previously considered as cathartic in so far as they provided a vent for popular excitement. Lion-baiting was outlawed in Austria by Joseph II and Charles IV of Spain, who had always viewed bullfighting with repugnance, continued the work of his father Charles III, who had reduced the number of bullfights to twelve a year, by issuing orders banning the *corrida*. A decade later, in 1801, the famous *torero* Pépé Hillo was gored to death and the royal favourite, Godoy, urged the King to abolish 'these bloody spectacles'. Bullfights were eventually outlawed in 1805, making Godoy the object of universal opprobrium. The experiment was never repeated. To curry popular favour, Ferdinand VII had bullfighting reinstated in 1808, along with other measures such as lowering the price of tobacco and making wine more accessible to the populace at large. As Godoy observed: 'No-one was given bread; bulls were offered instead. The unfortunate common people thought they had been well requited.'[169]

The forces of conservatism, thoroughly alarmed by Jacobinism, remained nonetheless divided. English game laws were the toughest in

Europe at the end of the eighteenth century but few landowners were prepared to countenance legal restrictions that threatened both their leisure and their social position. Besides, those enlightened aristocrats in France who had waived their privileges with such nonchalance by calling for the abolition of the game laws had been rewarded with either exile or death. Reform might prove equally sanguinary in Britain. When the first animal protection bill ever, to abolish bull-baiting, was introduced in 1800, so few Members of Parliament bothered to attend that it was easily defeated. Of the eleven bills introduced between 1800 and 1835 against various forms of cruelty to animals, most failed. Charles James Fox, sympathetic to reform, opined that poaching was no worse than purchasing parliamentary seats.[170] In 1809, a motion against cruelty to animals proposed by Lord Erskine was upheld in the Lords but defeated in the Commons, and when he tried to reintroduce it a year later it was again rejected. Erskine was a genuine animal lover, keeping as pets several dogs, a goose, a macaw, and two leeches which he named after famous contemporary surgeons.[171] Not surprisingly, many contemporaries considered the British to be crueller to animals than other Europeans: Lady Morgan, after travelling in Italy in the early nineteenth century, observed 'that all domestic animals are more amiable and intelligent on the continent, than with us: it may be they are better treated; for nothing tames like kindness'.[172] In 1835, the naturalist Edward Jesse reckoned that, 'of all the nations of Europe, our own countrymen are, perhaps, the least inclined to treat the brute creation with tenderness', an opinion seconded by Queen Victoria herself in 1868 when she commented, 'the English are inclined to be more cruel to animals than some other civilized nations are.'[173]

The most determined group in favour of abolition was the Clapham Sect, led by William Wilberforce, who were opposed to all blood sports and shared the belief that men became worse than beasts by attending such spectacles. In the Commons, the MP William Windham attacked the Sect: 'If to poverty were to be added a privation of amusements, he knew nothing that could operate more strongly to goad the mind into desperation, and to prepare the poor for that dangerous enthusiasm which is analogous to Jacobinism.'[174] Sidney Smith agreed: 'Any cruelty may be practised to gorge the stomachs of the rich, none to enliven the holidays of the poor'[175] and, in the *Rights of Woman*, Mary Wollstonecraft justified popular dominion over animals on the basis that cruelty satisfied a need 'to revenge the insults that they are obliged to bear from their superiors'. Kindness to animals was seen as a luxury the poor could ill afford. The only bill that was not rejected before 1833 was the Martin Act of 1822, banning the abuse of horses and cattle but not outlawing bull-baiting. The idea of the working classes tormenting the noble horse was perceived as an egregious class affront.

The upshot of all this resistance to legislation was the creation of the SPCA in 1824, founded not by the Clapham Sect but by a Jew, Lewis Gompertz, who, despite his proven financial ability during the society's early years, was forced to resign in 1830 as a 'public relations liability'. The greatest fillip to its success was the backing in 1835 of the Duchess of Kent and Princess Victoria. Thanks to their patronage the first Cruelty to Animals Act was passed in 1839. When Queen Victoria ascended the throne in 1837, she granted the society permission to add the royal prefix.[176] In 1879 Edward, Prince of Wales, became the first royal patron, a position subsequently occupied by the Queen herself. In her Jubilee address of 1887, Victoria cited, 'with real pleasure, the growth of more humane feelings towards the lower animals'[177] and suggested a medal be minted in honour of those who had played such a prominent part in the society's activities. Noticing that the cat failed to feature among the animals, she demanded that the omission be rectified because the cat was a much misunderstood animal. A cat promptly appeared on the extreme righthand of the medal. Lord Abercare, President of the RSPCA in 1886, praised the reigning Monarch: 'The Society does not possess a more active member than the Queen herself. Many things that escape less observant eyes attract her attention and prove her to be a vigilant apostle of humanity.' To mark the centenary of the society's foundation, George VI, then Duke of York, addressed the International Humane Congress in London in 1924 with the words: 'it is common knowledge that when this Society was founded it had a great urgent problem to solve in bringing home to the general public the grave fact, then not sufficiently realised, that in the treatment of animals it was possible to be careless even to the point of brutality. The Society had to protect and foster a love of animals in the hearts of those who had hitherto been apathetic, and I believe the reason that today so many people are genuine animal lovers can largely be traced to the beneficent educational activity of the RSPCA.'[178] By the time Axel Munthe was invited to address the society in 1934, another distinguished guest, Bernard Shaw, showed remarkable prescience in questioning whether the time had not arrived for the formation of a 'Society for the Protection of Mankind. On all sides, I notice the most thorough, conscientious and systematic schemes afoot to exterminate the human race.'[179]

Victoria also patronised the Dogs' Home in Battersea, established in 1860, and it was thanks to her personal intervention that dogs were kept two days longer than the law required.[180] The Queen allowed none of her own dogs to be destroyed and spurned all docking and cropping; she was also an ardent anti-vivisectionist. When anti-rabies hysteria reached one of its many peaks in 1867, and the Metropolitan Streets Act introduced compulsory muzzling for all unled dogs, she personally urged that 'muzzles, except in the case of very savage dogs, should not be used'.[181] The Prince of Wales was equally sympathetic to animals and both he and Alexandra were so opposed to ear-cropping that in 1895, when Edward was patron of the Kennel Club (a position he had occupied since 1875), he protested against the practice to the Secretary: 'The letter was almost a royal command. The Club immediately banned the exhibition of dogs with cut ears.'[182] Edward also dispersed the royal pack of bloodhounds which had been in existence for seven hundred years because of his aversion to the hunting of tame deer. Alexandra would allow no gun to be fired near the gardens at Sandringham and was deeply opposed to foxhunting. She used artificial bait when fishing and condemned society ladies who wore osprey feathers.[183]

No Cruelty to Animals Act has superseded that passed in 1911, which remains the basis for all prosecutions. With the collapse of so many royal houses by 1918, those that survived sought a lower profile, and the method of personal intervention favoured by Queen Victoria and Edward VII became an anachronism. The act was carefully phrased to allow the continuation of vivisection; only 'unnecessary abuse of animals' was outlawed. Notwithstanding the Badgers Act of 1973, banning badger-baiting, and the 1988 Protection of Animals (Amendment) Act, making it an offence to advertise or attend animal fights, both baiting and fighting are on the increase. The dog licence, introduced in 1878, at a cost of seven shillings and sixpence per animal, was abolished in 1988 as too expensive to administer; 350,000 stray dogs are now destroyed annually in Britain.

Jan Wyck: A Dutch Mastiff. *The word 'pug' dates from the eighteenth century.*
This one was known as Old Vertue.

CHAPTER FIVE

The Origins
of the Species

T HE EXCHANGE OF GIFTS between royal courts was a practice
of ancient origin based on establishing sound mercantile, diplomatic and dynastic relations between princely houses. While large
dogs were prized as highly as horses for their use in hunting and war, lapdogs were luxury commodities from earliest times, admired as much for
their novelty value as for their capacity for undemanding companionship.
Merchants and breeders able to gratify their royal benefactors could expect
to be lavishly rewarded. From the Renaissance the horses, weapons and
suits of armour that had constituted the principal medieval commodities
of exchange were progressively superseded by medals, portraits and dogs.
Princes were interested in conspicuous display, in enhancing the prestige of
their kingdoms and — increasingly — in the exotic, tastes stimulated by the
voyages of discovery and the reopening of trade routes with the East. Pets,
having no function, were *ipso facto* the ultimate luxury. Furthermore, from
the fifteenth century, princes established greater privacy within their
palaces and these privy quarters lent themselves to the keeping of pets to a
far greater extent than had the castles of medieval kings. Gifts were also
sentimental, and pet dogs and cats were exchanged between betrothed and
married monarchs, princes, lovers and favourites.

237

TRADE WITH THE EAST

The export of dogs from Europe to China almost certainly began with the establishment of the overland silk route in the second century BC. In exchange for silk the Greeks and Romans provided goods unavailable in China, including Melitiae, tiny dogs bred on the island of Malta and already very popular in the West. Pliny claimed that Caesar deplored the neglect suffered by children whose mothers spent more time fawning over their pets than attending to their parental duties. The dogs were shipped to Byzantium – or Fu Lin, as the Chinese called the city – before continuing by land to the Far East. The few robust enough to have survived the rigours of the journey would have been all the more appreciated for their rarity. In ancient China all

treasures, whether pearls, jade or unusual animals, had to be offered in the first instance to the emperor. The dogs he selected were entrusted to the palace eunuchs, who also supervised the breeding programmes. The only recognised standards were those illustrated in 'dog-books' where the ablest court artists painted idealised portraits. The best specimens from a litter were presented to the emperor by the chief eunuch. A favoured courtier might be given permission to keep a dog but terrible punishments were inflicted on anyone who dared to remove one of the imperial dogs from the palace precincts.

Eunuchs at the Chinese court strove to attain the idealised Pekingese as represented in the imperial 'dog-books'.

It was at the same period, the second century BC, that lions reached China for the first time in her history, travelling from India by the overland trade route north of Tibet known as the Sinkiang. The lion had been associated with the Buddhist god of learning since at least 260 BC, when Asoka, the Emperor of India, converted. The subjection of the King of the animal creation symbolised the subordination of the fiercest passions to the gentle Buddha. The Buddhist Chinese subsequently whelped the Maltese dogs with an indigenous dog, possibly the pug, to produce a breed resembling the lion as closely as possible. The result was the Pekingese, although it was not so named until the Chinese established their capital in Peking in the twelfth century. The dogs' growth was modified by various means: puppies were kept in close-fitting wire cages until they reached maturity, deprived of exercise in order to reduce their appetite, and physically manipulated and massaged over an extended period by the eunuchs in order to produce the shape that pleased their imperial master. To obtain short noses, the cartilages were broken by applying pressure with the thumbnail or by the use of chopsticks; tongues were forcibly stretched. They were bred in the imperial palace and even in the imperial ancestral temple until the practice was prohibited under the Ming Emperor Wan Li at the end of the sixteenth century. Until the nineteenth century, when the Dowager Empress frowned on such deformations, a large number of diminutive Pekingese were bred as 'sleeve' dogs and were carried about in the voluminous sleeves of the long robes worn both by women and mandarins. They were called *Wo*, meaning small, or *Na-pa*, possibly after their Byzantine origin.[1] Considerable superstition was attached to the colour and markings of the dogs bred in the imperial palace: those born with white ears promised riches and nobility for the owner; white dogs with yellow heads held out great hopes of prosperity; yellow dogs with white tails presaged official appointments at court in each generation; black dogs with white forelegs heralded the birth of many male heirs; yellow dogs with white forelegs brought good luck; white dogs with black heads meant good fortune as well as riches; white dogs with black tails ensured that each generation in a family would ride in chariots, a privilege granted only to a select few. A white blaze on the forehead had divine associations, imitating the shining white sphere between the eyebrows of the Buddha, and such dogs were almost guaranteed to find favour with the emperor. Pure white, so admired in Europe, was eschewed in the East as the colour of mourning.

The collapse of the Eastern Han Dynasty at the close of the second century AD was followed by four hundred years of fragmentation in China. By the time the country was reunited under the T'angs in 618 both the Greek and Roman empires had fallen. Malta, however, had become part of the Byzantine Empire in 395 and trade links with the East were reforged, albeit falteringly. The first written references to 'Fu Lin' dogs date from the seventh century. It was also at this period that Buddhism reached Tibet and Japan from China, where it had become the predominant religion in the fifth century. In 609 the Turcoman Emperor accompanied Yang Ti of the Sui Dynasty to Korea, marrying a Chinese princess on his return. His successor sent the first Emperor of the T'ang Dynasty, Kao Tsu, a dog and a bitch, both twelve inches long and six inches high, whose talents were immortalised in verse by the court poet, Li Po. It was claimed they could lead horses by the reins and hold torches in their mouths to light the way for their master when he returned home inebriated after a party.[2] Kao Tsu's grandson, Kao Tsung, gave Temmu, Emperor of Japan (reigned 672–86), small lion dogs which became known as chins after their country of origin. This was the period when Japan was remodelled on the pattern of T'ang China; lion-dogs were bred to resemble the Buddhist lion as closely as possible and to have 'butterfly heads, sacred vulture-feathered feet, and chrysanthemum tails'. White foreheads with a black spot in the middle were said to represent the sacred island of Japan. As the Japanese had never seen a lion, the similarity between the chins and their leonine prototype was

Detail of one of Alexandra's chins from the Country Life *photograph. Japanese spaniels were named 'chins' after their country of origin, China.*

understandably weak. In 732, when a Korean prince presented miniature dogs and other rare small animals to the Emperor Shomu, they were received with such enthusiasm by ladies at court that the price soon soared. By c. 990, when Ichijo was given four dogs, they had achieved a quasi-divine status, and two were placed on lavish cushions either side of the Emperor's divan. Nor did their popularity wane: in 1860 the botanist Robert Fortune described Japanese lapdogs as 'hugely prized by natives and foreigners. They are small – some of them not more than nine or ten inches in length. They are remarkable for snub-noses and sunken eyes and are certainly more curious than beautiful. They are carefully bred; they command high prices even amongst the Japanese, and are dwarfed, it is said, by the use of saki – a spirit to which their owners are particularly partial.'³ None of these chins reached the West before 1854 when the Tokugawa Shogunate toppled and the country was finally compelled to open its gates to foreign trade. The President of the United States and Queen Victoria were the first beneficiaries, receiving four and two chins respectively.⁴ Queen Alexandra was devoted to the breed, and was given one by the Mikado. They were known as Japanese spaniels in the West where their novelty and charm were early captured by painters like Renoir and Manet.

From 878, when China closed her doors to foreigners, until the country's conquest by the Mongols in the thirteenth century, few travellers penetrated her frontiers. Princes of the Mongol Yuan Dynasty were nonetheless received in papal audience in Rome and some forty bishoprics were established by Franciscan missionaries in the Celestial Kingdom. At least seven embassies took place between Constantinople and Peking and a limited traffic in small dogs probably continued, although Marco Polo made no mention of having observed any during his travels. When the ailurophile Mings succeeded the Mongol Yuan Dynasty in 1368, contact between Europe and China was initially severed. The Manchus, who succeeded in 1644, again exhibited a preference for dogs over cats, and Tibetan terriers were presented by the ruling dynasty of Lhasa as part of their annual tribute after the country's conquest by China the following year. They were bred in the old Buddhist monasteries. The larger terrier-Pekingese crosses were used by the Chinese to guard the kennels and in dogfighting. By 1822 eight different varieties of imperial Pekingese had been evolved, superintended by four thousand eunuchs. These leonine creatures were deemed particularly appropriate to the Manchus, a dynasty named after Wen Shu, the Manjusri Buddha, god of learning, and were still being regularly presented as late as 1908, when the Dalai Lama gave several specimens to the Dowager Empress, who was constantly seeking to stress the divine basis of Manchu power and kept at least one hundred dogs as her personal pets.

It was only in the wake of the voyages of discovery during the fifteenth century that mercantile relations were re-established with the Ming Dynasty. Commercial considerations notwithstanding, one of the early purposes of voyagers had been to search out the monstrous human races long alleged to populate the distant corners of the globe, tribes like the Cynocephali, reputed to have dogs' heads. As a result of extensive travel, Renaissance anthropology attained new levels of objectivity. Ships set sail with artists and apothecaries on board, and the fruits of their investigations were bound in lavishly illustrated volumes, given a wider degree of accessibility by the newly invented printing presses. The first man to write a connected account of the natural history of the New World was Gonzalo Fernandez de Oviedo y Valdes (1478–1557). Beginning his career as a page to Prince Juan, the son of Ferdinand and Isabella, he was sent to America in 1513 as inspector of mines and served the Crown in various capacities. His *General and Natural History of the Indies* was first published in 1526. The exotic novelties brought back by the travellers were housed in cabinets of curiosities, much in vogue throughout the sixteenth and seventeenth centuries, and assembled by both Renaissance princes and natural historians. The Holy Roman Emperor Rudolf II and Philip II of Spain, as well as Gesner and Aldrovandi, were avid collectors. The Russian Tsar, Peter the Great, purchased the cabinet of the Dutch apothecary, Albertus Seba (1665–1736) in 1617, and it formed the nucleus for the first Museum of Natural History in Russia.

By 1600 all the major European powers had a commercial foothold, not only in the Far East but also in Russia and the Levant, through the multifarious trading companies established in the course of the previous century. The Mediterranean market, already specialising in luxury goods, received a further fillip during the boom years of the sixteenth century. The Italian wars of 1490–1530, and the fact that Italy had long had the widest commercial network in Europe, led to Italian becoming the most widely understood language on the Continent until superseded by French in the seventeenth century. The combination of prosperity and luxury produced a taste for superfluity, stimulated by the exotic flora and fauna brought back on ships from the East. Nor did the fauna consist exclusively of exotic creatures with which princes happily supplemented their expanding menageries. In 1492 Columbus found small Melitiae-type dogs in Cuba which he presented to the Spanish court in 1493 along with six Indians waiting to be baptised, live parrots and stuffed animals.[5] On Hispaniola (Haiti) another species of dog was discovered, called Cori, and raised in the native homes. Of all colours and both smooth and long-haired, they were used in hunting despite being considered inferior to those brought from Spain. By 1597 Thomas Platter noted all varieties of novel merchandise in Marseilles harbour, including 'monkeys, strange animals',[6] and Jan Brueghel's *Allegory of Sight*, painted in 1617, an inventory of visually appealing commodities, included lapdogs. Dr Caius referred in 1576 to 'a newe kinde of dogge brought out of Fraunce ... for we Englishe men are marvailous greedy gaping gluttons after novelties, and covetous corvorauntes of things that be seldom, rare, straunge, and hard to get'.[7] Tabby cats also reached England for the first time in the early 1600s; valued at five pounds each, they soon replaced the old English cat which was blue and white.[8] Archbishop Laud was one of the first to own one in the 1630s, the decade that saw the invention by John Harrison, a Leeds merchant, of the cat-flap. According to Daniel Defoe, cats were ubiquitous by the reign of Charles II.

For Eastern potentates, addicted to the chase, the ownership of a fierce hunting dog represented the acme of happiness. Traders were granted extensive privileges in exchange for such specimens, particularly mastiffs and water spaniels, British and Irish dogs that had long enjoyed a reputation for ferocity. Caesar's contemporary, Strabo, had described England as a country producing 'corn, cattle, gold, silver and iron, which also form its exports, together with skins, slaves and dogs of a superior breed for the chase'.[9] Mastiffs, scenting hounds and greyhounds were exported to Rome through the agency of the *Procurator Pugnacium*, whose job was to obtain the best specimens. These remained the most popular breeds for 1500 years. In 1614, General Saris of the East India Company, who had introduced English breeds to Japan, wrote home: 'The fittest things for the owld Kinge wilbe a vest of delicatt fine blacke cloth lyned through with black coniskins made sweet; to his sonne a fair headpec and gorgett, a box of all such thinges as ar belonging to a faulconer, quayle calls, a mastife, a water spaniell and a faire grayhound.'[10] In the same year, the governor of Surat requested the East India Company to send as presents to the Great Mogul, Jehangir (ruled 1605–27), 'looking-glasses, figures of beasts or birds made of glass, mastiffs, greyhounds, spaniels and little dogs'. Mastiffs were admired both for their ferocity and their efficacy in guarding the falcons' mews. Problems were presented by the long sea route, however, and many died *en route*. Sir Thomas Roe, English ambassador to the Great Mogul, recorded that this potentate had expressly asked for some of these dogs because an Englishman who had previously been chief factor at his court had given him one of such ferocity it had killed both a leopard and a wild boar, whereas some large dogs dispatched by the Shah of Persia had refused the combat. According to Roe, the Great Mogul threw malefactors to the dogs.[11] In 1615, Jehangir was so desperate to acquire a brace of Irish greyhounds that he promised Roe 'on the Word of a Prince he would gratify me, and grant me more Privileges than I should think of asking'.[12] Again, in 1614, only one of the mastiffs sent by James I to the Shah of Persia was still alive on arrival but, as it proceeded to kill a leopard and a bear that the Shah's own dogs had refused to fight, the company factor wrote back reassuringly: 'the King was exceedingly pleased . . . two or three mastiffs, a couple of Irish greyhounds, and a couple of well-fed water-spaniels would give him great content.'[13] The Persians also liked lapdogs. The company factor wrote in 1617 demanding in the next delivery 'a suit of armour, two young and fierce mastiffs and, above all, as many little dogs, both smooth and rough-haired, as can be sent. His women, it seems, do aim at this commodity.'[14] The ferocity of English mastiffs was universally recognised; Abraham Ortelius in 1598 claimed 'nowhere else can be found dogs either as large or as savage', and Stow reported how 'other forraine writers do affirme that there are in Englande beasts of as great courage, as the Lion, namely the Mastiffe Dog'.[15]

Dogs were among the commodities imported into Europe by the Dutch East India Company in the late sixteenth century through their principal station at Nagasaki, opened exclusively to Dutch trade in 1570. After the decline of Antwerp as a port, east and west India trade passed through Amsterdam, where a dog market was established to meet demand. The author James Howell was a visitor in 1619, describing it disapprovingly as 'a kind of public mart for those commodities, notwithstanding their precise observance of the Sabbath'.[16] In the 1677 painting of *The Dog Market* by Abraham Hondius (1638–95) sixteen different breeds can be identified and the array of dog-collars in the foreground illustrates the types available at the time. A clearly affluent lady is seen accompanied by her black page purchasing toy spaniels. The market was flourishing in 1639 when John Evelyn toured the Low Countries,[17] and one of the most popular breeds on offer was the pug, not least because of its royal associations; Henri IV owned one called Soldat at the time of his death in 1610.

Known in Chinese as the Lo-chiang, pugs were a fashionable breed at the Chinese court from the beginning of the eighth century until 1153, when the Chinese capital moved from Hsianfti to Peking. The Chinese introduced the breed into Japan, where the first black pug was bred as early as c. 900. On their introduction to the Netherlands, pugs were referred to as Chinese mastiffs, being far larger than the present strain, and then as Dutch mastiffs when they reached England during the reign of William III. The word 'pug', which appears to have been first applied to the breed in the 1720s, derives from *pugnaces*, for in Japan they had been fighting dogs. They were still known as the Dutch pug in the nineteenth century. The Japanese had expelled the English East India Company in 1623 and the Portuguese in 1637, leaving the Dutch in a uniquely privileged commercial position. Pets may also have been among the goods imported to Europe from China at this period and considered a great novelty. The physician of Louis XIII recorded four occasions between 1610 and 1611 when the young King went to admire 'merchandise coming from China'.[18] For his birthday in 1606 his father, Henri IV, had given him a dog which he named Lion and whose appearance was considered so ugly by his nurse that she urged him to get rid of it.[19] It may have been one of the lion-dogs at the breeding of which the Chinese were so adept.

Detail of the pug from the Largillière painting of Louis XIV and His Heirs. This was the pug of the Duc de Bourgogne, the King's grandson.

The Dutch and English East India Companies continued to trade in dogs until their dissolution in 1799 and 1873 respectively. Officers stationed in the Far East eventually took up breeding as a hobby; Captain Lukey's brother had a kennel of Maltese dogs which he bred in Manila, two of which, Cupid and Psyche, he shipped back to England in 1841 for Queen Victoria. Unfortunately, they did not take kindly to the long sea voyage and were considered unpresentable on arrival. Other officers brought back their personal pets when they retired, thus introducing breeds thitherto unknown. Gilbert White made the first reference to a chow-chow in his fifty-eighth letter to Thomas Pennant, written in 1781:[20]

Detail of Plumpy the chow. Chows were first seen in England in the late eighteenth century.

My near neighbour, a young gentleman in the service of the East India Company, has brought home a dog and a bitch of the Chinese breed from Canton; such as are fattened in the country for the purpose of being eaten: they are about the size of a moderate spaniel; of a pale, yellow colour, with coarse bristling hairs on their backs; sharp upright ears, and peaked heads, which give them a very fox-like appearance. Their hind-legs are unusually straight, without any bend at the hock or ham, to such a degree as to give them an awkward gait when they trot. . . . Their eyes are jet black, small and piercing; the insides of their lips and mouths of the same colour, and their tongues blue.

EUROPEAN TRADE

Notwithstanding the interest manifested by European Renaissance princes in acquiring ever swifter hunting dogs, lapdogs rapidly became equally desirable. Despite their religious prejudice against dogs, there is plenty of evidence to suggest there were dogs at the Sublime Porte after its capture by the Turks in 1453. Indeed, the earliest reference in European literature to a pet dog is a letter from Theodore Gaza, a native of Thessalonica and Professor of Greek at Ferrara, to Sultan Mehmed II (reigned 1451–81), which he sent together with a gift of a toy dog: 'When his master is at home, he remains at home; and when he goes out, the dog goes out with him, and neither the length of a journey nor the rough country, nor thirst, nor storm, nor heat will deter him from following his master everywhere. And while he follows, he sometimes runs forward, and sometimes runs back to his master, and at other times plays about and wags his tail and does everything he can to sport pleasantly with him. If his master calls him, he approaches; and if he threatens him, cowers to the ground; and if he strikes him, shows no resentment.'[21] History fails to relate whether the Sultan kept the animal, and the phrasing of the letter would certainly suggest such dogs to have been thitherto unfamiliar, despite Constantinople's historic importance in the traffic of dogs between Malta and China. A hundred years later they were no longer a rarity: the Venetian ambassador at the Sublime Porte recorded in 1583 that the Sultan, Murad III, had received the representative of Elizabeth I and 'presented her Majesty with a most beautiful watch set with jewels and pearls, two pretty lapdogs . . .'[22] In 1594 Elizabeth's ambassador wrote at the behest of the Venetian government requesting 'two great sporting dogs' on behalf of the Sultan, and in 1607 the Venetian representative at the English court wrote that he would execute the order of his serenity the Doge to buy 'two big fierce dogs' to be sent to Constantinople as a present from the Venetian government to the Sublime Porte; the dogs were duly dispatched in 1609. In 1662, the Levant Company wrote from London to the Earl of Winchelsea, ambassador to Constantinople: 'Being some time past minded by your Secretary, and knowing also that such things may be of use there, and no unacceptable present; we send by these ships, two large and comely Irish Greyhounds, to be disposed of as your Excellency may see occasion.'[23]

Italy had maintained a close relationship with Islam since the Crusades, and there had been constant commercial intercourse between the harbours of the eastern and southern Mediterranean. Borso, first Duke of Ferrara (ruled 1450–71), had such a reputation for wealth and grandeur that Moslem princes sent him presents in the belief that he ruled the entire peninsula. He loved hunting and his hounds and falcons were reckoned the best in Italy; he owned no fewer than seven hundred pure-bred horses. When the Emperor Frederick III visited Italy in 1452, Borso lavished gifts of coursers and falcons upon him. The traffic in dogs between the courts of Renaissance Italy and the rest of Europe began in earnest towards the close of the fifteenth century when the struggle for mastery of the peninsula between France and the Holy Roman Empire brought rulers into close personal contact with the splendours of the Italian princely courts for the first time. For the following hundred years this influence would be paramount. Commynes, who accompanied Louis XII to Italy, described gifts as a way of diverting the attention of princes and preventing them from interfering in the affairs of foreign countries. Most of the dogs exchanged during the Renaissance were hunting breeds, and there is little doubt that they were given with a view to mollifying the occupying rulers and courting strategic alliances. In 1499 Isabella d'Este, wife of Francesco II of Mantua, sent dogs and falcons, which she had bred herself, to Louis XII, who had invaded Milan. For the same reason she sent a pair of dogs to Cesare Borgia in 1503. Louis XII's forces were finally driven from Italy in 1512 and defeated by an Anglo-Imperial alliance in 1513 at the Battle of Guinegate.

The reign of Louis' successor, Francis I, was marked by rivalry with the Emperor Charles V. The numerous gifts, canine and otherwise, dispatched by Henry VIII to these two monarchs were propitiatory and reflected the treacherous diplomacy of the time, which consisted in switching allies at the crucial moment. English greyhounds and mastiffs were highly esteemed at this period throughout Europe. Dogs had been presented to the French court on earlier occasions: as early as 1461 Edward IV had marked the accession of Louis XI by sending five mastiffs through his ambassador Thomas Langton, and Henry VII dispatched hounds to Louis XII. While allied to the Emperor, Henry VIII sent four hundred dogs to Charles V, 'each garnished with a good yron collar', and they proved such good warriors during the pacification of Valencia in 1521 that their valour was held up as an example to the imperial troops. In 1526, Wolsey abandoned the Anglo-Imperial alliance and signed the Treaty of Cognac with France; Francis received from Henry VIII 'eight very handsome sporting dogs'. In exchange, 'xx corons of the somme of four pounds, thirteen shillings, and four pence' was paid by Henry 'to a frencheman in Rewarde for bringing of a brase of Greyhoundes fro the Frenche king to the king's grace to Eltham'.[24] In 1540 Henry's envoy to the King of France described how the constable took me to the King's dinner, whome we found speaking of certain 'masties' you gave him at Calais, and how long it took to train them; for when he first let slip one at a wild-boar, he spied a white horse with a page upon him, and he took the horse by the throat and they could not pluck him off until he had strangled it. He laughed very heartily at telling this, and he spoke of the pleasure he now takes in shooting with a cross-bow, desiring to have a hound that would draw well to a hurt deer. Your Majesty's father sent to King Louis a very good one of a mean sort. I hear you could not do him a greater pleasure than send him such a hound.[25]

The 'masties' Francis referred to would have been given to him in 1532 when the English and French monarchs met at Calais and Boulogne. In the suite of Anne Boleyn travelled the wife of Arthur Viscount Lisle, subsequently posted to Calais as Lord Deputy. She acquired a small dog, Purquoy, of a breed still unfamiliar in England, which she was asked to relinquish to the Queen in no uncertain terms: John Husee, a member of the King's retinue, wrote to Lady Lisle on 7 January 1534, 'But Madam, there is no remedy, your ladyship must needs depart with your little Purquoy, the which I know well shall grieve your ladyship not a little.'[26] Lady Lisle did not delay and Purquoy was delivered to the Queen by 20 January when the ambassador to France, Sir Francis Bryan, wrote to Lord Lisle asking him 'to give hearty thanks on my behalf for her little dog, which was so proper and so well liked by the Queen that it remained not above an hour in my hands but that her Grace took it from me'.[27] It was reported back to Lady Lisle that Anne Boleyn 'setteth much store by a pretty dog, and her grace delighted so much in little Purkoy [sic] that after he was dead of a fall there durst nobody tell her grace of it, till it pleased the King's Highness to tell her Grace of it. But her Grace setteth more store by a dog than by a bitch, she saith.'[28] Purquoy had died later that same year, and Lady Lisle was on the point of dispatching another when she heard of Anne Boleyn's disgrace.

In 1540, Francis I became aware of Henry's desire to put an end to his political isolation in Europe and was hinting at the possibility of an alliance. Instead, Henry allied with Charles V in 1544. On 9 December 1545 his lord deputy sent four greyhounds from Ireland, but not before writing to their supplier, James Hancock of Dublin, reproaching him for wilful obstinacy which might disappoint the King as to certain dogs intended for a nobleman in Spain which he, the deputy, had promised: the Marquis of Defarrya wanted an annual delivery of 'two Goshawkes and four greyhounds, and forasmuch as the said Duke hath done the King acceptable service in his Wars, and that the King is informed that the said Marquiss beareth to him especial good will, he therefore grants the said suit, and commands that the Deputy for the Time being shall take order for the delivery of the said Hawks and Greyhound unto the order of the said Marquiss and his son, and the longer liver of them yearly; and that the Treasurer shall pay the charges of buying the said Hawks and Hounds'.[29] In 1548, a year after Henry's death, Charles V's sister, Mary of Hungary, received 'greyhounds and running dogs' while the French Queen was reported to be 'the gladdest woman in the world' as a result of the 'hobbies, greyhounds, hounds and great dogs' dispatched from the English court that same year.

Elizabeth I continued to send canine gifts to foreign courts. In 1559, the year following her accession to the throne, the envoy of the Duke of Mantua wrote home: 'the Queen did act thus with the French Lords to whom she gave gifts more than splendid, viz, To Monsieur Montmorency . . . divers dogs – mastiffs, great and small, hounds [scurieri], and setters – a quantity of every sort' which had been reared at the Isle of Dogs, royal kennels since the time of Edward III. These were sent in recognition of the treaty of Câteau-Cambrésis which secured peace with France. She dispatched mastiffs to Charles IX which turned out to be extremely savage; one killed a cow belonging to one of the royal laundresses, who insisted on generous compensation.[30] Elizabeth presented her Master of the Horse, the Earl of Essex, with one hundred of these ferocious dogs to assist him in his war in Ireland, one of which he gave to the Duke of Württemberg, who was visiting England in 1592. Mastiffs frequently appear in Bavarian royal portraiture of the late sixteenth century. Privy purse expenses under Henry VIII indicate that he regularly paid twenty shillings (approximately £300 in today's currency) for a mastiff between 1529 and 1532, a relatively insignificant sum, suggesting there was no scarcity.

In 1604 the Treaty of London concluded many years of war between Spain and England. The Duke of Lerma, royal favourite and virtual ruler of Spain under Philip III, wanted peace in order to extricate the country from her financial difficulties. Peace meant renewed contacts with the Continent and facilitated the exchange of breeds. Mastiffs from the famous kennel at Lyme Park in Cheshire were among the gifts presented to the King of Spain: 'Sixe stately Horses, with saddles and saddle clothes very richly and curiously embroidered, that is to say three for the King and three for the Queene Two Crosse bowes with Sheffes of Arrowes Foure fowlling pieces with their furniture very richly garnished and inlaid with plates of gold A Cupple of Lyme hounds of singular qualities.'[31] The dog in Velásquez's *Las Meninas*, painted in 1656, is their descendant.

In 1606, dogs had been sent to Louis, the French Dauphin, then aged five, by James's eldest son Henry, Prince of Wales, who wrote: 'Monsieur and brother, having heard that you have begun to ride, I thought it would give you pleasure to receive a pack of small dogs which I send in order to express my desire that we may follow in the footsteps of the Kings, our fathers in whole-hearted and firm friendship.'[32] In 1614 the Venetian representative reported to the Doge that James had sent 'palfreys, dogs for hunting lions, arquebuses and sables and crossbows' to Philip III, whose daughter's hand he sought in marriage for his second son, Charles. The negotiations broke down and, in 1618, when negotiating the marriage of Charles, Prince of Wales since the death of his brother Henry, his mother Queen Anne sent six horses and forty hounds to Louis XIII, renowned since infancy for his love of the chase. The Stuarts had succeeded the Tudors in 1603 and were anxious to forge dynastic alliances with the principal continental powers.

Irish wolfhounds, or greyhounds, were also in great demand throughout Europe, where wolves continued to menace the entire continent until the eighteenth century. They were dispatched to the King of Poland in the mid-seventeenth century and, under Charles II, the Levant Company sent some to the ambassador in Constantinople in the hope of obtaining favours from the Sultan. The prohibition on their export in 1652 ensured that Irish wolfhounds were particularly sought after under the Protectorate and Oliver Cromwell gladly obtained them for loyal supporters. In June 1653 Dorothy Osborne wrote to her fiancé Sir William Temple, son of the Master of the Rolls in Ireland, asking him to persuade his father to send one: 'I have one that was the Generalls but tis a bitch and those are alway's much lesse then the dog's, I gott it in the time of my favour there and it was all they had. H.C. [Cromwell's second son, Henry] undertook to write to his Brother Fleetwood [husband of Cromwell's daughter, Bridgit] for another for mee, but I have lost my hope there. Whomsoever it is that you imploy hee will need noe other instructions but to gett the biggest hee can meet with, 'tis all the beauty of those dogs or of any indeed I think, a Masty [mastiff] is handsomer to mee then the most exact litle dog that ever Lady playde withall.'[33] In September, before this commission could be honoured, Dorothy Osborne received a brace from Cromwell's son, Henry: 'I must tell you what a present I had made mee to day two of the finest Young Ireish Greyhounds that ere I saw, a Gentelman that serv's the Generall sent them mee they are newly come over and sent for by H.C. hee tels mee but not how hee gott them for mee.'[34]

Such was the unrivalled reputation of these English and Irish dogs in the sixteenth and seventeenth centuries that they became analogous with the British nation. In *Henry VI* Part I, Talbot says:

> They call'd us; for our fiercenesse, English dogges,
> Now, like to Whelpes, we crying run away.

And in *Henry V*, Rambures says: 'That island of England breeds very valiant creatures; their mastiffs are of unmatchable courage.' Honoré de Courtin, one of the ambassadors dispatched by Louis XIV to the court of Charles II in 1665 to negotiate an Anglo-French alliance, claimed: 'The English are like their own mastiffs, which as soon as they see other dogs throw themselves upon them and throttle them if they can – and then go back home and lie down and go to sleep.'[35] Carolus Linnaeus (1707–78) designated the mastiff *Canus anglicus* and John Gay lauded 'a mastiff of true English blood' in one of his celebrated *Fables*.

The potential ferocity of a dog did not diminish the affection many princes came to feel for them: the wolfhound portrayed alongside Charles V by Seisenegger in 1532 was his pet and almost certainly of Irish origin; the mastiff in *Las Meninas* was clearly a court dog, perfectly relaxed with the Spanish royal family. They symbolised strength without menace and divinely invested authority. Monarchs loved animals and they loved hunting – the gift of a dog could not fail to please. By the end of the seventeenth century, the

A mastiff bitch and puppy by an English amateur artist of the eighteenth century. Foreigners likened mastiffs to the British, alternately aggressive and lazy.

fashion for large dogs, at the breeding of which the Tudors and Stuarts had excelled, had waned. Pets might still accompany their royal masters to war but they would never again engage in battle as they had in the sixteenth century. The ascendancy of Versailles further undermined the popularity of large dogs. The French court during the seventeenth and eighteenth centuries displayed a marked preference for smaller breeds like the papillon and the Bolognese, a preference that would be emulated throughout Europe. Dynasties believed themselves firmly established and preferred baroque allegory to enhance the image of their power. The small dogs in royal portraiture of this period – in so far as they had any symbolic importance whatsoever – were there to indicate that the succession was secured and the dynasty firmly rooted. The upsurge of popularist movements throughout Europe in the wake of the French Revolution, and the threat to monarchies which they posed, led to the politicisation of dogs in the nineteenth century and a burgeoning fixation with the pure-bred 'national' dog.

In December 1844 King Louis-Philippe gave Victoria a French Pyrenean mountain dog, Gabbas, painted by Thomas Musgrove Joy the following year.

The dog proved extremely savage and bit the Queen badly in the arm, for which it was punished by exile to the Zoological Society. Similarly, in the 1860s the British breeder Mr Jennings of Pickering was paid handsomely for a Talbot hound, Welcome, by Prince Napoleon, who relished its French ancestry. In 1866, the year of the Treaty of Prague whereby Schleswig-Holstein passed, as a province, from Danish to Prussian rule, Bismarck sent Edward, Prince of Wales, a Russian dog, a Samoyed, probably the first specimen of the breed in England. Edward had married a Danish princess, Alexandra, three years previously, and she would have been mortified to receive a specimen of the Prussian chancellor's favourite breed, known in Germany as the *Deutsche Dogge* – but elsewhere as the Great Dane. Edward was also notoriously anti-German and pro-Russian. The Great Dane was a very ancient breed, known in the Middle Ages as the alaunt, probably after the Alauni, a Scandinavian tribe. Alternatively it may have been descended from the Molossi, the dogs described by Gratius in the first century AD as coming

T. M. Joy: Study of Gabbas, the Pyrenean mountain dog given by King Louis Philippe to Victoria, which bit the Queen.

from Epirus, formerly Molossus, and which Virgil praised in his *Georgics*. They were certainly familiar dogs in Renaissance Italy; the heraldic device of Gianfrancesco Mantua and his successors was a muzzled *cane alano*, designed by Pisanello, and dogs clearly identifiable as Great Danes appear in many paintings of the period. The only certainty about the breed is that it did not originate in Germany, and the British dog establishment rejected Prussian pressure to have the dog renamed. Before the 1860s, *Deutsche Dogge* had been but one of the many names by which the breed had been known in Germany — *Grosse Dogge* and *Dänische Dogge* were also in common usage. In 1883 HRH Prince Albert Solms, later the Kaiser's Lord Chamberlain, wrote to the editor of the *Kennel Gazette* suggesting that the Great Dane Club, then in the process of its formation, be called the Great German Dogge Club. The recommendation was spurned.[36] There may have been an element of black humour behind the decision of the Tsar to send Edward a Pomeranian, Beaty, shortly after Bismarck's gift of a Samoyed; Pomeranians, of the same spitz family as the Samoyed, were considered by the Russians to have originated in Siberia. Since the acquisition by Prussia of Swedish Pomerania in 1815 at the Treaty of Vienna, the spitz had been progressively collared as a German dog. Bismarck had purchased the Junker estate of Varzin in Pomerania in 1867. That the breed was so much admired at the Saxon court was largely due to the marriage in 1853 of Prince Albert to Caroline Vasa, daughter of Gustavus, Prince of Sweden. Countries laid claim to breeds in much the same way as they did territories, some with more justification than others. The Mikado sent Alexandra a Japanese spaniel, which the Queen named Togo; Tsar Nicholas II sent her a brace of borzois in 1893, the same year as he exhibited eighteen of his dogs at Cruft's. In Japan and Russia, as in China, ownership of imperial breeds was the exclusive prerogative of the ruling families who nonetheless occasionally offered them as gifts.

GIFTS OF GRACE AND FAVOUR

Gifts of animals from princes to commoners were considered a great honour. Count Esterhazy explained to his wife in a letter from Russia, where he was living in exile during the French Revolution: 'If between individuals, little presents sustain friendships, on the part of sovereigns they reflect true interest; they are often lavish with people to whom they are indifferent, either out of gratitude for services rendered, or for political reasons; but as they only give trifles to those whom they genuinely like one should be particularly appreciative.' Catherine the Great had given him a 'miniature black greyhound, with a white nose and tail, called Dido and very pretty'.[37] Bismarck was another beneficiary of imperial largesse. Such was the fame of his dog Tyras that when it died in 1889 the news was transmitted across the world and the Kaiser, feeling it incumbent on him to give him another on his birthday, applied to his minister, Botticher. When the new dog arrived Bismarck thought it wiser not to mention its protruding ribs and generally poor condition to the Kaiser when he came to congratulate him on his birthday. The firm that had supplied the dog subsequently asked permission to describe themselves as 'Dog Dealers to Prince Bismarck'.

Catherine the Great was introduced to greyhounds by her English physician Dr Dimsdale, who had presented her with a brace earlier in her reign. The bitch had her first litter in the Empress's bedroom, and thus was founded the noble breed of Russian greyhounds. Dimsdale, who had inoculated Catherine and her son Paul, was amply rewarded both materially and honorifically, becoming a baron of the empire. So legendary was Catherine's devotion to these dogs, which she tended personally and which accompanied her whenever she walked in the park at Tsarskoye Selo, that Pushkin even referred to them in his story *The Captain's Daughter*, where the Empress is described as sitting in the gardens with 'a little white dog of English breed' which she promised the heroine, Marya Ivanovna, 'did not bite'.[38]

Queen Victoria's already enormous retinue of dogs was further augmented when John, the brother of her physician, Sir James Reid, presented her with a Chinese chow in the 1890s. Reid became a regular visitor to the royal kennels and enjoyed long conversations with the kennelman. Victoria, in turn, gave Reid a three-month-old white Pomeranian puppy named Vicky, which stayed at Ellon, the family home, with Reid's mother. 'When she saw photographs of Vicky the Queen always complained that she was "too fat"',[39] a criticism she levelled at most of the dogs she encountered while herself generally opting to ignore medical advice counselling a reduction in her calorific intake. Similarly, Queen Victoria of Sweden, daughter of Frederick I, Grand Duke of Baden, paid tribute to the services, friend-

Hans Mielich: Ladislas of Fraunberg, Count of Haag. *Mielich was court painter to Albert V, Duke of Bavaria, who ordered the arrest of Ladislas in 1557—8. The leopard was the Count's pet and shared his confinement.*

Antonis Mor: Cardinal Granvelle's Dwarf, *c. 1550. Mor was in the service of Antoine Perrenot de Granvelle, Bishop of Arras, from 1548.*

ABOVE *Portrait by J. Heintz the Elder of the Hapsburg Emperor Ferdinand II with his dwarf and his dog. Ferdinand was twenty-six when he sat for this picture*

LEFT *Tiberio Titi:* The Medici Dogs with the Court Dwarf in the Boboli Gardens, Florence. *The dynasty's devotion to dogs was legendary and ended only with the line itself in the mid-eighteenth century.*

Diego Velásquez: Las Meninas, *1656. There are two dwarfs in the foreground,
Maribarbola and Nicolas de Pertusato, or Nicolasito, the latter with his foot on the mastiff.
Nicolas entered the royal household in 1651. It was possibly his insolence that led to the
wholesale removal of dwarfs from court after the accession of Philip V in 1700.*

ABOVE *Pisanello:* **The Vision of St Eustace.** *The picture records the dogs of Leonello d'Este, Duke of Ferrara.*

LEFT *Philip de László: study of a borzoi for the equestrian portrait of Kaiser William II, including a pencil sketch of the eventual portrait. De László made several studies for the official portrait of the Kaiser, painted at Wilhelmshöhe in the summer of 1909.*

Friedrich Wilhelm Keyl: Looty, 1861. This was one of the Pekingese looted from the Summer Palace and presented to Queen Victoria by an officer in the British Army.

Pekingese of the Imperial Palace. Only the ablest court artists were permitted to paint these idealised portraits of the Emperor's dogs.

Mazo's painting of the Hunt of the Tabladillo at Aranjuez, *1666, incl*

...ortraits of the same dwarf and mastiff as appear in Velásquez's El Inglés.

Madame de Pompadour with her spaniel Mimi, by François Boucher, 1759. Between 1747 and 1764 Madame de Pompadour was Boucher's most enthusiastic patron and he instructed her in the art of etching.

ship and love of animals she shared with her physician-in-ordinary, Axel Munthe, by giving him towards the end of his life Gorm, a German sheep-dog puppy which she had obtained from the Karlsruhe kennels run by her father. This was her second canine gift to her doctor for, while still Crown Princess, before 1907, she had given him a Lapland dog, Tappio.

Royal susceptibility to pets made them easy prey for ambitious subjects hoping to further their own interests. Children were discouraged from accepting gifts from strangers, and when, in 1608, the Dauphin Louis formed an attachment to two ostensibly stray *chiens d'Artois* he did not hesi-tate to return them to their owner when the latter presented himself at Fontainebleau offering them as a gift to the seven-year-old Prince. The Empress Eugenie who, unlike Louis, had not been raised to occupy a throne, fell into just such a trap when she accepted two turtle-doves from a young girl who, after a hiatus of six months, approached her for a position at court. In consequence, the Empress 'was very reluctant to grant petitions under cover of presents and refused them without compunction'.[40] Courtiers and favourites, familiar to their sovereigns, frequently gave them pets: Potemkin gave Catherine the Great a kitten and Fersen obtained a dog in his native Sweden for Marie Antoinette. George IV's daughter, Charlotte, was given a dog by a lady at court but it cannot have greatly fur-thered her career as the Princess expressed disappointment that it was not a pug. Queen Victoria received a great many including a Scottish deerhound, Hector, from Dundas in 1835, a Sussex spaniel puppy, Tilco, a gift from the Earl of Albemarle in 1838, and the large dog from Kashmir, Minka, presented by Lady Bloomfield in 1847, who had obtained it from Prince Wassiltchikoff, president of the Conseil de l'Empire in St Petersburg. Bout, a 'Cashmere pug', was given to the Queen by Lord Hardinge in 1848. She received an Eskimo dog from Captain Wemyss in 1843. In 1873 she was given a greyhound, Giddy, by Lord Lurgan, which died in 1882 and was painted by Charles Burton Barber in 1874. One of the Queen's all-time favourites was the collie Noble IV (being the fourth of that name in her possession), a gift from Lady Charles Innes-Kerr, daughter-in-law of the Duchess of Roxburghe, in 1872. The King's host in Ireland, Lord Dudley, presented Edward VII with an Irish terrier puppy in 1903 and he later received a chow-chow from Sir Henry Knollys, the brother of his private assistant, which had been brought no fewer than twelve thousand miles to Sandringham by a captain in the Indian army. Queen Alexandra was known to have a particular penchant for the Pekingese and received specimens as birthday gifts from both Lady Algernon Gordon Lennox and Mr Alfred Rothschild. She named the latter Xerxes.

Queen Victoria's Pekingese, aptly named Looty, was a gift from Captain John Hart Dunne of the 99th Regiment, a soldier serving in the Anglo-French army which had invaded China in 1860 to enforce the Treaty of Tientsin. One of the clauses of the treaty had stipulated that the Chinese should refrain from considering all foreigners as being descended from dogs and themselves alone as being human. When the invading forces stormed the Summer Palace they discovered five Pekingese dogs in the apartments of the aunt of the Emperor Hsien Feng. The smallest – it was probably a sleeve Pekingese – was taken by Dunne and given to the Queen, who had the bitch portrayed by Friedrich Wilhelm Keyl in 1861, sitting beside a Chinese vase. By way of thanks, Queen Victoria paid Keyl fifteen guineas to paint a replica for Captain Dunne. The dog evidently thrived in captivity at the royal kennels and lived until 1872.

Of the other four Pekingese taken by Admiral of the Fleet, Lord John Hay, two were given to the Duchess of Wellington, and the other brace to the Duchess of Richmond, who bred them at Goodwood. When fresh blood was needed for an outcross, Alfred de Rothschild tried through his agents in China to secure a palace dog, but he could obtain none despite efforts lasting two years. He discovered that the dogs were rigidly guarded and that theft was rigorously punished. By the time of the Boxer Rebellion in 1900, only spaniels, pugs and poodles were found at the imperial palace by the occupying allied forces: the Pekingese had gone with the court to Si-gnanfu.[41] Nonetheless, in 1896 Douglas Murray succeeded in smuggling out a brace, Ah Cum and Mimosa, in a box of hay placed inside a crate containing Japanese deer. These Pekingese were mated with the Goodwood dogs. Pekingese had in fact become readily obtainable from 1865, when a monthly fair lasting six days was first held in the Chinese capital selling the dogs deemed unworthy for the Emperor and Dowager Empress. The Duc de Morny, Napoleon III's half-brother, acquired several in the 1860s, possibly from French soldiers in the army of Gros who had joint command with Elgin of the invading forces in 1860. Palace associations lent cachet to the breed, however, and also inflated the price. Whether any of the Pekingese exhibited at the Peking Palace Association Shows in the early twentieth century were authentic descendants of the imperial Chinese dogs remains a moot point.

The Dowager Empress had never given away a Pekingese before her return to the capital in 1902 after the quelling of the Boxer Rebellion. Being unprecedented, the gift of imperial dogs to the representatives of those foreign powers to whom she owed her restoration was considered a unique honour. Both George Brown, British Consul in Shanghai, and Mrs Conger, wife of the American Minister in Peking, received a brace. It was on the recommendation of the latter that the American artist Katherine Carl was given the commission to paint the Empress's official portrait in 1903. In her revealing account of life in the closing years of dynastic China, Carl omitted to mention that none of the beneficiaries of the Dowager Empress's largesse was able to breed from their prestigious dogs as each Pekingese had been carefully doctored expressly to protect the purity of the imperial strain:[42]

On one of our walks, her dogs were brought out by their attendant eunuchs. Dogs are great favourites with all the Chinese, and especially with the Empress Dowager. She has some magnificent specimens of Pekingese pugs and a sort of Skye terrier. The pugs are bred with great care and have reached a high state of perfection, their spots being perfectly symmetrical and their hair beautifully long and silky, and they are of wonderful intelligence. The King Charles spaniels are said to have been bred out of the first of these dogs ever carried to Europe. The Empress Dowager has dozens of these pets, but she has favourites among them, and two are privileged characters. One of these is of the Skye variety, and is most intelligent and clever at tricks. Among other tricks, he will lie as dead at Her Majesty's command, and never move until she tells him to, no matter how many others may speak to him. Her other favourite she loves for his beauty. He is a splendid, fawn-coloured Pekingese pug, with large, pale-brown, liquid eyes. He is devoted to her, and she is very fond of him, but as he was not easily taught, even as a puppy, she called him 'Shadza' (fool). Her dogs all have most appropriate names, given by herself. They know Her Majesty's voice and will obey her slightest word.

The Empress Dowager does not care for the small sleeve-dog; she hates the thought of their being stunted by being fed only on sweets and wines. She says she cannot understand animals being deformed, at man's pleasure. The day we first met the dogs in the garden was the first time I had seen them. They rushed up to Her Majesty, not paying the slightest attention to anyone else. She patted their heads and caressed and spoke to her favourites. After a while they seemed to notice that a stranger was present, and they bounded over toward me. Some of them growled and showed other evidences of displeasure, some seemed surprised almost to fear; but as the instinct of a dog never deceives him as to who is his friend this was all soon changed to friendly greetings. I bent down to caress them, and forgot my surroundings, in my pleasure at seeing and fondling these beautiful creatures. I glanced up, presently, never dreaming Her Majesty had been paying any attention to me, as I was standing at a little distance behind her, and I saw on her face the first sign of displeasure I had noticed there. It seems her dogs never noticed anyone but herself, and she appeared not to like her pets being so friendly with a stranger at first sight. Noticing this, I immediately ceased fondling them, and they were presently sent away. It was but a momentary shadow that passed over her face, and I quite understood the feeling. One does not like to see one's pets too friendly with strangers, and I had been tactless in trying to make friends with them at once.

A few days later, on another of our walks, some young puppies were brought out to be shown the Empress Dowager. She caressed the mother and examined critically the points of the puppies. Then she called me up to show them to me, asking me which I liked best. I tried not to evince too much interest in them this time, but she called my attention to their fine points and insisted upon my taking each of them up. She seemed to be ashamed of her slight displeasure of the day before, and to wish to compensate for it.

The dogs at the Palace are kept in a beautiful pavilion with marble floors. They have silken cushions to sleep on and special eunuchs to attend them. They are taken for daily outdoor exercise and given their baths with regularity. There are hundreds of dogs in the Palace, the young Empress, the Princesses and Ladies, and even the eunuchs, having their own. Some of the eunuchs are great fanciers and breeders of them. One of them still breeds the sleeve-dog. Her Majesty's known dislike to these latter is probably the cause of fewer being bred in the Palace now than formerly, and the race is slowly dying out. All the other dogs in the Palace, except Her Majesty's, are kept in the apartments and courts of their owners, and are not seen by her.

The pavilion at the Summer Palace where the Empress Dowager's dogs were kept was near her Throneroom, and also near the pavilion she had set aside for me. When the Court was taking its siesta, I used to go out where the dogs were basking in the sun in their court and look at and play with these interesting little animals. I was free to do as I pleased and no-one but the dogs' guardian eunuch saw me there.

Among the younger set, of these pampered pets, was one that caught my fancy – one of those which had been brought for Her Majesty to look at in the garden. He was a beautiful white-and-amber-coloured Pekingese pug. He soon learned to know me and would come running to me when I crossed the threshold of the court. Not long after I had discovered where the dogs were kept and had been paying them my daily visits, one night, when we had finished dinner at Her Majesty's table, one of her eunuchs brought in this very little dog and put it in my arms, saying, Her Majesty had presented it to me from her own kennel! She had evidently learned of my visits to the dogs, though none of the eunuchs around her person had seen me go there, at least so I thought! I was delighted to own this beautiful animal, and when the Empress Dowager came into the Throneroom from her own apartments, I went up to her and kissed her hand and thanked her for it. She seemed much pleased that I had liked it, and remarked that she had heard it was my favourite of her dogs, that I was to call him 'Me-lah' (Golden Amber), from the colour of his spots. Her Majesty and the Princesses were all much amused at the way he followed me around, not leaving my side for an instant, nor paying any attention to their frequent efforts to attract his attention. From that day, he became my constant companion and faithful friend.[43]

Having won the confidence of the Empress, Carl was commissioned to paint her unofficial portrait with two of the favourite imperial Pekingese, Shadza and Hailo, for which the latter wore 'gala costume', consisting of 'two huge chrysanthemums tied in his hair over his ears'. The Empress apparently 'took the liveliest interest in the painting of the dogs' portraits, and seemed to think it much more wonderful to paint these little animals, so that they were recognisable, than to make a likeness of herself'.[44]

Sentimental Gifts

The exchange of canine and feline gifts between members of royal families was a matter of course generally prompted by purely sentimental and affective impulses. The necessity for forging dynastic alliances frequently entailed the definitive separation of parents from their children and siblings from each other. Even after the invention of the steamship and the railway had revolutionised travel, royal families were only rarely reunited. Contact was maintained through voluminous correspondence and the exchange of presents, of which pets – and their portraits – constituted a large proportion. Anne of Cleves in 1548, Henrietta Maria in 1627 and her daughter, Henrietta, Duchesse d'Orléans in 1670, all sent dogs to their royal, canophile brothers. Frederick the Great accompanied his gift of a bichon to his sister, Queen Louisa Ulrica of Sweden, in 1772 with a poem of his own composition, 'To a Bitch':

> How I envy you, Oh bichon! your imminent good fortune,
> My heart would like to snatch from you
> The destiny which places you in the Queen's hands,
> And which devotes you to her service,
> Ah! if heaven were to grant
> That I might be transformed into your shape,
> I would before all else take your place;
> To serve her, admire her, would be my joy.[45]

Queen Victoria received a large number of dogs from her relations. She had so many by the age of nineteen that Lord Melbourne warned she would be 'smothered with dogs'. One of her earliest pets, Dash, had originally belonged to her mother, the far from disinterested gift of Sir John Conroy in 1833. Three months later Princess Victoria appropriated the spaniel and, for Christmas that year, she gave it 'three india-rubber balls and two bits of gingerbread decorated with holly and candles. Dash showed his devotion by jumping into the sea and swimming after her yacht; when she was ill he spent 'his dear little life' in her room.[46] Edwin Landseer received his first royal commission when asked to paint Dash's portrait in 1836. Victoria's cousin, Alphonse Mensdorff, gave her two Hungarian Transylvanian sheepdogs aged five months in 1843; the Crown Prince of Prussia sent Fermach, a pug, in 1845; the dachshunds Dalkiel and Waldina were gifts from her Coburg relations, as were Vulcan, a German boar-hound, and Briach the mastiff. The German nobility had a virtual monopoly of dachshunds and were reluctant to part with a puppy unless it be to a relative. The best were bred by the King of Hanover in the north and the Grand Duke of Baden at Eberstein Schloss in the south. It was from the latter that Victoria received Waldmann in 1872. The dogs the Queen cherished above all others were those she received from Prince Albert, such as Dandie Dinmont, a birthday present in 1842, which died in 1858 aged nineteen. Victoria loved all things Scottish; in 1858, she gave her mother a Skye terrier called Boz which remained the Duchess's constant companion until her death in 1861 when the Queen took it under her wing. Boy, a smooth-haired dachshund, painted by Keyl in 1861, had belonged successively to Charles, Prince of Leiningen, the Duchess of Kent and the Queen. Similarly, Nero, the large black dog of the Prince Imperial, had belonged initially to his father Napoleon III, a gift from the Russian ambassador to Paris after the Crimean War. Jean-Baptiste Carpeaux, the Prince Imperial's drawing master from 1864, sculpted a statue of the eleven-year-old boy with Nero in 1867. The gift of animals – or animal-related artefacts – to children could have ulterior, albeit not necessarily sinister, motives. During her state visit to Napoleon III, her ally in the Crimean War in 1855, Queen Victoria noted in her journal[47] how 'the Emperor and Empress had a table covered with toys they had brought for the children: a doll and trousseau, beautiful soldiers for Arthur, a panorama, games, a beautiful little picture of a dog *en Gobelin* for Vicky, and finally, two beautiful models of the nine-pounders the Emperor has himself invented, and which he showed off with great pleasure. He is so very quiet, good-natured and unassuming and natural, if one may use such a word.' Victoria and Albert gave many pet dogs to their children, including the Skye terrier, Corran, named after Corran Ferry where the Prince had acquired it, to the Duke of Edinburgh. Brought from Scotland in 1863, it died in 1877 and was painted by Charles Burton Barber in 1872.

Royal Appropriation

In 1599, the capricious mistress of Henri IV, Henriette d'Entragues, Marquise de Verneuil (1579–1633), took such a fancy to the miniature greyhound of the King's High Constable, Montmorency, that he had little choice but to give it to her. Henri wrote to thank him 'for your beautiful bitch ... which I immediately sent to mademoiselle d'Entragues, who received it with all the grace befitting he who gave it to me and her beauty; and she is already busily occupied in arranging its marriage with her dog'.[48] Catherine the Great recalled in her memoirs how she too had had to forfeit a treasured pet when it transferred its affections elsewhere. In 1750, twelve years before she ascended the throne, she was given a 'small English poodle' by her husband, the Grand Duke Peter. The gift was bestowed at a time when the Empress Elizabeth's favourite, Ivan Ivanovich Shuvalov, had attracted the opprobrium of all the court.

> I gave the dog into the charge of a stoker in our service named Ivan Ushakov. I do not know how it occurred to the other servants to call the dog Ivan Ivanovich after him.
>
> This poodle was indeed an amusing animal; he walked on his hind paws like a human being most of the time and was exceedingly playful; my women and I dressed him every day and the more he was dressed up the more playful he became. He sat with us at table, with a napkin round his neck and ate very neatly from his plate; then he would turn his head and ask for a drink, yapping at the man who stood behind him. Sometimes he would climb on the table to get what he wanted, a cake or a biscuit or something of the sort, which always made everyone laugh.
>
> As he was small he did not annoy anybody and was allowed to do as he liked, because he never abused the liberty he enjoyed and was extremely clean. This dog served to entertain us all the winter. The next summer I brought him to Oranienbaum. When Chamberlain Saltikov the younger arrived there with his wife, she and all the other ladies of our Court did nothing but sew clothes and devise hair-styles for my poodle; they all wanted to have him. Finally, Madame Saltikov took such a fancy to him that he became entirely devoted to her and when she went away the poodle would not let her go, nor she the poodle, and she begged me so much to let her take him that I gave him to her. She took him under her arm and went straight to the country to her mother-in-law, who was ill at the time: seeing her arrive

with the dog and behaving quite insanely with him, the old lady wanted to know the pup's name. When told it was Ivan Ivanovich, she could not help expressing her astonishment in front of several Court ladies who had come to see her from Peterhof. The ladies came back to court and three or four days later the whole town and the Court were seething with the rumour that all the young ladies who disliked M Shuvalov each had a white poodle which they had called Ivan Ivanovich to ridicule the Empress's favourite, and that they made these poodles do heaven knows what and dressed them up in the same light colours which Shuvalov himself affected.

Matters went so far that the Empress let the young women's parents know that she found it impertinent that they allowed their daughters to behave in such a way. The poodle at once changed his name but was made as much of as before in the Saltikovs' house where he stayed until his death, cherished by his masters, in spite of the Imperial reprimand.

It had, in any case, been the merest gossip, for only one dog – a black one at that – had been really called by that name and nobody had thought of M Shuvalov when giving it to him.

As to Madame Choglokov [Catherine's lady-in-waiting], who did not like the Shuvalovs, she pretended not to notice the dog's name, though she had often heard it, and given him many a little cake, laughing at his absurdities and pranks.[49]

BREEDERS

Ever since the Crusades there had been a continuous traffic between the eastern and western Mediterranean. Arab horses and greyhounds, exchanged against the luxury goods in the production of which the Italian peninsula excelled, were highly prized by the rulers of the city-states for use in sport and war. During the Renaissance the taste for the exotic broadened the horizons of these princes to include the toy dog, unfamiliar since pagan times. The works of the classical natural historians, freshly translated by humanist scholars, provided important information on breeding methods which proved to be of a type used by the Chinese since time immemorial.

In his *Zoology*, written in the third century AD, Aelian stated that to keep them small toy dogs were shut up in boxes where they were fed on the choicest dishes and that these boxes were lined with sheepskins so that by some osmotic process they too would produce litters with shaggy coats. By the beginning of the sixteenth century many paintings attest to the popularity of the Maltese in the city-states of northern Italy. Carpaccio and Titian include them in their works, the latter famously in his portraits of Federico Gonzaga and Philip II of Spain. Both painters were natives of Venice, the city to which Isabella d'Este sent her agent Brognolo to procure Syrian and Tibetan cats, bred in the convents, and where she most probably acquired some of her little dogs as well, such as her favourite Aura.[50] Catherine de Medici obtained her dogs from Venice after becoming Queen of France in 1533.

As a result of Charles VIII's invasion of the peninsula in 1494–5, many Italians settled in Lyon, where they specialised in the provision of luxury goods for which they enjoyed an unrivalled reputation. Lyon thus became the earliest Renaissance city in France. The ultra-royalism of the city, and her advantageous geographical position at a time when much of France was under English domination, ensured that the links between Lyon and Paris were very strong. The annexation of Provence in 1481 facilitated commerce in the Mediterranean and, as Renaissance merchants required no passports and those serving the French Crown were exempt from toll and guild regulations, handsome profits were guaranteed. The *chiens de Lyon* were immensely popular at the courts of Catherine de Medici's sons and their royal consorts; Mary Stuart, Queen of Francis II, favoured them and had them shipped to her when she returned as a widow to Scotland in 1561. The early naturalist Konrad Gesner (1516–65) saw Maltese dogs on sale at one of the fairs held in the city four times a year. Although the religious wars that beset France between 1562 and 1598 led to the fairs being transferred to Chalons and to Lyon's eclipse by Bologna, E. Topsell recorded that the sale of these dogs still continued a decade later:

a little French dog, for about Lyons in France there are store of this kind and sold very deare, sometimes for ten crownes and sometimes more. They are not above a foot long and always the lesser the more delicate and precious. Their head is like the head of a mouse, but greater, their snowt sharpe, their ears like that of a cony, short legs, little feete, long taile, and white colour, and the haires about the shoulder longer than ordinary is most commended. They are of pleasant disposition and will leape and bite without pinching, and bark prettily, and some of them are taught to stand upright, holding up their forelegs like hands to fetch and carry in their mouths that which is cast unto them. There are some wanton women which admit them to their beds, and bring up their young ones in their own bosomes, for they are so tender that they seldome bring above one at a time, but they loose their life.[51]

As a result of the religious wars these *chiens de Lyon* were subsequently bred in Bologna where they became known as *bottoli*. Ulisse Aldrovandi (1522–1605), a native of Bologna where he was professor of botany and and later of natural history at the university, testified to their being sold there. He reported that a *bottoli* puppy was sold to a Bolognese monk for four hundred livres and that they were fed by duchesses in the peninsula from gold vessels.[52] It was, however, as the centre of the trade in small spaniels that Bologna excelled. These Bolognese were bred commercially as early as 1545 when Anne, future wife of the Prince of Orange, purchased one, and Henri III brought some back to France after his flight from Poland

through Italy in 1574. It was in the seventeenth century, however, that they achieved the pinnacle of their glory. The Bolognese breeder Giovanni Maria Filipponi supplied many courts, but none as lucratively as that of the French King Louis XIV. For twelve years his freight of dogs was carried in crates by mule across the Alps and presented for inspection to the King, who had first choice and paid handsomely for a specimen that particularly pleased him.[53] While Filipponi enjoyed the most celebrated custom there were other breeders

Detail of the spaniel from Largillière's **Louis XIV and his Heirs.** *The Bolognese at the French court were bred by Giovanni Maria Filipponi and carried by mule to Versailles in crates.*

in Bologna, including the Mendicants, whose methods John Evelyn described disapprovingly when he visited the city in 1645:[54] 'Many of the religious men nourish these lap-dogs which the ladies are so fond of and which they here sell. They are a pygmy sort of spaniel, whose noses they break when puppies; which, in my opinion, deforms them.' But their popularity with the French King was a guarantee of the breed's rise to stardom, for there was no greater arbiter of fashion by the late seventeenth century than the court of Versailles. Bologna's reputation as a centre of dog-breeding was still strong in the 1780s when William Beckford described the city as 'that celebrated mart of lap-dogs and sausages'.[55]

In Venice, in Bologna and also in Paris, pet dogs and cats were bred in convents and monasteries, where the industry represented an important source of revenue. Henri III of France was not beyond stealing them when he wanted to augment his already enormous collection. L'Estoile noted how, in November 1575, the King went 'by carriage, with the Queen his wife, through all the streets and houses of Paris appropriating the little ladies' dogs [*petits chiens damarets*] which happily depart with them; similarly goes to all the convents in the outskirts of Paris on a like quest for dogs, to the great regret and annoyance of the ladies to whom the dogs belong'.[56] In the thirteenth century cats had been ordained the only animals to be allowed in nunneries but, when Pope Innocent VIII issued his bull against sorcerers in 1484, they became associated with devil-worship and were replaced by small, feline dogs, devoid of satanic association but as suited as their ill-fated predecessors to life within the palace. Hence the presence at the effeminate court of Henri III's predecessor and brother, Charles IX, of wild dogs, no larger than cats and called Adives, originally from India, which the King imported at enormous expense from Asia.[57]

Physiological advances and political events combined to break the Italian monopoly. The Huguenots were soon adept at imitating their techniques and, with the Revocation of the Edict of Nantes in 1685 and their subsequent expulsion from France, they brought their skills to the countries that offered them sanctuary. As these countries were necessarily Protestant, northern Europe had soon achieved mastery in this field. From their London base in Spitalfields, the Huguenots proved immensely successful at breeding the French dogs with which they were most familiar and, despite competition from the Blenheim strain, the French toy spaniel remained a popular species at court and among the aristocracy until the nineteenth century. Pets were given French names to match their nationality; Queen Charlotte's was called Badine. But if, in England, French toy spaniels had become the height of fashion, in France it was the King Charles spaniel which was most admired. The curly King Charles spaniel was most probably bred from the Spanish truffle dog imported to England under Charles I. Henrietta, sister of Charles II, took several with her to France when she married the King's brother, the Duc d'Orléans, in 1661, and by the reign of Louis XV they had become so popular that courtiers sent agents to England to procure specimens.[58] On 19 January 1766 Horace Walpole wrote to his friend Anne Pitt from Paris relating how he had met the Princesse de Talmond, a Polish relative of the French Queen, who 'did not know what to say to me, and dismissed me with begging I would get her a lap-dog'.

Monasteries and convents had specialised in the breeding of the toy dogs that were found so appealing by the aristocracy and at court. During the Renaissance, Italian ducal families themselves bred dogs to extremely high standards, particularly in Mantua, Ferrara and Florence. Catherine and Marie de Medici, through their marriages to French kings, introduced a taste for royal dog-breeding to the Valois and Bourbon courts. Charles IX, Catherine's son, bred miniature white greyhounds which he occasionally bestowed as gifts; he gave no fewer than six to Madame de Sipierre, the wife of his first tutor. On marrying Henri IV in 1600, Marie de Medici took great pride in rearing white spaniels which she gave away as presents, particularly to her relatives among the Italian ducal houses. Italian influence ensured that the previous concentration on hunting breeds no longer predominated and small dogs found favour at courts across Europe with both kings and queens. In England, aristocratic breeders broadened their interests from the thoroughbred racehorse which had previously been their chief concern to include livestock and dogs – a process facilitated by the spread of enclosure. The kennels maintained by many noble English families since the fifteenth century nevertheless remained almost exclusively occupied by hunting dogs of such calibre that they were widely admired on the Continent. Lady Lisle, the wife of the Lord Deputy of Calais in the reign of Henry VIII, was constantly approached for specimens of her white greyhounds and mastiffs. These she supplied to dignitaries on both sides of the Channel, and one of her principal clients was the Constable of Francis I, Duc Anne de Montmorency. White greyhounds were particularly sought after at this period, and the brace that features in the painting of the *Field of Cloth of Gold* was a gift to Henry VIII from his brother-in-law, the Duke of Suffolk, in 1536.[59] The Leghs at Lyme Park, with their particular strain of mastiffs, were probably the most famous English breeders of the late six-teenth century. The Leghs had been breeding these dogs since at least 1415, when a Lyme mastiff fought at the Battle of Agincourt.

Supplying the court with dogs brought favours; in 1584 Sir Piers Legh gave a Lyme mastiff to the Earl of Leicester, favourite of Elizabeth I, who wrote to acknowledge the gift:

Ffor yor hounde and for yor hynde, sent me by yor Servante, I do right hartely thank you; I perceyve you will not forget me and assure yor selfe that as occasion shall serve, I will not be unmyndefull of yor Continewall remembrance of me. And so praying you to make assured accompt, with my right harty commendacons, and lyke thankes, I bid you ffarewell

ffro the Courte the XIXth

of November, 1584.

Yor very louinge frend

R. Leycester

I thanke you very hartiley Sr Piers for yor hounde and will requyte you the loose of him with as good a thinge.[60]

The Lyme Park kennels were to supply mastiffs across the globe until the family's Jacobite sympathies lost them favour at the Hanoverian court. Leicester's position at court as principal dispenser of political patronage made him a frequent recipient of propitiatory gifts: in 1562, Shane O'Neill, a descendant of the ancient kings of Ireland, had sent him two Irish wolfhounds with the request that he exert influence on his behalf with Queen Elizabeth. One of these dogs, Boye, can be seen in the portrait of the Earl painted c. 1564 by an anonymous artist of the Anglo-Netherlandish school. Behind the garter arms in the painting are two Ionic columns, the emblem of the Hapsburg Emperor, Charles V, and the pose of the dog is clearly modelled on Titian's portrait of the Emperor with his Irish wolfhound. Attempts to curry favour through the gift of dogs did not always succeed, however, and when Brian O'Rourke from Connaught arrived in Glasgow in 1591 with four Irish wolfhounds to be presented to James VI, he was seized as a rebel on the instructions of Elizabeth I.[61]

At the end of the seventeenth century, James II obtained his springer spaniels from the kennels of the Duke of Norfolk, presumably because he only wanted dogs of unquestionable Catholic faith, and for a long time they were known as Norfolk spaniels. So notorious was James's devotion to one particular spaniel, Mumper, that when in 1682 his ship, the *Gloucester*, went down in Yarmouth Roads, James was accused of abandoning all but his dogs and his priests. Mumper was said to have struggled with Sir Charles Scarburgh for a plank, but they both survived and the latter acted as Charles II's chief physician at his death in 1685. The story was probably fabricated to belittle the Stuarts. Norfolk fed inferior spaniels to his eagles, and when a stranger who happened to witness this slaughter asked if he might be allowed to keep one the Duke allegedly replied: 'Pray, sir, which of my estates should you like to have?'[62] Clumber spaniels were named after the Nottinghamshire estate of the Duke of Newcastle, where he bred them from the original dogs given to him by the Duc de Noailles shortly before the French Revolution. Newcastle's kennels supplied Prince Albert with Clumbers when he started his breeding programme.

After a hiatus of some two hundred years, European princes of the nineteenth century once again turned their personal attention to breeding animals. The enormous interest in natural history generated in the course of the eighteenth century had coincided with an increasingly secular attitude to scientific experimentation and a weakening of theological orthodoxy, with its insistence on an unbreakable Great Chain of Being. In France, in 1773, an attempt to cross a mastiff with a she-wolf proved as fruitless as a similar experiment made by Buffon to cross foxes and bitches. Royal breeding programmes of the nineteenth century applied eugenics to the strengthening of pure-bred pedigree stock and, unlike their aristocratic subjects, were not exclusively preoccupied with hunting dogs. Queen Victoria and Prince Albert were notoriously catholic in their canine tastes. One of the breeds she particularly admired was the pug, the archetypal pet

Field of the Cloth of Gold. *The greyhounds in the picture, only given to Henry VIII in 1536, cou*
King by the Duke of Suffolk, but the most famous greyhound breeder of the period was Lady Lisle, wife

have attended the famous meeting between Henry VIII and Francis I in 1520. They were given to the Lord Deputy of Calais.

in so far as it served no practical purpose whatsoever, and she started her pug breeding programme with Olga, Pedro, Minka, Fatima and Venus. Virtually all Victoria's dogs, irrespective of their country of origin, had impeccably noble and royal credentials. Her basset hounds were all descended from a brace, Babil and Bijou, presented to her by the Comtesse de Paris, wife of the claimant to the French throne, who bred them herself in exile at Stowe in Buckinghamshire. Many of Victoria's German relatives were highly competent breeders, patronised by royal families across the Continent. The King of Württemberg had a prestigious kennel at Stuttgart which specialised in toy spaniels. Louise-Sophie, sister-in-law of the future Kaiser William II, recalled how 'One day on my way to my music lesson in Stuttgart I met a man with a Bologna dog and several puppies. I had always wanted a little white dog and my mother having given her permission (and the money) I went again to Stuttgart and bought one, thus realising one of the dreams of my early life. I called my little pet Stutto, and he accompanied me to Glienecke on my marriage.'[63] The King of Hanover, the Grand Duke of Baden, Prince Edward of Saxe-Weimar and Prince Karl of Prussia all shared a deep personal interest in breeding dogs.

Prince Karl's first wife had been the sister of Tsar Nicholas I, and it was doubtless through her that he developed his interest in borzois, becoming the breed's first champion in Germany. Until the abolition of serfdom in 1861, borzois had been bred exclusively by members of the Russian aristocracy and were virtually unknown outside the empire. Thereafter, many of the kennels had to be dispersed and some of the dogs were acquired by breeders in England, Germany and the USA. In England, the kennels of the Duchess of Newcastle at Clumber soon established a reputation as the most prestigious. Those owned and bred by the British royal family originated as gifts from the Tsar in the 1870s when the 'Imperial Association for the Propagation of Hounds and Regulation of Hunting' had been formed to save the breed from the extinction with which it had been threatened by the events of 1861. From 1873 borzois were bred by members of the imperial family, and principally by the Grand Duke Nicholas Nicholaevich, at whose kennel in Perchino were raised the best specimens, far finer than those of the Tsar. Occasionally offered to fellow sovereigns as gifts, borzois could be purchased for extremely high prices, inflated by

Philip de László: study of a borzoi. The artist worked on the dogs both from photographs and life. The finished painting remains untraced. The Kaiser, who never owned a borzoi, nonetheless regarded them as more suitable than his dachshunds for an official portrait.

their association with the Russian monarchy and, unlike other surviving members of the imperial family, Grand Duke Nicholas was able to live very comfortably after fleeing from Russia in 1917 on the proceeds of the sales of borzois he had made in the preceding years. Notwithstanding his personal preference for dachshunds, the Kaiser decided to be painted alongside a borzoi when he commissioned an official portrait from Philip de László in 1909, and had a brace sent up to Wilhelmshöhe from Chemnitz in Saxony for the artist to use as models. The elegance and prestige of the breed made it a more fitting companion for an emperor in a portrait destined for public display.

Queen Victoria's kennels, and those of the Prince of Wales at Sandringham, together with the entry of some of their dogs at the newly founded dog shows, enormously influenced the anglophile Indian princes under the Raj. The Maharajahs of Patiala, Jhind, Darbhanga and Junagadh all bred dogs and competed to procure the best specimens from

Cruft's. The kennels of the Maharajah of Jhind were considered the best in the country in the 1930s, each dog being valued at several thousand pounds sterling. He held an annual Dog Week which attracted dog fanciers from across the Subcontinent. Royal interest in dog-breeding remains undiminished in Great Britain, where HM the Queen rears Labradors, Pembrokeshire Welsh corgis and dorgis – dachshund/corgi hybrids. The Sandringham strain of black Labradors was founded by Queen Alexandra in 1911. When she died in 1925 George V changed the affix from Wolferton to Sandringham. George VI re-established the kennel, 'closed' by Edward VIII in 1936, with half a dozen golden Labradors. In 1968 the buildings were replaced by smaller wooden structures accommodating up to forty dogs which are both bred and named by the Queen herself, and which she occasionally presents to heads of state or fellow sovereigns: in the 1970s she gave Giscard d'Estaing, the French President, Sandringham Samba, and the King of Spain's Labradors are from the same kennel. The original royal corgi was purchased by George VI, when Duke of York, in 1933. Named Golden Eagle, it bore the affix of the Rozavel kennels in Surrey, where it had been born. Three years later a mate was provided, a bitch called Jane. Susan, the corgi given to Princess Elizabeth in 1944, became the matriarch of a dynasty still flourishing to this day. Although a breed of ancient lineage, the corgi was a relatively rare pet until royal patronage rescued it from the doldrums. The first dorgis were the result of cross-breeding one of the Queen's corgis, Tiny, with Princess Margaret's dachshund, Pipkin. Not only do few aristocrats interest themselves in breeding any longer but, with the dorgi, the Queen has pioneered a movement away from the current obsession with pedigree.

Notes

CHAPTER I

1. Munthe, Axel, *The Story of San Michele* (London, 1990), pp. 52–3.
2. Windsor, Edward, Duke of, *A King's Story* (London, 1951), p. 192.
3. Palatine, Princess: *Letters of Madame, Duchess of Orleans.* 2 vols, trans G. S. Stevenson (London, 1924). 2.85–6.
4. Quoted in Castelot, André, *Napoleon*, trans. Robert Baldick (London, 1960), p. 183.
5. Héroard, Jean, *Journal*, 2 vols (Paris, 1868). 1.187.
6. Quoted in Stone, Lawrence, *The Family, Sex and Marriage in England 1500–1800* (London, 1979), p. 120.
7. Frédéric II, *Oeuvres historiques*, 30 vols (Berlin, 1846–56). 27.183.
8. Maylunas, Andrei and Mironenko, Sergei, *A Life Long Passion. Nicholas & Alexandra. Their Own Story* (London, 1996), p. 473.
9. Ibid, p. 478.
10. Ibid, p. 404.
11. Fraser, Antonia, *Mary Queen of Scots* (London, 1970), p. 200.
12 & 13. Windsor, op. cit., pp. 6, 11.
14. Hardinge, Lord, *My Indian Years 1910–1916* (London, 1948), p. 95.
15. Sophia, Electress of Hanover, *Memoirs*, trans. H. Forester (London, 1888), p. 3.
16. Fischer, Henry W., *The Private Lives of William II and his Consort. A Secret History of the Court of Berlin* (London, 1904), p. 145.
17. Wilhelmine, Frédérique, Sophie, Margrave de Bareith, *Mémoires*, 2 vols (London, 1812). 1.329.
18. Ibid. 1.329.
19. Pepys, Samuel, *Diary*, 11 vols, ed. Latham & Matthews (London, 1970). 8.452.
20. Palatine, op. cit. 1.41.
21. Ibid. 2.118.
22. Ibid. 1.26.
23. Ibid. 1.27.
24. Ibid. 1.130.
25. Ibid. 1.196.
26. Catherine the Great, *Memoirs*, trans. Moura Budberg (London, 1955), p. 227.
27. Ibid, p. 283.
28. Fulford, Roger (ed.), *Your Dear Letter: Private Correspondence of Queen Victoria & the Crown Princess of Prussia, 1865–71* (London, 1971), p. 205.
29. Ibid, pp. 90, 115.
30. Ibid, p. 343.
31. Paoli, Xavier, *My Royal Clients* (London, 1911), p. 354.
32. Haslip, Joan, *The Lonely Empress* (London, 1965), p. 85.
33. Larisch, Marie-Louise, Countess Larisch von Wallersee-Wittelsbach, *Secrets of a Royal House* (London, 1935), pp. 138–9.
34. Palmer, Allen, *The Twilight of the Hapsburgs* (London, 1994), pp. 149–50.
35. Haslip, op. cit., p. 219.
36. Ibid, p. 330.
37. Ormathwaite, Lord, *When I Was at Court* (London, 1937), pp. 82–3.
38. Hervey, Lord, *Memoirs* (London, 1984), p. 12.
39. Solnon, Jean-François, *La Cour de France* (Paris, 1987), p. 170.
40. L'Estoile, Pierre de, *Journal du Règne de Henri III* (Paris, 1943), p. 187.
41. Frédéric II, op. cit. 27.8.
42. Gooch, G. P., *Frederick the Great* (London, 1947), p. 114.
43. Héroard, op. cit. 2.230.
44. Ibid. 1.431.
45. Hartmann, C. H., *Charles II & Madame* (London, 1934), p. 43.
46. Palatine, op. cit. 1.65; 1.131; 2.185.

47. Sévigné, Madame de, *Correspondance*, 3 vols (Paris, 1974). I.616.
48. Pepys, op. cit. 4.112.
49. Catherine the Great, op. cit., p. 300.
50. Ibid, pp. 249–50.
51. Ibid, p. 297.
52. Motteville, Madame de, *Memoirs*, 3 vols (London, 1902). I.46.
53. Palatine, op. cit. 2.209.
54. Ibid. I.220.
55. Hausset, Madame de, *Mémoires* (Paris, 1882), p. 87.
56. Ibid, p. 51.
57. Dufort de Cheverny, Comte de, *Mémoires*, 2 vols (Paris, 1909). I.93.
58. Hausset, op. cit., p. 59.
59. Burnet, Bishop, *History of my own times*, 6 vols (London, 1833). I.472.
60. Motteville, op. cit. I.224–5.
61. Solnon, op. cit., p. 286.
62. Ibid, p. 344.
63. Ibid, p. 315.
64. Palatine, op. cit. I.168.
65. Pepys, op. cit. 7.201.
66. Lenotre, G., *Versailles au temps des Rois* (Paris, 1934), p. 122.
67. D'Orléans, A. M. L., Mademoiselle de Montpensier, *Memoirs* (Paris, 1848), p. 72.
68. Evelyn, John, *Diary and Correspondence*, 4 vols (London, 1850). 3.261.
69. Motteville, op. cit. I.70.
70. Windsor, op. cit., p. 287.
71. Pope, Alexander, *Correspondence*, 5 vols, ed. George Sherburn (Oxford, 1956). I.75.
72. Carré, Henri, *Jeux, Sports et Divertissements des Rois de France* (Paris, 1937), p. 127.
73. Pepys, op. cit. 8.421.
74. Burnet, op. cit. I.170.
75. Waliszewski, K., *Peter the Great* (London, 1898), p. 196.
76. Frédéric II, op. cit.17.183.
77. Alexander, Grand Duke, *Always a Grand Duke* (New York, 1995), p. 173.
78. Collier, V. W. F., *Dogs of China & Japan in Nature and Art* (London, 1921), p. 12.
79. Commynes, Philippe de, *Memoirs* (London, 1972), pp. 392–3.
80. Volker, T., *The Animal in Far Eastern Art* (Leyden, 1950), p. 46.
81. Varé, Daniele, *Last of the Empresses* (London, 1936), pp. 224–5.
82. Carré, op. cit., p. 12.
83. Héroard, op. cit. 2.132.
84. Thomas, Keith, *Man & the Natural World 1500–1800* (London, 1983), p. 274.
85. Alexander, op. cit., p. 270.
86. Hartmann, op. cit., p. 324.
87. Palatine, op. cit. I.92.
88. Sévigné, op. cit. 2.342–3.
89. Solnon, op. cit., pp. 43–4.
90. Freville, A. F. J., *Histoire des Chiens Célèbres*, 2 vols (Paris, 1796). I.173–4.
91. Richelieu, Maréchal Duc de, *Mémoires*, 2 vols (Paris, 1889). 2.146–7.
92. Fraser, op. cit., p. 220.
93. Ibid, p. 531.
94. Tanner MS in Maxwell Scott, *The Hon. Mrs: The Tragedy of Fotheringhay*, (London, 1895), p. 235.
95. Steegmuller, Francis, *La Grande Mademoiselle* (London, 1959), p. 116.
96. Ibid, p. 128.
97. Arneth, A. R. von, *Maria Theresa und Marie Antoinette. Ihr Briefwechsel. 1770–1780* (Vienna, 1865), p. 42.
98. Soderhjelm, Alma, *Fersen et Marie Antoinette* (Paris, 1930), pp. 101–2.
99. Ibid, p. 246.
100. Lenotre, G., *The Last Days of Marie Antoinette* (London, 1907), p. 173.
101. Soderhjelm, op. cit., p. 349.
102. Ibid, p. 342.
103. Hue, F., *Dernières Années du Règne et de la Vie de Louis XVI* (Paris, 1816), p. 465.
104. Delille, J., *Oeuvres*, 15 vols (Paris, 1824). 12.23.
105. Gooch, G. P., *Catherine the Great and Other Studies* (London, 1954), p. 19.
106. Salm-Salm, Princess, *Ten Years of My Life*, 2 vols (London, 1876). 2.129.
107. Paoli, op. cit., p. 139.
108. Vorrès, Ian, *The Last Grand Duchess* (London, 1964), p. 86.
109. Ibid, p. 103.
110. Ibid, p. 115.

111. Maylunas & Mironenko, op. cit., p. 442.

112. Ibid, pp. 594–5.

113. Chauchavadre, Paul, *Because the Night was Dark* (London, 1966), p. 487 and Radzinsky, Edvard, *The Last Tsar* (London, 1992), p. 333.

114. Maylunas & Mironenko, op. cit., p. 635.

115. Radzinsky, op. cit., p. 103.

116. *The Sokolov Investigation of the Alleged Murder of the Russian Imperial Family*, trans. John F. O'Conor (London, 1972), p. 105.

117. Bluche, F., *Louis XIV* (Paris, 1990), p. 587.

118. Reid, Michaela, *Ask Sir James* (London, 1996), p. 209.

119. Stoeckl, Baroness de, *Not All Is Vanity* (London, 1950), p. 245.

120. Bloch, Michael, *The Duchess of Windsor* (London, 1996), p. 215.

121. Dufort de Cheverny, op. cit. I.323.

122. Walpole, Horace, *Correspondence*, ed. W. S. Lewis, 48 vols (Oxford, 1967–83). 39.370.

123. Stephanie, HRH Princess, *I Was to Be an Empress* (London, 1937), p. 49.

124. Ibid, p. 263.

125. Brézé, Jacques de, *Les Dits du Chien Souillard* (Paris, 1959), p. 57.

126. Frédéric II, op. cit. 12.205–6.

127. Ibid. 27.179–83.

128. Héroard, op. cit. I.346.

129. Munthe, Gustaf and Uexkull, Gudrun, *The Story of Axel Munthe* (London, 1953), p. 102.

130. Morrow, Ann, *Highness. The Maharajahs of India* (London, 1987), p. 244.

131. Reverdil, E. S. F., *Struensee et la cour de Copenhague 1760–1762. Mémoires* (Paris, 1858), pp. 7–8.

132. Chapman, H. W., *Caroline Matilda Queen of Denmark 1751–1775* (London, 1971), p. 95.

133. Fischer, op. cit., p. 264.

CHAPTER 2

1. Clark, Kenneth, *Animals and Men* (London, 1977), p. 48.

2. Knecht, A. J., *Renaissance Warrior & Patron: The Reign of Francis I* (Cambridge, 1944), p. 447.

3. Incontri, Maria Luisa, *Il Piccolo Levriero Italiano* (Florence, 1956), p. 42.

4. Ibid, p. 28.

5. Cartwright, Julia, *Beatrice d'Este. Duchess of Milan* (London, 1903), p. 38.

6. Crowe, J. A., and Cavalcaselle, G. B., *Life and Times of Titian*, 2 vols (London, 1877). I.395.

7. Cartwright, Julia, *Isabella d'Este. Marchioness of Mantua 1474–1539*, 2 vols (London, 1903). 2.137.

8. Carré, op. cit., p. 125.

9. Pope, op. cit. I.75.

10. Jesse, G. R., *History of the British Dog*, 2 vols (London, 1856). 2.348.

11. Millar, Oliver, *The Tudor, Stuart & Early Georgian Pictures in the Collection of HM the Queen* (London, 1969), p. 98.

12. Leitch, Virginia, *The Maltese Dog* (London, 1953), p. 23.

13. Jesse, op. cit. 2.228.

14. Ibid. 2.190.

15. Daly, Macdonald, *Royal Dogs* (n.d.), p. 34.

16. Leitch, op. cit., p. 27.

17. Sophia, Electress, op. cit., p. 13.

18. Ailesbury, Thomas, Earl of, *Memoirs*, 2 vols (London, 1890). I.45.

19. Ash, Edward C., *Dogs. Their History and Development*, 2 vols (London, 1927). I.308.

20. Pepys, op. cit. I.158.

21. Palatine, op. cit. I.121.

22. Collier, op. cit., p. 167.

23. Beckford, William, *Dreams, Waking Thoughts and Incidents* (London, 1891), p. 114.

24. Campardon, Emile, *Madame de Pompadour et la cour de Louis XV* (Paris, 1867), p. 320ff.

25. Rosenblum, Robert, *The Dog in Art* (London, 1988), p. 18.

26. Hare, Augustus J. C., *The Life and Letters of Frances, Baroness Bunsen*, 2 vols (London, 1879). 2.40.

27. Victoria, Queen, *Leaves from a Journal in the Highlands* (London, 1868), p. 33.

28. See Millar, Oliver, *The Victorian Pictures in the Collection of HM the Queen* (London, 1992).

29. Mallet, V. (ed.), *Life with Queen Victoria; Marie Mallet's Letters from Court 1887–1901* (London, 1968), p. 57.

30. Stocker, Mark, *Royalist & Realist. The Life and Work of Sir Joseph Edgar Boehm* (London, 1988), p. 87.

31. Ponsonby, Sir Frederick, *Recollections of Three Reigns* (London, 1951), p. 143.

32. Stoeckl, op. cit., p. 108.

33. Secord, William, *Dog Painting 1840–1940* (London, 1992), p. 302.

34. Hardinge, Lord, *Old Diplomacy* (London, 1949), p. 97.

35. Paoli, Xavier, op. cit., pp. 214–5.

36. Souhami, D., *Mrs Keppel & Her Daughter* (London, 1997), p. 66.

37. Ibid, p. 93.

38. Wheeler-Bennett, Sir John, *Knaves, Fools & Horses. Europe between the Wars* (London, 1974), p. 173.

39. Cayzer, Bea, *The Royal World of Animals* (London, 1989), p. 33.

40. Stoeckl, op. cit., p. 108.

41. Secord, op. cit., p. 279.

42. Megnin, Pierre, *Le Chien: Histoire, hygiène, médecine* (Paris, 1877), pp. 66–9.

43. Mallet, op. cit., p. 88.

44. Allen, Charles, *Lives of the Indian Princes* (London, 1984), p. 51.

45. Secord, op. cit., p. 333.

46. Clark, op. cit., p. 46.

47. Collier, op. cit., p. 136.

48. Boylan, Clare, *The Literary Companion to Cats* (London, 1994), p. 89.

49. Collier, op. cit., p. 135.

50. Barrow, Sir John, *Travels in China* (London, 1804), p. 141.

51. Collier, op. cit., p. 141.

52. Maylunas & Mironenko, op. cit., p. xviii.

53. Thomas, Keith, *Religion & the Decline of Magic* (London, 1971), p. 539.

54. Sands, William Franklin, *At the Court of Korea* (London, 1987), p. 104.

55. Carl, Katharine A., *With the Empress Dowager of China* (London, 1906), p. 55.

CHAPTER 3

1. Campbell, Lorne, *Renaissance Portraits* (New Haven, Connecticut, 1990), p. 132.

2. Carré, op. cit., p. 121.

3. Ibid, p. 121.

4. Jesse, op. cit. 2.185.

5. Incontri, op. cit., p. 68.

6. Jesse, op. cit. 2.134–5.

7. Fraser, op. cit., p. 220.

8. Shyllon, F. O., *Black Slaves in Britain* (London, 1973), p. 9.

9. Carré, op. cit., p. 119.

10. Ibid, p. 121.

11. Incontri, op. cit., p. 65.

12. Kete, Kathleen, *The Beast in the Boudoir* (California, 1994), pp. 84–6.

13. Morrow, op. cit., p. 245.

14. Leitch, op. cit., pp. 348–9.

15. Montgomery, John, *Royal Dogs* (London, 1962), p. 66.

16. Ash, op. cit. 1.59.

17. Ibid. 2.618.

18. Marco Polo, *The Travels* (London, 1958), p. 142.

19. Buchan, John, *Lord Minto* (London, 1924), p. 246.

20. Menzies, S., *Royal Favourites*, 2 vols (London, 1865). 1.177.

21. Incontri, op. cit., p. 64.

22. Daly, op. cit., p. 49.

23. Ibid, p. 93.

24. Batiffol, L., *La Vie Intime d'une Reine de France. Marie de Medici* (Paris, 1906), p. 96.

25. Ibid, p. 97.

26. Ibid, p. 97.

27. Ibid, p. 146.

28. Héroard, op. cit. 2.89; 2.159.

29. Ibid. 2.168.

30. Carré, op. cit., p. 132.

31. Dufort de Cheverny, op. cit. 1.122.

32. Ibid. 1.119.

33. *Memoirs of the Comtesse de Boigne* (London, 1907), 4 vols, 1.54–5.

34. Batiffol, op. cit., p. 146.

35. Richelieu, op. cit. 2.137.

36. Catherine the Great, op. cit., p. 82.

37. Daly, op. cit., pp. 91–2.

38. Hale, John, *The Civilisation of Europe in the Renaissance* (London, 1994), p. 179.

39. Campardon, op. cit., p. 77.

40. Ibid, p. 357.

41. Barrow, op. cit., p. 232.
42. Reid, op. cit., p. 150.
43. Stone, op. cit., p. 62.
44. Evelyn, op. cit. 2.207.
45. Ailesbury, op. cit. 1.87.
46. Frédéric II, op. cit. 27.218.
47. Campan, Madame J. L. H., *Memoirs of Marie Antoinette* (London, 1903), pp. 462–3.
48. Catherine the Great, op. cit., p. 133.
49. Ibid, pp. 36–7.
50. Yusupov, Prince, *Lost Splendour* (London, 1996), pp. 35–6.
51. Fischer, op. cit., p. 198.
52. Topham, Anne, *Chronicles of the Prussian Court* (London, 1926), p. 48.
53. Fischer, op. cit, pp. 33–5.
54. Allen, Charles, *Plain Tales from the Raj* (London, 1975), p. 197.
55. Incontri, op. cit., p. 60.
56. Boucher, J., *La cour de Henri III* (Paris, 1986), p. 20.
57. Incontri, op. cit., p. 67.
58. Campardon, op. cit., p. 364.
59. Victoria, op. cit., pp. 118–19.
60. Maylunas & Mironenko, op. cit., p. 199.
61. Windsor, Duchess of, *The Heart Has Its Reasons* (London, 1956), pp. 362–70.
62. Quoted in Incontri, op. cit, p. 59.
63. Carré, op. cit., p. 125.
64. Héroard, op. cit. 1.266.
65. Ibid. 2.12.
66. Ibid. 1.202.
67. Carré, op. cit., p. 128.
68. Ibid, p. 132.
69. Ibid, p. 132.
70. Doran, Dr John, *Lives of the Queens of England*, 2 vols (London, 1855). 1.56.
71. Haslip, op. cit., p. 94.
72. Morgan, Lady, *The Book of the Boudoir*, 2 vols (Paris, 1829). 2.33.
73. Victoria, Queen, *More Leaves from the Journal of a Life in the Highlands* (London, 1884), p. 146.
74. Cayzer, op. cit., p. 12.
75. Victoria, *More Leaves*, op. cit., p. 268.
76. Montgomery, op. cit., p. 17.
77. Alexandra, Queen of Yugoslavia, *For a King's Love* (London, 1956), p. 105.
78. Carré, op. cit., p. 125, and Kete, op. cit., p. 154.
79. Fraser, op. cit., p. 220.
80. Batiffol, op. cit., p. 97.
81. Leighton, Robert, *Complete Book of the Dog* (London, 1922), pp. 286–94.
82. Dixey, A. C., *The Lion Dog of Peking* (London, 1932), p. 145.

CHAPTER 4

1. Jesse, op. cit. 2.187.
2. Batiffol, op. cit., p. 96.
3. Jesse, op. cit. 2.257.
4. Ibid. 2.292–3.
5. Evelyn, op. cit. 4.219.
6. Daly, op. cit., p. 50.
7. Ash, op. cit. 1.111.
8. Frederick the Great, *Die Briefe Friedrichs des Grossen an seinen vormaligen Kammerdiener Fredershof 1926*, ed. Johannes Richter (Berlin, 1926), p. 54.
9. Munthe, op. cit., p. 66.
10. Ibid, p. 404.
11. Ibid, p. 60.
12. Ritvo, Harriet, *The Animal Estate* (London, 1990), p. 195.
13. Ash, op. cit. 1.112.
14. Ibid. 1.67.
15. Jesse, op. cit. 2.62–3.
16. Ibid. 2.108.
17. Carré, op. cit., p. 128.
18. Sévigné, op. cit. 1.184.
19. Héroard, op. cit. 2.43.
20. Ibid. 1.412.
21. Ritvo, op. cit., pp. 171–4.
22. Ibid, p. 170.
23. Munthe, op. cit., p. 67.
24. Montgomery, op. cit., p. 33.
25. Yusupov, op. cit., pp. 118–19.
26. Cayzer, op. cit., p. 65.
27. Alexandra, op. cit., pp. 66–7.
28. Carré, op. cit. 121.
29. Ibid, p. 128.
30. Virgil, *Georgics*, trans. Dryden (London, 1772), p. 416.
31. Harris, Sir James, *Diaries and Correspondence*, 4 vols (London, 1844). 1.142.
32. D'Houville, Gérard, *L'Impératrice Josephine* (Paris, 1925), p. 66.
33. Bruce, Evangeline, *Napoleon & Josephine. An Improbable Marriage* (London, 1995), p. 194.
34. Maylunas & Mironenko, op. cit., p. 505.

35. Reid, op. cit., pp. 60–1.
36. Mallet, op. cit., p. 74.
37. Ponsonby, op. cit., p. 241.
38. William II, Kaiser, *My Early Life* (London, 1926), p. 276.
39. Munthe, op. cit., p. 52.
40. Ibid, pp. 279–80.
41. Munthe and Uexkull, op. cit., p. 49.
42. Lestrange, Robert, *Les animaux dans la littérature et dans l'histoire* (Paris, 1937), p. 127.
43. Batiffol, op. cit., p. 96.
44. Palatine, op. cit. 1.224.
45. Ibid. 2.22.
46. Walpole, Horace, *Reminiscences* (London, 1924), p. 107.
47. Frédéric II, op. cit. 13.12.
48. Clark, op. cit., p. 16.
49. Quoted in Boylan, op. cit., p. 5.
50. Plutarch, *Lives*, 6 vols (London, 1823). 3.363.
51. Beckford, op. cit., p. 180.
52. Cartwright, *Isabella*, op. cit. 1.135.
53. Ibid. 2.55–6.
54. *The Life of Benvenuto Cellini*, trans. John Addington Symonds (London, 1918), pp. 104, 108.
55. Carré, op. cit., p. 126.
56. Chateaubriand, *Mémoires d'outre-tombe*, 3 vols (Paris, 1973). 1.151.
57. Incontri, op. cit., p. 74.
58. Frédéric II, op. cit. 27.204.
59. Ibid. 26.288.
60. Wilhelmine, op. cit. 2.262–3.

61. Palatine, op. cit. 1.226.
62. Ibid. 1.143.
63. Gosse, Sir Edmund (trans.), cit. Lady Aberconway, *Dictionary of Cat Lovers* (London, 1950), p. 248.
64. Millar, Delia, in *Country Life*, 11 February 1988.
65. Ibid.
66. Reid, op. cit., p. 61.
67. Windsor, op. cit., p. 14.
68. Cayzer, op. cit., p. 54.
69. Millar, Delia, op. cit.
70. Stoeckl, op. cit., p. 163.
71. Incontri, op. cit., p. 64.
72. Maylunas & Mironenko, op. cit., p. 223.
73. Morrow, op. cit., p. 60.
74. John Chamberlain of Ware Park quoted in Chalmers, Patrick, *The History of Hunting* (London, 1936), p. 300.
75. D'Eon, Chevalier, *Memoirs*, trans. Antonia White (London, 1970), p. 171.
76. Dufort de Cheverny, op. cit. 1.367–9.
77. Windsor, op. cit., p. 294.
78. Bloch, op. cit., pp. 116–17.
79. Cayzer, op. cit., p. 53.
80. Brooke, HH the Hon. Lady Sylvia, Ranee of Sarawak, *Queen of the Headhunters* (London, 1970), pp. 10–11.
81. Reginald Pole quoted in Weir, Alison, *Children of England* (London, 1996), p. 16.

82. Windsor, Duke of, op. cit., p. 292.
83. Thomas, *Man & the Natural World*, op. cit., p. 60.
84. Lytton, Lady, *Toy Dogs* (London, 1911), p. 42.
85. Lestrange, op. cit., p. 270.
86. Ibid, p. 40.
87. Héroard, op. cit. 2.9.
88. Lenôtre, G., *Le Roi Louis XVII* (Paris, 1921), p. 91.
89. Campan, op. cit., p. 135.
90. Menzies, op. cit. 2.529.
91. Catherine the Great, op. cit., p. 159.
92. Ibid, p. 211.
93. Evans, E. P., *The Criminal Prosecution & Capital Punishment of Animals* (London, 1988), p. 19.
94. Jesse, op. cit. 2.213–4.
95. Thomas, *Man & the Natural World*, op. cit., p. 98.
96. Jesse, op. cit. 2.352.
97. Dale-Green, Patricia, *The Cult of the Cat* (London, 1963), p. 12.
98. Thomas, *Man & the Natural World*, op. cit., p. 109.
99. Héroard, op. cit. 1.74.
100. L'Estoile, Pierre de, *Journal de Henri IV*, 3 vols (Paris, 1948). 1.456.
101. Thomas, *Man & the Natural World*, op. cit., p. 78.
102. Frédéric II, op. cit. 27.29.
103. Hibbert, Christopher, *The Rise and Fall of the House of Medici* (London, 1979), p. 80.

104. Bertrand, L. M. E., *Philippe II et l'Escorial* (Paris, 1929), pp. 150–1.

105. Dale-Green, Patricia, *The Cult of the Dog* (London, 1966), pp. 81–2.

106. Scott, Eva, *Prince Rupert* (London, 1889), p. 81.

107. Palatine, op. cit. 2.139.

108. Burckhardt, Jacob, *The Civilisation of the Renaissance in Italy*, 2 vols (London, 1878). 2.14.

109. Ibid. 2.338.

110. L'Estoile, *Henri III*, op. cit., p. 321.

111. Jesse, op. cit. 2.191.

112. Ibid. 2.192.

113. Ibid. 2.192.

114. Miall, L. C., *The Early Naturalists. Their Lives and Work 1530–1789* (London, 1912), p. 83.

115. Evelyn, op. cit. 1.255.

116. Ibid. 1.216.

117. Pepys, op. cit. 7.245–6.

118. Jesse, op. cit. 2.358.

119. Ibid. 2.366.

120. Thomas, *Man & the Natural World*, op. cit., p. 159.

121. Ibid, p. 185.

122. Jesse, op. cit. 2.194.

123. Collier, op. cit., p. 45.

124. Jesse, op. cit. 2.208.

125. Rye, W. B., *England as Seen by Foreigners in the Days of Elizabeth and James I* (London, 1865), p. 46.

126. Evelyn, op. cit. 2.27–8.

127. Jesse, op. cit. 2.350–60.

128. Rye, op. cit., pp. 215–16.

129. Héroard, op. cit. 1.227.

130. Ibid. 2.83.

131. Longworth, Philip, *Alexis. Tsar of all the Russias* (London, 1984), p. 54.

132. Ibid, p. 189.

133. Stone, op. cit., p. 162.

134. Thomas, *Man & the Natural World*, op. cit., p. 157.

135. Gilmour, Ian, *Riot, Risings & Revolution. Government and Violence in 18th Century England* (London, 1993), p. 201.

136. Evelyn, op. cit. 2.46.

137. Collier, op. cit., p. 83.

138. Collier, op. cit., p. 17, and Volker, op. cit., p. 51.

139. Jesse, op. cit. 2.187.

140. Longworth, op. cit., p. 189.

141. Dale-Green, *Cult of the Dog*, op. cit., p. 44.

142. Ash, op. cit. 1.303.

143. Fréville, op. cit., p. 44.

144. Mallet, op. cit., p. 114.

145. Lewes, George, *The Life of Goethe* (London, 1938), pp. 449–50.

146. McManners, John, *Death & the Enlightenment* (Oxford, 1985), p. 156.

147. Besterman, Theodore, *Selected Letters of Voltaire* (London, 1963), p. 149.

148. See Hastings, Hester, *Man & Beast in French Thought of the 18th Century* (London, 1936).

149. Thomas, *Man & the Natural World*, op. cit., p. 171.

150. Schmitt, op. cit., p. 140.

151. Dale-Green, *Cult of the Dog*, op. cit., p. 146.

152. Thomas, *Religion*, op. cit, p. 440.

153. Thomas, *Man & the Natural World*, op. cit., p. 275.

154. Davis, Arthur, *The Kaiser I Knew* (London, 1918), p. 285.

155. Thomas, *Man & the Natural World*, op. cit., p. 51n.

156. Ibid, p. 104.

157. Megnin, op. cit., pp. 181–5.

158. Posner, Donald, *Watteau* (London, 1973), p. 285.

159. Fogle, Bruce, in *Country Life*, 7 September 1995.

160. Munthe and Uexkull, op. cit., p. 98.

161. Munthe, op. cit., p. 314.

162. Jesse, op. cit. 1.288.

163. Volker, op. cit., p. 45.

164. Hardinge, op. cit., p. 75.

165. Volker, op. cit., pp. 44–5.

166. Sansom, Sir George Bailey, *A History of Japan*, 3 vols (London, 1958–64). 3.134.

167. Hastings, op. cit., p. 18.

168. Kete, op. cit., pp. 5–6.

169. Hilt, Douglas, *The Troubled Trinity. Godoy & the Spanish Monarchs* (Alabama, 1987), p. 131.

170. Gilmour, op. cit., p. 202.

171. Thomas, *Man & the Natural World*, op. cit., p. 120.

172. Morgan, op. cit., p. 32.

173. Ritvo, op. cit., p. 126.

174. Lansbury, Coral, *The Old Brown Dog* (Wisconsin, 1985), p. 27.

175. Gilmour, op. cit., p. 202.

176. Ritvo, op. cit., p. 129.

177. Thomas, *Man & the Natural World*, op. cit., p. 150.

178. Montgomery, op. cit., p. 69.
179. Munthe and Uexkull, op. cit., p. 161.
180. Montgomery, op. cit., p. 15.
181. Ritvo, op. cit., p. 192.
182. Montgomery, op. cit., p. 22.
183. Ibid, pp. 39–40.

Chapter 5

1. Ash, op. cit. 2.617.
2. Collier, op. cit., p. 127.
3. Ibid, pp. 179–80.
4. Ibid, p. 177.
5. Miall, op. cit., p. 59.
6. Hale, op. cit., p. 175.
7. Jesse, op. cit. 2.44.
8. Thomas, *Man and the Natural World*, op. cit., p. 109.
9. Jesse, op. cit. 1.346.
10. Ash, op. cit. 2.625.
11. Collier, op. cit., p. 46.
12. Jesse, op. cit. 2.303.
13. Collier, op. cit., p. 82.
14. Ibid, p. 82.
15. Jesse, op. cit. 2.206.
16. Howell, James, *Familiar Letters* (London, 1774), p. 26.
17. Evelyn, op. cit. 1.23.
18. Héroard, op. cit. 1.148; 2.39–41; 2.73.
19. Ibid. 1.172.
20. White, Gilbert, *Natural History & Antiquities of Selborne* (London, 1994), p. 250.
21. Vesey Fitzgerald, B. S., *The Domestic Dog* (London, 1957), p. 80.

22. Collier, op. cit., p. 125.
23. Jesse, op. cit. 2.351–2.
24. Ibid. 2.188.
25. Collier, op. cit., p. 60.
26. Byrne, Muriel St Clare (ed.), *Lisle Letters*, 6 vols (London, 1981). 2.21
27. Ibid. 2.30.
28. Ibid. 2.331.
29. Ash, op. cit. 1.214.
30. Carré, op. cit., p. 125.
31. Newton, Lady Evelyn, *The House of Lyme* (London, 1917), p. 42.
32. Héroard, op. cit. 1.170.
33. Osborne, Dorothy, *Letters to Sir William Temple* (London, 1987), p. 92.
34. Ibid, p. 133.
35. Hartmann, op. cit., p. 155.
36. Ash, op. cit. 1.255.
37. Esterhazy, Comte Valentin, *Nouvelles lettres à sa femme* (Paris, 1909), p. 20.
38. Pushkin, *The Captain's Daughter* (Salisbury, 1978), p. 459.
39. Reid, op. cit., p. 110.
40. Carette, *My Mistress, the Empress Eugenie or Court Life at the Tuileries* (London, 1889).
41. Leighton, op. cit., p. 281.
42. Warner, Marina, *The Dragon Empress. Life and Times of Tz'u-Hsi 1835–1908* (London, 1972), p. 255.
43. Carl, op. cit., pp. 52–6.
44. Ibid., p. 173.

45. Frédéric II, op. cit. 13.90.
46. Longford, Elizabeth, *Victoria RI* (London, 1964), p. 46.
47. Victoria, *Leaves*, op. cit., p. 42.
48. Dussieux, L. (ed.), *Henri IV: Lettres Intimes* (Paris, 1876), p. 315.
49. Catherine the Great, op. cit., pp. 188–9.
50. Cartwright, *Isabella*, op. cit. 1.135.
51. Ash, op. cit. 1.145.
52. Ibid. 2.659.
53. Ibid. 2.635.
54. Evelyn, op. cit. 1.194.
55. Beckford, op. cit., p. 191.
56. L'Estoile, *Henri III*, op. cit., p. 85.
57. Megnin, op. cit., pp. 25–6.
58. Dufort de Cheverny, op. cit. 1.40.
59. Byrne, op. cit. 3.321. The more recent attribution of the painting is c. 1545, See Thurley, Dr Simon, *The Royal Palaces of Tudor England* (Yale, 1993).
60. Newton, op. cit., p. 41.
61. Jesse, op. cit. 2.145.
62. Ibid. 1.176.
63. Louise-Sophie, HRH Princess Friedrich Leopold of Prussia, Princess of Schleswig-Holstein, *Behind the Scenes at the Prussian Court* (London, 1939), p. 36.

Index

Figures in italics indicate black and white photographs; those in bold refer to colour plate sections following.

Picture Acknowledgements

BLACK AND WHITE ILLUSTRATIONS:
Author's collection: I, 191, 196, 197; Bildarchiv Museum Schloss Fasanerie: 92 (detail); Private collection 17 (detail) 201; The British Library: 210; The British Museum: 46 (detail) 58, 59, 79, 238 (detail); Christie's Images Ltd 1999: 6; Cooper-Hewitt, National Design Museum, Smithsonian Institute/Art Resource, NY, photo: Andrew Garn: 188; Country Life Picture Library: 107, 110, 118, 226 (detail), 240 (detail), 246 (detail); Dunham Massey, National Trust Photographic Library/ John Hammond 236, 253; © English Heritage Photographic Library: 11 (detail), 94; Private collection, England: photograph courtesy of Hazlitt, Gooden & Fox: 142 (detail); Glasgow Museums: The Burrell Collection © Glasgow Museums: 82 (detail); Kunsthistoriches Museum, Vienna: 50 (detail), 80, 126, 179 (detail); Museo del Prado – Madrid 68, 75 (detail) 76, 87, 143, 145, 146 (detail), 215 (detail); Réunion Musées Nationaux © photo RMN 73 (detail), 83 (detail), 84 (detail); Museo degli Argenti, Florence © QUATTRONE: 84; Musee Condé, Chantilly (Giraudon) 160 (detail), 134; National Museum, Stockholm: 29 (detail), 168; by courtesy of the National Portrait Gallery, London: 95, 113, 115 (detail), 175 (detail); Patrimonio Nacional, Madrid 1995: 97, 158; Private collection 275; The Royal Collection © Her Majesty The Queen: 22, 43, 81, 82 (detail), 88 (detail), 90, 101, 104, 105 (detail), 109, 111, 144 (detail) , 203, 254, 272, 273; Staatliche Schlosser und Garten, Potsdam, Sans Souci: 38; courtesy of the trustees of the V&A: 92 (detail), 99, 149 (detail); © National Trust, Waddesdon Manor: 9; reproduced by permission of the Wallace Collection, London: 2-3, 37, 85 (detail), 245 (detail), 267 (detail); Wellcome Institute Library, London: 178.

COLOUR PLATES:
Section one:
Louis XIII of France by Elle (© English Heritage Photographic Library); Emperor Joseph I by Benjamin Von Block (Kunsthistoriches Museum, Vienna); Elizabeth Charlotte of the Palatine attributed to J. B. Ruel ("Bildarchiv Museum Schloss Fasanerie bei Fulda"); Anne of Denmark by Paul Van Somer (The Royal Collection © Her Majesty The Queen); Queen Mariana of Spain by Juan Bautista Martinez del Mazo (© National Gallery, London); Charles I, Henrietta Maria and their two eldest children, 1632 by Sir Anthony Van Dyck (The Royal Collection © Her Majesty The Queen); Portrait of Ferdinand VI by Jean Ranc (© Museo del Prado – Madrid); Frederico Gonzago, Duke of Mantua (1500-40) by Titian (© Museo del Prado – Madrid); Empress Eugenie on the beach at Trouville by Eugene Boudin (1824-98) (Glasgow Museums: The Burrell Collection © Glasgow Museums); Très Riches Heures du Duc de Berry (Musée Condé, Chantilly: Giraudon); Charles I and Henrietta Maria departing for the Chase by Daniel Mytens (The Royal Collection © Her Majesty The Queen); Grand Portrait en pied de Madame Adeleide de France (1732-1799) by Jean Marc Nattier (©photo RMN).

Section two:
Infante Felipe Prosper by Diego Velásquez (Kunsthistoriches Museum, Vienna); Three Eldest Children of Charles I by Anthony Van Dyck (The Royal Collection © Her Majesty The Queen); Five Children of Charles I after Anthony Van Dyck (by courtesy of National Portrait Gallery, London); Princess Sophia Matilda of Gloucester by Sir Joshua Reynolds (1723-92) (The

Royal Collection © Her Majesty The Queen); La Famille de Louis de France, fils de Louis XIV, et le 'Grand Dauphin' en 1687 by Pierre Mignard (1612-1695) (© photo RMN); Charles II being presented with a pineapple by Hendrik Danckerts (courtesy of the trustees of the V&A); The Family of Frederick, Prince of Wales by George Knapton (1698-1778) (The Royal Collection © Her Majesty The Queen); Louis XIV and his Heirs by Nicolas de Largillière (reproduced by permission of the Wallace Collection, London); Queen Charlotte by Sir Thomas Gainsborough (1727-1788) (The Royal Collection © Her Majesty The Queen); Maria Louisa of Naples by Joseph Dorffmeister (Kunsthistoriches Museum, Vienna); Portrait of Madame de Pompadour's dogs after Bachelier painting of Iñes and Mimi on gold box by Louis Roucel (© National Trust, Waddesdon Manor; Photo: Mike Fear).

Section three:
Queen Victoria with Victoria, Princess Royal, and Albert Edward, Prince of Wales by Sir Frances Grant (1830-1878) (The Royal Collection © Her Majesty The Queen); Eos by Sir Edwin Landseer (1803-1873) (The Royal Collection © Her Majesty The Queen); Princess Alice Asleep by Sir Edwin Landseer (1803-1873) (The Royal Collection © Her Majesty The Queen); Albert, Edward Prince of Wales and Prince Albert by Franz Xaver Winterhalter (The Royal Collection © Her Majesty The Queen); Papier-mâché tray decorated after Landseer's painting of the dogs Hector, Nero and Dash and the Parrot Lory by Jennens and Betteridge (The Royal Collection © Her Majesty The Queen); The Bitchhound Nursing her Pups by J. B. Oudry (Musée de la Chasse et de la Nature, Paris); Fino and Tiny by George Stubbs (1724-1806) (The Royal Collection © Her Majesty The Queen); Queen Victoria at Osborne by Sir Edwin Landseer (1803-1873) (The Royal Collection © Her Majesty The Queen); Jemmy Shaw Canine Meeting, R. Marshall (The Kennel Club Picture Library); Cats and Dogs Belonging to the Queen by Charles Burton Barber (The Royal Collection © Her Majesty The Queen); Marco by Charles Burton Barber (The Royal Collection © Her Majesty The Queen); Queen Alexandra and her three Eldest Grandchildren and Dogs by Fred Morgan (1856-1927) and Thomas Blinks (1853-1910) (The Royal Collection © Her Majesty The Queen); Her Majesty Queen Elizabeth II, Michael Leonard (by courtesy of the National Portrait Gallery, London).

Section four:
Ladislaus of Fraunberg, Count of Haag by Hans Mielich (Princely Collections, Vaduz Castle); Le nain de Granville by Morvan Dahorst Anthonis (1519-1575) (Louvre © photo RMN); Emperor Ferdinand II by Josef Heintz the elder (Kunsthistoriches Museum, Vienna); Medici Dogs in the Boboli Gardens, Florence by Tiberio Titi (Private Collection, England. Photograph courtesy of Hazlitt, Gooden & Fox); Las Meninas by Diego Velázquez (© Museo del Prado – Madrid); The Vision of Saint Eustace by Pisanello (© National Gallery, London); Study of a Borzoi for The Equestrian Portrait of Wilhelm II (private collection); Looty by Frederich Wilhelm Keyl (1823-1871) (The Royal Collection © Her Majesty The Queen); Pekingese of the Imperial Palace (© The British Museum); Hunt of the Tabladillo at Aranjuez by Mazo (© Museo del Prado – Madrid); Madame de Pompadour by François Boucher, 1759 (reproduced by permission of the trustees of the Wallace Collection, London).